Bindi

Bindi

The Multifaceted Lives of Indo-Caribbean Women

Edited by ROSANNE KANHAI

UWIPRESS

UNIVERSITY OF THE WEST INDIES PRESS

Jamaica • Barbados • Trinidad and Tobago

University of the West Indies Press
7A Gibraltar Hall Road   Mona
Kingston 7   Jamaica
www.uwipress.com

ISBN 978-976-640-238-9

A catalogue record of this book is available
from the National Library of Jamaica.

Book and cover design by Robert Harris.
Set in Fairfield Light 11/15 x 24.
Printed in the United States of America.

Contents

        Ms Mastana Bahar 2000 / 141

        GABRIELLE JAMELA HOSEIN

SECTION THREE: SURVIVAL AND CREATIVITY

6   Women as Invisible Healers: Traditional Midwives
        in Trinidad and Tobago / 165

        KUMAR MAHABIR

7   Identity, Activism and Spirituality in the Art
        of Bernadette Persaud / 180

        BRENDA GOPEESINGH

8   Breaking with Tradition: Hybridity, Identity and
        Resistance in Indo-Caribbean Women's Writing / 208

        ANITA BAKSH

9   Beyond Fragile Homes: Indo-Trinidadian Women
        Constructing Habitable Narratives / 225

        PAULA E. MORGAN

        Contributors / 249

INTRODUCTION

Bindi

The Multifaceted Lives of Indo-Caribbean Women

– ROSANNE KANHAI –

ITS NAME DERIVED FROM the Sanskrit *bindu*, which translates as "a drop", the traditional bindi is a round dot pasted on a Hindu woman's forehead just above and between the eyebrows. Historically, the colour and material of the bindi were coded according to age and gendered roles: sandalwood for young girls, vermilion for married women, ash for widows. The origins of the bindi are shrouded in antiquity. Indian folklore suggests that the vermilion dot, accompanied by a stripe of vermilion powder along the centre part of a married woman's hair, is a vestige of the goddess Kali's smearing her face with the blood of her (male) victims. Since these red markings are first applied during the marriage ceremony, they may be symbolic of the female blood in sexual initiation, menstruation and childbirth. According to the chakra system, the bindi marks the third eye or sixth chakra of focused attention and insight; this interpretation is also applicable to men, for whom the bindi is of subtle sandalwood.

In the Caribbean the ancient folkloric connotations of the bindi are hardly important. It was historically part and parcel of Hindu religion and culture to add embellishment to religious rites and celebrations such as weddings. The basic materials were cheap and easily available, but it was special in application. At religious rites the sandalwood bindi was offered as a blessing, usually from an older man or woman to a younger man or woman, from a parent or grandparent to a child or from a pundit to a devotee. It bestowed spiritual

love, purification and healing. On festive occasions the pasting and wearing
of the red bindi was a celebration of femininity. Women and girls laughed
together as they primped and preened, teased each other, shared jewellery or
helped each other tie and fasten their saris; healing happened at the social
level. The widow ash was not worn in the Caribbean, but a black dot, made
of soot paste collected by burning ghee, was applied during illness and for
protection from the evil eye. Typically this black bindi was put on children,
both male and female, as they were thought to be more vulnerable to malevolence, but it could be worn by adults during particularly trying periods. The
black bindi was a reminder of the ever-present threat of illness or misfortune.
It was applied as part of healing and purification rituals carried out within the
structure of family and community in a comprehensive process that included
herbal medicines, massages, prayers and offerings to the divine. Thus the various aspects of the bindi symbol balanced and intersected with each other as
Hindus grappled with the exigencies of life. Common to all bindis was the
importance of a visually prominent marking as a symbol of healing and affirmation within family and community, and in the presence of the divine.

In contemporary times, the bindi has become mainstreamed internationally
as a fashion accessory for women. Its position remains the same, but shapes
vary from vertical lines to triangles or ovals. Bindis now come in a diversity of
fabrics, colours and materials – such as mirrors, sequins or glitter – and can
be glued to the forehead or applied with body paint. There has been an
increase in public bindi-wearing by Hindu and Hindu-descended women. As
well, bindis are now worn by non-Indian women who have converted to Hinduism and in a more playful manner by female movie and pop stars and fashion models of various ethnicities, religions, sexualities and ages.

I see this trend as indicative of the power of the bindi to escape cultural
boundaries and to effectively belong to all women. Certainly a Muslim or
Christian woman may reject the bindi, but in its easy movement from sacred
to secular practice, from experiential to philosophical knowledge and from
individual to universal divinity, the bindi rejects no one. Just as fashion cannot
be owned by any one cultural group, the eternal female, represented in the
earth goddess Kali, is beyond culture. The contemporary bindi carries a hint
of exoticism but is not a symbol of otherness. It is not rigidly coded according
to age and gender roles but instead it playfully matches fabrics, jewellery or
hairstyles.

With specific regard to the history and cultural politics of the Caribbean, the bindi is symbolic of the mainstreaming of Indian fashion in popular culture and, more broadly, the endurance of Indian-derived religions, artefacts and customs. Within the context of this collection, I expand the symbol of the bindi to refer to all that is visually Indian in the Caribbean, including the Hindu *jandhi* and the Muslim veil; the architecture of both mosques and mandirs; Hindu and Muslim names, festivals and foods. Historically many non-Indo-Caribbeans have not understood the differences between Muslim and Hindu religious and cultural practices, since Indian entry into the Caribbean was not segregated according to religion. To stretch the bindi symbol across religious lines is to be true to the shared history of Indians of different religious backgrounds in the Caribbean, and to capture the reality of some shared cultural habits. Some stereotypes – both positive and negative – have been applied to Indo-Caribbeans across religious lines, including Christians. In fact, many Indo-Caribbean Christians retained some Hindu- or Muslim-derived practices and were effectively bi-religious, blurring the boundaries between religion and culture. In colonial thinking, what was Indian was pagan, backward and perhaps malevolent. In contemporary times, however, both suspicion and curiosity have been replaced by relative acceptance.

While the current mainstreaming of the bindi symbol is analogous to the mainstreaming of Indo-Caribbean peoples and practices, the bindi's predominant appearance as a woman's decoration brings Indo-Caribbean womanhood to the fore. This collection invokes the complexity and flexibility of the bindi as a discursive space registering the multifaceted ways in which Indo-Caribbean women of different religious backgrounds have shaped their lives and come to understand themselves – and to be understood as ever-evolving hybrids of Eastern and Western influences within the Caribbean.

This collection is a sequel to *Matikor: The Politics of Identity for Indo-Caribbean Women*,[1] a seminal anthology by and about Indo-Caribbean women now in its second printing. *Matikor* used as its theoretical lens the *matikor* – a secretive, exclusively female, celebratory, sexualized dance activity on the eve of a Hindu wedding. The collection *Matikor* lifted the veil of secrecy yet retained the exclusively female quality; it expanded the focus on sexualized dance to include various forms of scholarly, personal and creative expression. *Matikor* marked the self-conscious coming into voice of the first generation of Indo-Caribbean women researchers and artists as they publicly articulated their experiences and thoughts. Utilizing fiction, personal narratives and scholarly analyses, Indo-Caribbean women plumbed their sordid group history for insights into their own development and explored their gender and ethnic marginalization as places of empowerment and creativity.

Matikor came at a time of consciousness-raising in Indo-Caribbean communities; *Bindi* evaluates the effects of this movement for women. In the decade between the two collections there has been a significant upsurge in creative and research activities by and about Indo-Caribbean women. Novels published include Ramabai Espinet's *The Swinging Bridge*; Joy Mahabir's *Jouvert*; Niala Maharaj's *Like Heaven*; and Lakshmi Persaud's *For the Love of My Name*, *Sastra* and *Raise the Lanterns High*. Poetry collections include Rajandaye Ramkisson-Chen's *Mirror Eye* and Rosanne Kanhai's *Rage and Renewal* and *The Green Face Man*. Patricia Mohammed's *Gender Negotiations among Indians in Trinidad, 1917–1974* and Brinda Mehta's *Diasporic (Dis)locations: Indo-Caribbean Women Writers Negotiate the "Kala Pani"*, scholarly texts that focus on Indo-Caribbean women, are now part of the conceptual base for gender studies in the Caribbean.[2] Sheila Rampersad, whose passionate voice resonates in *Matikor,* has developed as a recognized journalist at Trinidad and Tobago's *Sunday Express*. Brenda Gopeesingh, whose *Matikor* personal narrative marked her coming into voice, is a feminist activist in Trinidad's Hindu Women's Organisation and a valuable independent researcher, as evidenced in her work for this collection.

Matikor can be seen in the hands of many students at the University of the West Indies. As never before, bachelor's, master's and doctoral theses either focus on or include Indo-Caribbean women. Undoubtedly the fertile intellectual and creative environment from the late 1980s to the present has spawned a second generation of more confident Indo-Caribbean women researchers and artists. Indo-Caribbean women's experiences have also become a subject to be handled seriously by Caribbean researchers and artists. Unlike *Matikor*, which was designed to be exclusively by Indo-Caribbean women contributors, *Bindi* invited contributions from men and women of all ethnicities. Indo-Caribbean women no longer need a private space in which to find their voices, and *Bindi* honours the recognition by Caribbean thinkers that Indo-Caribbean women's lives are valid material to be studied.

The bindi, rooted as it is in ancestry yet dynamic in its adaptability to culture and style, is wrought on the one hand from Indo-Caribbean women's respect for ancestral influences and on the other hand from the daring and creativity to utilize these influences as places of strength from which to move forward in progressive, creative ways. The pride and boldness of the bindi – not to be missed in the centre of the forehead – is an outward manifestation of the inner intellectual and spiritual strengths upon which Indo-Caribbeans draw to take advantage of available opportunities and influences. Every woman's expression of herself is a facet of the bindi; the possibilities for invention are infinite. This is not confined to women of Indian descent but extends to every woman who dares to make her own statement. Fashion is an integral part of womanhood; in lean times or in plenitude, a woman is conscious of how she puts herself together to face the world. It is appropriate that an eternal and universal facial marking of femininity forms the title of this women's collection.

Bindi begins where *Matikor* ends, by a suggesting to Caribbean communities and to other communities that include the Caribbean a way forward in their search for insights on how post-colonial societies have developed. Indeed the boom town of European conquest and colonization, the Caribbean was a space of convergence for various groups in a process that resulted in a veritable melting pot of cultures. They came from Africa, Asia and Europe: slaves, indentured workers, planters, slave-owners, administrators, soldiers, buccaneers, merchants, artisans and many others who were part of the *toute bagai* relocated to lands where the indigenous people had been all but wiped out. In that seething cauldron of cruelty and power, creativity and ingenuity, happenstance and ambition, Caribbean cultures developed. The African and Asian victims of colonialism resisted from the onset and never let up, yet solidarity among these groups was neither enduring nor widespread. As colonialism ran its course and the wheels of post-colonialism got off to a slow, unsteady start, nationalist discourses grappled with issues of power and power-sharing. Indo-Caribbeans do not have a regional critical mass with which to make demands, but they are not easily ignored in the countries where their populations are significant. Theirs has been a nagging voice insisting that national independence was more complex than a simple handover of power from white to black hands. Additionally, those hands were predominantly male, creating a double marginalization for Indo-Caribbean women.

This group is one model of global living that reveals how women are positioned within the experiences of relocation of peoples and the negotiation of inter- and intra-group relationships. As the European powers straddled the world in the eighteenth and nineteenth centuries, the colonial process that brought people of vastly different cultural backgrounds together did not always favour harmonious interactions, and many post-colonial societies are still grappling with resulting cultural tensions. Indians entered the Caribbean in the mid-nineteenth century as indentured labour for colonial plantations. Most were placed in Trinidad, Guyana and Suriname, with smaller groups on other Caribbean islands and in Belize. Indians met newly emancipated Africans and, particularly where there were larger numbers of Indians, ethnic hostilities began – in the context of colonial divide-and-rule – that endure after the colonial period.

Pre- and post-independence national politics exploited and aggravated ethnic and cultural schisms. In Trinidad, the Afro-Trinidadian–based political party that negotiated independence in the late 1950s and early 1960s developed structures of power together with a discourse of black affirmation that resulted in comparative marginalization of the Indo-Trinidadian community from the process of decision making and the construction of national identity and culture. Not until 1995 was there an Indo-Trinidadian based government whose stint (1995–2001) challenged but did not significantly transform the political and cultural landscape. In May 2010 the People's Partnership, led by an Indo-Trinidadian woman, Kamla Persad-Bissessar, and anchored in the Indo-Trinidadian community was elected. It remains to be seen if this multi-racial, multi-party coalition can effectively plumb the ethnic complexity of Trinidad. In Guyana, ethnic-based political parties have taken turns governing; however, there is a history of ethnic violence, its victims predominantly Indo-Guyanese in terms of personal injury and seizure and destruction of property. When, as recently as 2008, Afro-Guyanese criminals massacred Indo-Guyanese village men, women and children as they slept, dread of racial violence shook Indo-Caribbean communities and members of those communities living abroad. The Surinamese cultural mix includes numerous ethnic groups and political parties that produce the national discourse, but the Dutch colonial process of ethnic ghettoization seems to have left cultural traditions relatively intact in the Indo-Surinamese community. Recognizable Indo-Caribbean voices have not been heard in countries where there are smaller Indian-derived communities, so it is not possible to analyse how these groups define themselves.

The followers of Islam and Hinduism are small groups in this predominantly Christianized hemisphere, and the endurance of the bindi is symbolic of their resistance to religious engulfment. At the cultural level, westernization and Afro-dominated creolization have been dominant forces in the Caribbean. The pull to ethnic Indian purity is as much an unbroken (though sometimes fragile) connection with ancestry as it is an inevitable reaction against self-effacement. The bindi is a symbol of the hybridization of Indo-Caribbean women: neither absorbed by dominant cultural influences nor confined by the demands of ethnic loyalty. Every woman on every occasion designs her own bindi, and after each wearing it is washed away, to be joyously reconceptualized at another time. Obviously the historical guidelines for the wearing of a bindi have been flouted; its endurance is due to its adaptability to cultural currents and personal style. Each facet of the bindi – shape, colour, design, raw materials, the occasion – is in constant negotiation and re-creation, as are the choices that Indo-Caribbean women make in their lives.

It is difficult to evaluate the extent to which connections with India and, for Muslims, the Arab world – through missionary-type activities, professional and educational training, movies and trips to India or the Arab world – are sources of definition for Indo-Caribbean women. Surely there is influence, but no established pattern has been ascertained. Indo-Caribbean women's connections with Indian, South Asian, global Hindu or global Muslim diasporic movements are tentative and, to the extent that they do exist, are either unorganized or organized under the auspices of male leaders. However, the popularity of the bindi in the Caribbean is simultaneous with its popularity globally – evidence that Indo-Caribbean women are not cut off from the rest of the world – but here too they make their choices about what they accept. Just as there are no rigid boundaries to fashion, ideas and influences drift across social and political boundaries.

An underlying concern for any group of women across the globe is domestic violence, and this matter must be addressed in any women's collection. I use the term *domestic violence* to include all types of physical and emotional abuse that happens within the home, with varying levels of complicity from the community as a whole. Such abuses are not confined to any cultural group but do take place within cultural traditions and structures. The spectre of domestic violence haunts the pages of *Matikor*, and it forms an incessant backbeat to many *Bindi* chapters. One hopes that increased educational opportunities and economic mobility for both men and women will inevitably result in more harmonious domestic relations, but to date there is no adequate research to measure how much improvement has taken place in the Indo-Caribbean community. What we do know is that, for Indo-Caribbean women, staying within the ethnic community was not only historically mandated by colonial laws but also necessary for basic survival and for religious and cultural continuity. When women met with domestic violence or other types of physical and emotional trauma, they were compelled to develop coping structures within the domestic and community space. For the early generations of Indo-Caribbean women, one such strategy was to educate their daughters and therefore empower them to challenge or escape real or possible domestic violence. In conjunction with personal and family resistance, alertness, and determination to develop strategies and strengths to deal with life's vicissitudes, women need broader support systems to keep them safe.

There are also correlations between the well-being of Indo-Caribbean women and feminist consciousness-raising in the region. With regard to domestic violence, one can extrapolate that women's organized awareness and liberation contribute to a climate in which women are less likely to tolerate bodily harm to themselves and their families. Undoubtedly Indo-Caribbean women have benefited by the gains made by Caribbean feminism, even if cultural specifics did not always receive adequate attention. This does not mean that no women have been left behind in spaces of pain; a welcome trend would be to see privileged women developing legal and other structures to assist victims of domestic violence. Let me hasten to add that, in any group of women, it is not only the underprivileged who suffer from domestic violence. Silence is a major ingredient, hence the need for research, personal stories and fictional accounts. From such knowledge, strategies to combat domestic violence can be developed. Domestic violence is the black bindi of gendered pain that women wear in mourning for sisters past, present and future. Yet the power of the bindi, in its many manifestations, carries possibilities for healing and regeneration. A comparison can be made between the bindi and the Muslim veil, symbols that are steeped in religious and cultural gendering but which are public reclamations of ancestry and rituals of community and solidarity that give women the strength to improve their lives.

Economic growth in Trinidad has outstripped that of other Caribbean territories, thanks to Trinidad's petroleum industry. Educational, professional and entrepreneurial opportunities are more abundant, and it is not surprising that more works in this collection are by Trinidadians and about Trinidad. The Guyanese experience is far less present in this collection than it is in *Matikor*. I can surmise from my visit to Guyana to recruit contributors for *Bindi* that there has been a significant brain drain, not atypical of Caribbean societies but a great loss nevertheless. In the case of Suriname, language barriers have resulted in less interaction between Indo-Surinamese and Indo-Trinidadians, but there is neighbourly contact with Indo-Guyanese. It seems also that the feminist movement in Suriname is less organized than in the anglophone Caribbean, and there is less focused study on women. As well, this collection did not yield contributions from territories where there are smaller Indo-Caribbean populations. Certainly research on these communities would be valuable in giving additional insights. To invoke the bindi, there are many facets to the Indo-Caribbean women's experience, but not all are manifest at this time and in this space.

While the bindi comes alive in its constant movement and reconfigurations, because of the need for a convenient structure this collection is organized according to three of its aspects: the Indian ancestral religions in transformation; constructions of the Indo-Caribbean female self that draws on various influences in ongoing re-creations; and the artistic expression that emanates from these processes.

SECTION ONE: RELIGION IN A GLOBAL CONTEXT

There was a time when mainstream Western feminists assumed that women all over the world would follow their leadership in moving away from religion and into secularism in order to demand and secure gender rights. Undoubtedly misogyny is deeply embedded in the major religions of the world today, if not in theory then certainly in practice. However, religions have not lost female membership numerically; in some societies there has been growing religious fundamentalism in which women seem to support and propagate further erosion of opportunities for women's self-development. Explanations include the failure of Western capitalism (within which Western feminism developed) to provide better standards of living for the most impoverished women; the spiritual barrenness of the commoditization of all aspects of human life; the reclamation of ancestry as part of decolonization; and globalized militancy that invokes ethno-religious support. These factors are not all equally relevant to Indo-Caribbean women but are the context for understanding their gendered lives within religious communities.

Historically many Indo-Caribbean families were compelled to convert to Christianity for access to education and job opportunities, but ethics and habits drawn from their ancestry were maintained within the home. In Trinidad, however, by the 1990s there was public validation of Indian culture and overt insistence by the Indo-Trinidadian community that it define itself on its own terms. This included the mainstreaming of Hindu and Muslim religions and cultures and articulation by some Christianized Indo-Trinidadians of respect for values and practices derived from the ancestral religions. Simultaneously the Trinidadian economy picked up momentum, as did feminist awareness in the region. Indo-Trinidadian women, with a work ethic developed in the context of family and religious-based community, were poised to advance professionally and had developed the skills and confidence to critique gendered aspects of that same family and community support system. As keepers of traditional cultures, they were the ones who could speculate on the possibilities of gender empowerment within those cultures.

Through the lens of the bindi, crafted as it is from women's creative resistance and adaptability, Sherry Ann Singh's "Women in the Ramayana Tradition" (chapter 1) and Halima Sa'adia Kassim's "Rings, Gifts and Shekels" (chapter 2) show that Indo-Caribbean women no longer have to make the hard choice between religious traditions and secularized empowerment. Both Singh and Kassim are second-generation scholars who came of age under the influences of feminism and ethnic affirmation and within a comparatively oil-rich economy that encouraged business and professional training. These chapters critique the patriarchal dictates of Indian religions and trace a pattern of resistance by women who remained within the religion and developed subversive interpretations and performances of religious texts and practices.

Singh points out that, since the arrival of Hinduism in Trinidad, women have been vital in developing and maintaining the tradition of re-enacting the Hindu epic the *Ramayana*. They have played key roles in the evolution of this tradition as both mirror and metaphor of the Hindu experience in Trinidad. Traditionally only males performed the epic, and its plot and characters have been used to justify female subservience. Singh documents how Indo-Trinidadian women resisted and subverted these conventions as could only happen in a diasporic community where Indian traditions of gender oppression had lost some of their stranglehold. This chapter also explores the *Ramayana* epic as a vehicle through which Hindu Trinidadians connect to Hindu communities across the globe, in defiance of boundaries set up by colonization. A sense of belonging to a global Hindu community rather than a Western-led global empire is itself subversive; the challenge for women is how to simultaneously confront gendered oppression within Hinduism. The spirit of the bindi asks that this confrontation maintain beauty, creativity and playfulness.

In today's world, where Islam has come into international consciousness, Kassim's "Rings, Gifts and Shekels" offers a way of understanding gender within the Indo-Trinidadian Muslim community, by charting a history in which the leadership of this community rested on a few educated men who used their authority to deny women the right of *ijtihad* (independent judgement) which Islam accords its believers. However, because of the pervasiveness of Islam in all aspects of life, Muslim feminism must begin with Islam's core set of rights and entitlements for women (and men). Kassim does not separate gender in and of itself (as Western feminist logic would), but situates gender concerns within the issues that Muslims face globally, such as poverty and socio-economic inequalities, social and religious fundamentalism, varying levels of educational attainment, inter-religious marriages, sexually transmitted infections (including HIV and AIDS), domestic violence, homosexuality and polygamy. This discussion is a bindi of multiple facets: it puts Indo-Muslim Caribbean women at the focal point of global Islam, where past, present and future bounce reflections off each other. Kassim offers possibilities of how contemporary Indo-Muslim women can live Islam, moving far beyond their value in terms of rings, gifts and shekels.

SECTION TWO: CONSTRUCTING SELF IN PERSONAL NARRATIVES

The personal narratives in Shaheeda Hosein's "Unlikely Matriarchs" (chapter 3), Valerie Youssef's "Finding Self" (chapter 4) and Gabrielle Hosein's "No Pure Place of Resistance" (chapter 5) can be seen as women designing their bindis as maps of self-representation. These maps are accounts of how self has emerged within the social turbulence of the Caribbean with its seemingly contradictory pulls, all of which offer possibilities of self-creation. To claim self in the Caribbean is itself defiance of the torturous journeys of bondage that were the genesis of the Caribbean people. Wrenched from land, customs, culture and everything else that makes a person, groups of people made their entrance into the Caribbean in bondage. Africans (more so) and also Asians were denied the legality of even their own persons. The end of slavery, indentureship and eventually colonialism did not mean economic or political self-determination for the newly independent countries, nor for the region as a whole. Global hegemony remained in the hands of the Western powers, leaving no space for the leisure of slow organic development.

Individual, ethnic, national and regional self-determination intersect, fraught with ambiguities and contradictions in a sorting out of identity that forms and re-forms infinitely. Indo-Caribbean communities have experienced insider/outsider identity, and theirs is the challenge of how to enter national and regional spaces and bend them to include themselves. Gender adds a layer of complexity, for sometimes ethnic gender roles and customs can be contrary to national, regional and global models and movements. In Indo-Caribbean families it is often the foremother who pulls towards tradition but also provides nurturance for the push towards the advantages of modernization. The "girl-child" negotiates self within the varying structures of definition of womanhood that have evolved. Notwithstanding the tension between the personal narrative and this narrative as representative of the group, each story reveals aspects of the journey of self, which undoubtedly began with historic pain but has developed to bring healing, growth and creative understandings.

Hosein's "Unlikely Matriarchs" draws generously on oral narratives to discuss rural women in the post-indentureship period who were able to craft a latent matriarchy that embodied many of the qualities for which contemporary feminists strive. She explains how Indo-Caribbean women transformed the miserable living quarters allocated to them into places of nurturance and stability – vital to improving the standards of living of the community as a whole. Hosein goes into the domestic space to add to Caribbean feminist discourse the informal, intimate labour of foremothers who laid the foundations so that succeeding generations could grasp and build on the opportunities that became available in later years; this ethic of deferred satisfaction constructs an inter-generational, continuous female self. One of the strengths of this piece is the voice of the author herself. This chapter is indeed a narrative of self as the author explains how her love and pride for her grandmothers have had to struggle against the shame heaped on these women for imposed degradation.

Youssef's "Finding Self" focuses on the way in which contemporary women of Indian descent in Trinidad perceive their gender identity and how much that identity owes to traditions and history in the Indian subcontinent, religious belief systems and life experience as Trinidadians. Youssef's analysis rests on personal interviews with three Indo-Trinidadian female university students in their twenties, who were asked to talk informally about their sense of identity, their national and cultural loyalties and their gender roles and ambitions. Youssef's skilful analysis of the language they use reveals – sometimes in contradiction to their overt statements – the unresolved conflicts and ambivalence of women striving to reconcile the complex demands of tradition with their aspirations as twenty-first-century emancipated thinkers. Youssef calls for support of a complex womanhood in the making.

Hosein's "No Pure Place of Resistance" reflects on the author's participation in an Indo-Trinidadian beauty contest, Ms Mastana Bahar, as part of her process of understanding the dynamic between gender performance and selfhood. Hosein synthesizes this personal experience with academic research, with insights she has gained from writings by Caribbean (especially Indo-Trinidadian) feminists and with her continuing work in feminist theory and gender studies at the University of the West Indies, St Augustine, Trinidad. She arrives at an intellectual space where she does not wish to fit into fixed notions of identity. Hosein says, "Not only have I stopped trying to be an 'appropriate' Indian 'girl' and to manage ethnic or gender expectations, I have stopped maintaining a claim to a racialized, sexualized, feminized self." It would seem that we have come full circle here, beginning with the Indo-Caribbean woman's compulsion to articulate self in an environment that would deny her personhood, and ending with a rejection of ethnic and gender-determined self that can only be realized when ethnicity and gender are not under question.

SECTION THREE: SURVIVAL AND CREATIVITY

To sustain the metaphor of the bindi as all things visually Indo-Caribbean, creative expression is the public display of the Indo-Caribbean woman's consciousness, the development of which is explored in previous sections of this collection. As with the contemporary bindi, Indo-Caribbean women's art manifests aspects of indentureship and post-indentureship influences, the social environment of the broader Caribbean, and Westernization and globalization. These influences overlap and intersect.

In the early days Indo-Caribbean women put much of their creativity into physical survival as well as into religious displays and performances, as far as they were allowed by both colonial laws and conventions within their own communities. Some of the women artists who pushed boundaries at that time are part of the folk heritage of the community. One such group are the folk healers of Kumar Mahabir's "Invisible Healers" (chapter 6). With a keen anthropologist's eye, Mahabir documents and therefore validates women folk healers who trained themselves and gave service as midwives, masseuses and herbalists in a time when Western medicine was not affordable to many. Emotional and spiritual advisers in their own right, these women served the community as well as extended its boundaries; many an Afro-Trinidadian woman had her first contact with the Indo-Trinidadian community when she sought the services of a folk healer. Mahabir frames these traditional healers as survival artists who continue to treat mainly low-income women, creating a healing space where there is less cultural divergence and therefore more trust between healer and patient.

However, there is a disconnect between traditional community art forms and Western forms that require an individualized self and authorship. Ironically, art itself can bridge that gap. Indo-Caribbean women's use of Western art forms has involved a gradual and cautious negotiation, taking place when they achieve some measure of individuation. That individuation certainly comes from Western influences but also allows them to draw on grassroots experiences of art, in spite of the lack of continuity between traditional, community art and contemporary, individual art.

Eurocentric art forms such as painting, writing, music and sculpture evolved, generally speaking, among the educated, privileged class, and it was the perspectives of this class that were offered to Indo-Caribbean students (and their Afro-Caribbean peers). In that celebration of the colonial reality and the devaluation of their own, the tortured consciousness of the Caribbean artist developed. In colonial educational institutions Caribbean artists learned skills which they could combine with folk influences, thus bringing together perspectives from diametrically opposed socio-economic and racial spectra. It is not surprising that Indo-Caribbean women artists choose as subject matter the intersections of gender, ethnicity and income. I state the obvious in saying that these women kept secret much of their reflections, perceptions and pain during the educational process, and that beating the odds to emerge successfully could happen only with family and community support. Yet the woman artist knows she must use her talent to expose gendered and other forms of oppression. She must publicly critique family and community, in spite of its marginal status. She takes the risk of her work's being used to bolster negative racialized stereotypes about the community that nurtures her. Her art is also a medium for perceptions about her place in the national and regional tapestry of the Caribbean. Her work comes from deep love and commitment to expose the ugliness and celebrate the beauty of the subjects under study, all the while pointing a way forward for the ethnic and larger national or regional communities.

Significant influences in Indo-Caribbean women's creativity come from the strong Afro-Caribbean presence. Ironically, while Afros and Indos, particularly in Trinidad and Guyana, are in so many ways placed in antagonistic political relationships, in many village communities people have always lived together for their very survival. Over time the origins of cultural practices, including art forms, became blurred. Villagers engaged collectively in art forms such as the construction of blue-bottle trees, performances at pre- and post-funeral wakes, and oral engagement in folklore. All the way from Africa came Anancy, for example, surviving the Middle Passage and the plantation years to become part of the creative conscious of Caribbeans of all ancestral backgrounds. Anancy shared and took on attributes of trickster figures from other cultural streams. The teller of a "nancy story" has certain recognizable skills; how to utilize those skills in a literary form is the challenge for the writer. Afro-Caribbean cultural expression is undeniably part of the heritage of Indo-Caribbean artists. Perhaps the most outstanding example of intercultural participation in Trinidad is the annual Carnival, an undoubtedly Afro-dominated festival in which Indos of all ages and genders – beginning as young as four years old – participate and contribute at various levels. Here too is a wellspring of Indo-Caribbean women's creativity, but drawing from this well is not without tensions; the strong presence of Afro-Caribbean art has, to some extent, marginalized Indo-Caribbean cultural expression.

Another source of tension comes from Indo-Caribbean purists. For example, some dance teachers privilege classical Indian dance and denounce hybridized dance forms. But art will not be contained by any particular agenda. We can say that art is the bindi that belongs yet is elusive, and in its elusiveness lies its growth. Likewise Indo-Caribbean patriarchies may find that their women are affirmative about their ancestral cultures but refuse to be managed within an inherited hierarchy. Indo-Caribbean women artists are in a creative space where they can draw on, critique, experiment with and otherwise invent influences of Indian ancestry, Caribbean cultures and Western forms. This is the reality of diaspora: art is enriched by drawing from one or more cultural influences, and the artist resolves or foregrounds whatever contradictions there may be.

Brenda Gopeesingh's "Activism, Identity and Spirituality" (chapter 7) traces the development of the art of Bernadette Indira Persaud, an Indo-Guyanese painter who effectively redefined a basically Eurocentric Caribbean aesthetic by making indigenous themes and forms central to her work. This chapter, a study of the integration of identity exploration, social activism and spiritual growth, draws on Gopeesingh's conversations with the artist at her home in Chateau Margot, Guyana, in March 2007 and on several newspaper clippings, pamphlets and journals. To study Persaud's work is to observe her relentless search for truth, which begins with the contrast between the transcendent natural beauty of Guyana and the bizarre cruelty of colleagues and neighbours who carried out orders from the dictator Forbes Burnham. Persaud's passion for understanding delves deep into Hindu and Muslim art and philosophy and expands to critique global power structures. As Gopeesingh puts it, the Indo-Caribbean woman can draw on traditional forms yet interrogate the relevance of ancestral philosophical ideas, thus exploring the distance travelled from the ancestral home. The medium of art bridges Indian philosophies and Indo-Caribbean grassroots experiences within the global context.

Anita Baksh's "Breaking with Tradition" (chapter 8) analyses fictional texts by Indo-Caribbean women writers Jan Lo Shinebourne, Shani Mootoo and Lakshmi Persaud. Baksh uses border theory as a framework of analysis, because the Indo-Caribbean experience is one that is inherently produced by border crossing, most obviously the ocean crossing that carried Indians to the Caribbean. In their fiction, Indo-Caribbean women writers transgress the borders of public and private domains and challenge specified social roles.

Shinebourne's *The Last English Plantation* promotes a model of Indo-Guyanese identity in a borderland space where it is impossible to divide the different groups according to distinct racial and cultural borders, while Shani Mootoo's *Cereus Blooms at Night* takes on the issue of non-heteronormative sexual identity and examines the protagonist's madness as a psychic crossing between reality and the imaginary. At the level of language, borders are crossed when the oral are integrated into the literary texts. Fictional characters revel in the diversity of languages: colonial English, Sanskrit, Hindi, the Bhojpuri dialect brought by Indian indentureds, Indo-Creole and Afro-Creole. Indo-Caribbean women's fiction is a speaking bindi in its endless creativity and reflexivity.

Paula Morgan's "Beyond Fragile Homes" discusses the three most recent novels by Indo-Trinidadian women: Ramabai Espinet's *The Swinging Bridge*, Niala Maharaj's *Like Heaven* and Joy Mahabir's *Jouvert*. As Morgan explains, all these writers live in metropolitan centres; their characters grapple with a concept of home that must integrate the emigrant's relocation, the land of birth and that of ancestry. Responding to the contemporary social climate, these texts explore a concept of home that includes security and confidence in the state's capacity to keep its citizens safe. In a context of generational anguish over ethno-political marginalization in Trinidad, how does the emigrant reconcile this pain with that of separation from the cultural intimacy of the grassroots family and community? Morgan's strategy is to marry literary with cultural events as she expertly sorts through the many layered discourses that reveal gendered and class-motivated schisms in a community that has made significant, but uneven, socio-economic strides. If the earlier generations of writers saw themselves as exiled, these women consciously straddle different locations and participate simultaneously in various ethical and ideological systems. Thus Morgan's questions: "What ideologies, if any, should art legitimately express? Who is the artist representing in her work and to whom is this representation directed? What calibration of artistic expression would best accomplish this purpose?"

The chapter authors and the editor offer this collection as by no means exhaustive in its exploration of Indo-Caribbean women but as a contribution to understanding both the Caribbean and women in a global network where peoples and their cultural baggage are in constant movement. Indo-Caribbean women are presented as a group with a history of social and psychological rupture(s) in a region where trade winds are not the only currents that converge. To study this group is to examine how marginalized women have negotiated the after-effects of colonialism and the thrust of globalization. This collection utilizes as well as sharpens the lens of post-colonial feminism as it explores the role of women within and in resistance to Western hegemony. Indo-Caribbean women are situated within Indian indentureship as a prototype of post-slavery plantation labour that informs how labour arrangements in today's world have developed and are managed. The bindi, a symbol of the refusal to bow to various types of management, is a lens through which to view how women have survived, and the extent to which they can thrive and continually recreate themselves within and in spite of historical and cultural context.

NOTES

1. Rosanne Kanhai, ed., *Matikor: The Politics of Identity for Indo-Caribbean Women* (St Augustine, Trinidad: University of the West Indies School of Continuing Studies, 1999).

2. Ramabai Espinet, *The Swinging Bridge* (Toronto: HarperCollins, 2004); Joy Mahabir, *Jouvert* (Bloomington, Ind.: Authorhouse, 2006); Niala Maharaj, *Like Heaven* (London: Hutchinson, 2006); Lakshmi Persaud, *For the Love of My Name* (Leeds: Peepal Tree, 2000); Lakshmi Persaud, *Sastra* (Leeds: Peepal Tree, 2007); Lakshmi Persaud, *Raise the Lanterns High* (London: BlackAmber Books, 2004); Rajandaye Ramkisson-Chen, *Mirror Eye* (London: Hansib, 2001); Rosanne Kanhai, *Rage and Renewal* (St Augustine, Trinidad: University of the West Indies School of Continuing Studies, 2002); Rosanne Kanhai, *The Green Face Man* (St Augustine, Trinidad: University of the West Indies School of Continuing Studies, 2007); Patricia Mohammed, *Gender Negotiations among Indians in Trinidad, 1917–1974* (Basingstoke, UK: Palgrave, 2002);

3. Brinda Mehta, *Diasporic (Dis)locations: Indo-Caribbean Women Writers Negotiate the "Kala Pani"* (Kingston: University of the West Indies Press, 2004).

Religion in a Global Context

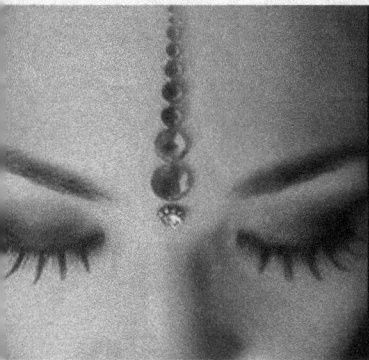

1

Women in the *Ramayana* Tradition in Trinidad

– SHERRY-ANN SINGH –

SOCIO-HISTORICAL CONTEXT

DURING THE PERIOD OF Indian indenture a total of 143,939 Indians migrated to Trinidad,[1] approximately 88 per cent of whom practised various facets of Hinduism. Of this number, 29 per cent were women and 71 per cent were men.[2] Despite the trying conditions experienced under the system,[3] about four of every five Indian immigrants chose to make Trinidad their permanent home at the end of their contracted periods of indenture.[4] From their very entrance into Trinidad society, Hindus were engaged in the practice of many aspects of their religion. This was especially so of the more private aspects, which could be observed within either the home or the immediate Hindu/Indian community. However, although Hindu immigrants "carried a slice"[5] of their society, and hence their religion, with them, their uprooting from the Indian context necessitated attempts at community and religious reconstruction.

In Trinidad, elements of religion were variously truncated, modified, diluted, intensified or excised. Thus, reconstitution and telescoping[6] – rather than transplanting – were two of the dominant processes that could be observed. These processes subsequently yielded a form of Hinduism in which some of the more visible and tangible elements were markedly modified. At the same time, however, the Hinduism which emerged was unarguably rooted in the broad philosophy and general tenets of many of the strands of Hinduism practised in India: the caste system, Hindu priesthood, the institution of marriage, gender roles and many of the religious rites, rituals and observances.

There was a remarkable degree of social, religious and cultural diversity within the immigrant population in Trinidad. This was evident in such areas as language, kinship ideology, social and economic structures, values, general attitudes, lifestyle and behaviour. This social and geographical diversity also underscored a "jumbled medley of beliefs, doctrines, rites, experiences, relationships, restrictions, polities, economies and orientations regarding matters supernatural and spiritual".[7] Specific regions in India yielded particular religious traditions which were inevitably transported – albeit often in highly attenuated forms – with the indentured immigrants to the Trinidadian context. Much of this diversity was situated in caste distinctions and in the presence of elements of both the Great and Little traditions of Hinduism.[8] However, by the beginning of the twentieth century most of these smaller traditions were being subsumed by the drive for a standardized form of Hinduism, namely the Sanatan Dharma strand of Trinidad Hinduism.

Following the abolition of indentured immigration in 1917, the Hindu community was able to intensify its efforts at community and religious reconstitution. By the 1920s a most discernible feature of Trinidad Hinduism was a move towards homogenization, along with a simultaneous and arguably paradoxical persistence of the many threads of Hinduism brought to Trinidad from the various geographico-cultural regions of India. Featuring most prominently in this context was the *Ramayana* (see the appendix for a synopsis of the *Ramayana* story). Perhaps the most celebrated product of the Trinidad Hindu community, V.S. Naipaul, described the *Ramayana* as something that "lived among us" and as "something I had already known".[9] From the very earliest days of Indian indenture in Trinidad, the *Ramayana* had established itself as the most popular Hindu religious text. It evolved from a collection of memorized verses and stories diffused through the oral tradition to a multitude of dimensions which simultaneously yielded to and reflected transformation in society. While the basic storyline and the characters remained the same, the symbiotic relationship between the society and the *Ramayana* tradition gen-

erated changes in interpretation, thematic emphasis, focus, style and modes
of presentation. However, it still managed to retain its tenets, themes and status as a religious and social doctrine.

THE *RAMAYANA* AND WOMEN IN A GLOBAL SETTING

Since the time of its inception in India before 500 BC, in the form of the Rama
stories,[10] the *Ramayana* tradition has undergone extensive variation and
change. Because of its intricate and intimate connection with the life of the
people, the *Ramayana* tradition can be found in almost every literary genre:
heroic, dramatic, lyrical, elegiac, tragic, comic and farcical poems or songs;
street and theatre dramas; epics; *kavyas* (ornate poetic compositions); *puranas*
(mythological stories); dance dramas and other performances; sculpture and
bas-reliefs; and mask, puppet and shadow plays of both the classical and folk
traditions.[11] In terms of the epic itself, almost three hundred tellings have
been recorded.[12] However, Valmiki's version of the Rama story has proven to
be fundamental to the *Ramayana* tradition. In the words of one scholar, "all
past inspiration had flown into this reservoir, and all later tellings have flown
from it".[13]

Each recension or literary genre inevitably exhibits numerous variations
based on the objectives of the particular composer, the historical and social
locations, religious affiliation, gender, and the political, cultural, chronological
and ideological contexts. The plethora of *Ramayana* versions in various Indian
languages exhibits regional and local shifts in emphasis and changes in minor
or major situations, actions and characterization. Recensions outside of India
also display variations that cater to and reflect the values, lifestyles and cultural nuances of the country and people concerned. Although the structure
and sequence of events may be the same (or at least similar), the discourse[14]
or actual retelling may differ greatly in relation to such matters as style, detail,
tone, texture and the importation and working of traditional, regional or folk
motifs into the story. While some tellings affirm the social, religious or political
status quo, others contest it. Diverse tellings render the *Ramayana* an apt
vehicle for accusing, justifying, mediating or debating issues pertaining to
social or political grievances. Interestingly, a substantial and long-standing
dimension of these tellings has been spun out of the experiences of women.

In India, many folk-songs of the Telugu women focus on a *Ramayana* tradition that questions the prevailing male dominance. Rama's integrity and actions as a husband are severely questioned, and grander male-dominated events such as war and coronation are sidestepped. Prominence is given to more female-oriented events and domestic matters such as child care and even the queen's morning sickness.[15] In an essay entitled "Grinding Millet but Singing of Sita", Usha Nilsson examines how women's *Ramayana* songs in the Awadhi- and Bhojpuri-speaking areas of northern India, far from following the *pativrata* (pious and faithful wife) ideal, contradict and resist the dominant male discourse as presented in the *Ramcharitmanas*. They also conceal hostility and tensions among women of different castes and social status.[16] Nilsson further reveals that when women of different economic and social strata sing the story of the *Ramayana* together, they follow the traditional storyline. However, when they meet in their separate groups, they sing about events close to their own life experiences. From such songs, new forms of the Rama-and-Sita story emerge which, while not questioning the divinity of the characters, emphasize their human aspects and frailties. The themes of these songs include marriage, childbirth, domestic tensions and quarrels, and they focus greatly on the trials and tribulations of Sita. The women's own world view and social commentary are brought into these songs, which often present contradictory accounts of selected events.

In contemporary times and, more specifically, within the context of the Indian diaspora, the *Ramayana* has both reflected and contributed to the transformation of Indian culture and society in various alien lands. For example, the Southall Black Sisters' 1979 Ramleela production in Greater London reflected the particular circumstances of their migration to Britain, reworking the *Ramayana* tradition through the conceptual categories of race, class, gender and colonialism.[17] The Southall Black Sisters were seen as the "only inside group that could mount a critique of sexist attitudes within their community to improve it, rather than attack it from the outside to disparage South Asian culture". Thus their 1979 Ramleela production sought to satirically question patriarchal attitudes and racism in the community, but in a spirit of affection and celebration. In this production women played all the parts – male and female – and their casting choices reflected a thwarting of traditional expectations. For example, while Sita was played by a tall Asian woman, Rama was portrayed by a short African-Caribbean woman. The critical edge of the production was supplemented by the use of a narrator and two jesters, who mediated between the events depicted and the audience. While the storyteller provided the background, commentary and significance of each scene, the two jesters would interrupt, pointing out topical parallels between the events in the play and events in the daily life of the audience, translating into various languages and questioning stereotypical gender roles and assumptions in the play. In an essay entitled "Charting the Journey", a participant in this production described it as "our own feminist version of Ramleela" which she contrasts with "the classic Hindu epic which depicts Sita, the central female character, as a subservient and devoted wife".[18]

John Kelly explored the notion of the *Ramayana* as Fiji's "fifth Veda".[19] He examined the political emergence and role of the *Ramayana* in Fiji's courtrooms, "the colonial concretisation of the *Ramayana* political imaginary", the *Ramayana* as a vehicle for self-identification, and the relevance of its themes of exile and the quest for *ramrajya* (a utopian state) to the Indian diaspora.[20] He argued that in Fiji, the *Ramayana* provided "models for moral behaviour". The majority of mainstream Hindus believed that emulation of Rama by Fiji Indian men and, more so, emulation of Sita by Fiji Indian women, would solve the islands' social problems. These diverse tellings indicate that, throughout history, a variety of female voices has been heard within the *Ramayana* tradition.

THE *RAMAYANA* IN TRINIDAD

Although the *Ramayana* tradition comprises several hundred varying written and oral interpretations, the *Ramcharitmanas* was the version brought to Trinidad by indentured Indians. Composed by the poet-saint Tulsidas around 1574, it has been central to the literary, cultural and religious heritage of India[21] and almost every other country of the Indian diaspora. Original in terms of neither plot nor theme, the *Ramcharitmanas* is rather an interpretation of the Valmiki myth of Rama, with influences and borrowings from other prominent texts of sixteenth-century India.[22] Since the beginning of the Indian presence in Trinidad, the *Ramcharitmanas* has occupied the unchallenged position of "*Dharmashastra* par excellence" in all facets of Trinidad Hinduism, providing "the major framework of the theological edifice of Hindu migrants".[23] So pervasive is this version that many refer to the author as the "father of Caribbean Hinduism".

During the period of indenture, the vast majority of the indentured immigrants (between 1876 and 1879, over 90 per cent) originated from the Uttar Pradesh and Bihar regions of India,[24] which were by then deeply immersed in the *bhakti* tradition, and hence permeated by Tulsidas's encapsulation of it. This can account for the *Ramcharitmanas* quickly becoming a religious, social, cultural and emotional anchor for the early indentureds, who found themselves in an alien and often hostile environment. The well-known and familiar story of the *Ramcharitmanas*, with its human interest and its largely ethical nature, attracts a larger audience than the *Bhagavad-Gita*'s pure philosophy and revelation.[25] Verses from the *Ramcharitmanas* can be set to music and sung, adding considerably to its appeal. The story is dramatic and loosely knit, and the narrative propels it in such a manner that both despite and because of its lack of active sermonizing, the philosophy hits home. The author's conception of *bhakti* possesses "deep appeal",[26] especially to a community entrenched in this (*bhakti*) tradition.

The specifically diasporic appeal of the *Ramcharitmanas* was based on a number of factors. Its focus on the *bhakti* tradition served as a link to the emotional and cultural ethos of the motherland. Its treatment of the exile theme provided immense solace and emotional support to the immigrants who, viewing their indenture as a type of exile, identified with the trials and tribulations in the text; they upheld Rama's dignity and endurance as an ideal worthy of emulation in their own situation. The idea of exile and return that runs deep in the text provided yet another point of identification and solace, since many, especially in the earlier phases of indenture, nurtured the hope of one day returning to the motherland. So intense is the diasporic appeal of the *Ramcharitmanas*, and so ingrained is the perceived analogy between Rama's exile in the *Ramayana* and the experience of Indian indenture, that Vijay Mishra aptly titled his study on the Indian experience in Fiji *Rama's Banishment*.[27]

The uncomplicated nature of the story, along with a clearly established dichotomy between good and evil, rendered it an appropriate authority in the Trinidad Hindu community's attempts at reconstruction and reconsolidation. Stories from the *Ramayana* impacted on Hindu – and sometimes non-Hindu – perceptions of the new environment to the extent that the significant unknown Other, or potentially threatening agents such as white colonial oppressors and Trinidadians of African descent, were sometimes referred to as "Ravan" (the villain of the story). In his study *The Development of the East Indian Community in British Guiana, 1920–1950*, Clem Seecharan confirmed that this was also the case in British Guiana, where stories from the *Ramayana* greatly influenced Hindu perceptions of the new environment, and where Forbes Burnham acquired the title of Ravan on account of his overtly anti-Indian policies.

The *Ramcharitmanas*'s focus on interpersonal relationships provided both positive and negative models for reconstruction of both family and community networks. The following extract from the *Sunday Guardian* is but one of numerous responses that support this function of the text: "*Ramayana* projects the highest values of righteous conduct that pertains to family life. There are portraits of the love between brothers, the duties of a wife, the relationship between father and son and the responsibilities of a king towards his subjects among other things."[28]

In Trinidad, as in many other countries of the Indian diaspora, the *Ramayana* has transgressed the boundaries of text to manifest itself as a larger, multi-dimensional tradition. This Trinidad *Ramayana* tradition can be defined as a collection of both conscious and unconscious remakings and interpretations (rather than one singular version) whose values, ideas and concepts have been influenced to varying extents by the history, experiences and attitudes of both the Hindu and wider Trinidadian society. It is informal in the sense that it has not yet assumed a written form; rather, its plausibility is entrenched largely in oral and visual modes of diffusion and transmission which have continuously fed on the written texts. It demonstrates that the *Ramayana*, by constantly informing and reflecting the Trinidad Hindu experience, can be deemed both mirror and metaphor of history and society, and thus Hindu socio-religious transformation. The *Ramayana* tradition in Trinidad comprises dimensions such as the Ramleela (a depiction of the Rama story in dramatic form), audio and visual recordings, literature, music, art and craft items, folksong, dance and dance-dramas, socio-religious festivals and observances, Hindu life-cycle rituals and, of course, the text itself as doctrine. This very dynamic and enduring tradition has had a symbiotic relationship with Hindu women in Trinidad; each has contributed to the shaping of the other in a number of salient ways.

WOMEN AND THE *RAMAYANA* IN TRINIDAD

The most long-standing dimension of the Trinidad *Ramayana* tradition is undoubtedly the Ramleela, the first performance of which was staged in 1888 in Dow Village, California, in Central Trinidad. Although modern technological, economic and educational advancements led to gradual changes in the drama's form, physical setting, grandeur and scale, the content remained relatively standard. Indeed, the dramatic form of the Ramleela served as a very effective means of incorporating uniquely Trinidadian issues and elements into the *Ramayana* tradition. Derek Walcott referred to the Ramleela performance in the village of Felicity in Trinidad as both a metaphor of history and a vital aspect of the Indian attempt at community reconstruction within the diasporic context.[29]

Social changes, directly related to the role and position of women, were persistently evident in the Ramleela. Before the 1960s the drama was performed solely by men, who undertook various preparatory acts such as a three-month fasting period (intended to purify both body and mind). Throughout the performance of the Ramleela the major actors lived together in *kutiyas* (temples or sheds provided by a supportive villager). These arrangements prevented the introduction of women actors before the 1960s. The absence of women in the Ramleela was compounded by socio-cultural constraints that relegated the woman largely to the home, the censorious attitude among Hindus towards female performers and public performances, and the ritual impurity assigned to menstruation. During the 1960s, however, female performers began their incursion into the Ramleela arena. At first their roles were minuscule and largely restricted to communal scenes where the entire audience could be integrated into the performance (such as when Bharat goes into the forest with an entourage to meet his brother Rama, Rama's return to Ayodhya, and even Rama and Sita's wedding).

By the 1970s, though, women were portraying major characters in many of the productions. The still widely perceived stigma of impurity associated with menstruation saw a predominance of pre-pubertal girls performing such parts, rather than adult women. By the 1990s, attitudes to this issue echoed wider attempts to navigate between the dictates of religious doctrine and traditional practices and a more rational and analytical approach to religious matters tempered by increasing infiltration of Western and secular considerations.

The major female roles were commonly portrayed by women (indeed it would now seem out of place to witness a man portraying female roles), with astute calculation and navigation of the menstrual cycle being a major deciding factor in the choice of the female actors. It is interesting to note that at a Ramleela performance in the village of Lopinot in 1995, all of the characters – both male and female – were portrayed by females, a possible metaphor for the increasing reversal of traditional gender roles among Hindus.

Scenes and tales from the *Ramayana* were also depicted in dance and dance-dramas by both visiting and local companies. In a 1992 article in the *Sunday Guardian,* the Shankar Kala Kendra's all-local production of a *Ramayana* ballet was praised as "one of the most detailed versions of the *Ramayana* ever staged in Trinidad . . . an eye opener in that it added authentic touches to hazy areas of that great Hindu scriptural text".[30] The National Council for Indian Culture facilitated several Indian productions and ballets of the *Ramayana* at its annual Divali celebrations at the Divali Nagar site.[31] Many of the performers were females who portrayed both male and female characters. In addition to such formal stage productions, the more informal Sarwan Kumar dance-drama[32] was embedded in the story of the *Ramayana*. Presented primarily in English, the dialogue and related anecdotes actively connected the story to contemporary life, inevitably lending a Trinidadian feel to the whole production. However, until its demise during the 1980s, the actors in this local dance-drama were solely men.

Women also contributed to various art forms which comprised the local *Ramayana* tradition. Scenes from the *Ramayana* were depicted on murals in public and private temples and at various socio-religious events. *Murtis* (images of a deity) and paintings in varying sizes of the major characters reflected the varying stages of artistic development. The sanctity that enshrouds the *Ramayana* tradition was evident even here. As reported in the *Sunday Guardian*, one female *murti* maker affirmed that "the making of the *murti* of *Shri Ram* is in itself a worship, a *Sadhana* [worship]".[33] Other handiwork reflecting motifs and scenes from the *Ramayana* included pottery and clay wind chimes.

Trinidadian writers, especially but not exclusively Indo-Trinidadians, contributed yet another dimension to the *Ramayana* tradition by drawing upon and working into their novels and short stories various aspects of the relationship between the *Ramayana* and Hindu women. In Seepersad Naipaul's *The*

Adventures of Gurudeva, the wife of the protagonist, who suffers brutal beatings by her husband, and her sisters-in-law ponder on yet resign themselves to their fate: "They had ever heard it taught by their fathers, by the elders of the village, as well as by the pundits who often read the Ramayana on evenings, that the husband was to the wife God, lord and master – all in one – and that a woman's highest virtue lay in her absolute submission to her husband's will – be that will of whatever complexion."[34] Yet, even as early as the 1930s and 1940s, there is a growing awareness of and dissatisfaction with the imbalance that has characterized husband–wife relations among Indians. One of the sisters-in-law opines: "It is all a very one-sided operation. They want us all to be like Sita – that is, to try as far as possible to be like her; but on the other hand, they are far from being like Rama . . . they do not even try. It is not fair."[35]

In her novel *Butterfly in the Wind*, Lakshmi Persaud emphasizes the role that interpretation of the *Ramayana* plays in the formation of morals and values, and refers to the notion that brides should be like "Rama's Sita". In *For the Love of My Name*, Persaud details how the *Ramayana* story has continued to influence the position and expectations of Hindu women and, seemingly paradoxically, how gradual but steady changes in their lives have generated variant approaches to related issues in the text. The female protagonist in the *Ramayana*, the self-sacrificing, loyal and obedient Sita, is depicted as the epitome of Hindu womanhood, and hence the ultimate model of female behaviour and values. Yet the female characters in Persaud's novel, drawing on their respective experiences and changing social contexts, vehemently question the treatment of Sita in the *Ramayana*, especially her having to undergo a fire test to prove her chastity. They ultimately recognize that "people are no longer like the heroes and heroines of the *Ramayana*, are they?"[36] In his *Yesterdays*, Harold Sonny Ladoo makes ample reference to the entire abduction image involving Rama, Sita and Ravan.[37]

Women have been the main propagators of various types of Indian folksongs in Trinidad. Such songs as *biraha, jhoomar, chowtaal* and *bhajans* comprised a salient aspect of the musical dimension of the local *Ramayana* tradition. While most carried religious connotations, those that were not restricted to solely religious settings but formed a vital part of wedding celebrations and other more secular forums sometimes de-emphasized the religious to highlight the more contextually suitable aspects. Such verses included, from a *biraha*, "*Raam ji ke bagiya / Sita ke phoolwaari / Latchiman devar rakhwaari*" [In Ram's flower garden Sita is the flower and Lakshman is the watchman], and "*Raamji ke shobha dekh Siyaji ke man lobhaa / Jhaak jharokha laagee nandani Janak ki* [The moment Sita saw Raam in Janakpur she fell in love], from a local classical song. Thus locally composed verses, while conferring the sanctity of the *Ramayana* onto the occasion but not directly invoking the religious dimension, somehow facilitated early inclusion of the *Ramayana* in settings where alcohol, ganja, meat-eating and hip-swaying were not uncommon. This inadvertently paved the way for a much later controversy surrounding the use of religious lyrics in secular forums, such as "chutney singing" and other cultural events.

By the late 1980s the emergence of what is termed chutney music from the confines of the home and immediate community into the public, non-Hindu eye led to contentious interplay between the religious and textual elements of this art form, as well as its increasing status as essentially secular entertainment. The most troublesome point was embedded in the juxtaposition of "wining" (in Trinidad this term refers to sexually suggestive gyrations of the hips), and the generally sensuous (some would say lewd) dancing that chutney music seems to evoke, with references to the *Ramayana* and other religious literature in the lyrics. Since this interplay of the religious and the secular has always been an integral aspect of local Indian folk music, one can surmise that the points of contention resided in contemporary socio-religious issues. These included concern about the public perception of Hindus, an increasing trend towards standardization, and a conscious or subconscious attempt to emulate the decidedly more clear-cut dichotomy between the sacred and the secular evident in the major Christian religions in Trinidad. A concerted move to institute more orthodox (one can surmise Brahminic) beliefs and systems into a traditionally diverse Hindu community also marked this conflict. Interestingly enough, while almost everyone will verbally disapprove of sensuous dancing to religious lyrics, many – probably intoxicated by both the rhythmic beat of the music and alcohol and not too concerned in the moment with separating the sacred from the profane – will participate in such activities. Though arguable, this type of duplicity is not unexpected within the context of the pervasive, fluid and diverse nature of Hinduism.

LIFE-CYCLE RITUALS

Both Hindu women and the *Ramayana* are important aspects of the major life-cycle rituals of birth, marriage and death which comprise the major socio-religious events in the lives of most Hindus. Changes in the rituals mirrored the evolution of the socio-religious aspect of Trinidad Hinduism and, by extension, changes in the attitude towards the *Ramayana*. Until the 1970s a vital aspect of the sixth- and twelfth-day birth rituals (*chhati* and *barahi* respectively) was the celebratory singing of songs by women to vigorous beating of the *dholak*, bottle and spoon, *lota* and spoon or coin, and *majeera*. Many of those songs depicted the birth and childhood of Rama and his brothers. A typical example is the following:

> *Are Brahma diye bardaan raja ghar beta bhaiyaa. . . .*
> *Kowsilya ghar Rama, Sumitra ghar Latchiman,*
> *Aur Kaikeyi Ghar Bharat Bhuwala, Raja ghar . . .*
> [God gave you a blessing, a gift of this child . . . .
> In Kowsilya's home, Rama; in Sumitra's home, Lakshman,
> And in Kaikeyi's home Bharat was born . . . .]

The celebrations almost always entailed consumption of alcohol and meat, in which the singers themselves often participated. This suggests that, from the very earliest stages of Trinidad Hinduism, there was a very blurred line between the religious and the secular, between the sacred and the profane, between prescribed orthodoxy and popular folk culture. By the 1970s an increasing preference for delivering babies in the hospital rather than at home resulted in rapid decline in the performance of this life-cycle ritual and, consequently, this aspect of the *Ramayana* tradition. There was a discordance between hospital birth and modern postpartum care for both child and mother and the traditional practices that surrounded home births. By the 1990s the sixth- and twelfth-day ceremonies were still sporadically observed, but the focus of the celebration was more on presenting gifts to the newborn. The live singing that facilitated the infusion of the *Ramayana* was replaced by a plethora of readily available pre-recorded chutney and Hindi film music.

The *Ramayana*'s impact on the Hindu wedding ceremony has been more substantial, enduring and diverse. While there was no direct reading of the text, the formal and informal discourse during the ceremony entailed elaborate descriptions of the marriage of Rama and Sita, emphasizing the divine couple as a role model for the newlyweds. Within this context, verses from the *Ramcharitmanas* were recited. The actual wedding vows did not originate in the *Ramayana* but rather from the Dharma Sastras; they were compiled into the Vivaah Padathi, or "Wedding Texts". However, it was not uncommon for the officiating priest, in order to augment the vows' cogency, to verbally situate them within the context of Rama and Sita's wedding in the *Ramayana*.

While there may not have been much variation in the choice of verses at wedding ceremonies, the points of emphasis were reworked, especially with regard to spousal relations. Before the 1970s, the prominence of some verses suggesting divine ascriptions to the persona and office of the husband and stressing total wifely dedication to him echoed the predominant character of Hindu husband–wife relations during that period. A good example is the following: "*Binu sram naari param gati lahaee. Pati vrata dharma chhaari chhal gahaee*" [Those wives who without guile take a vow of fidelity towards their husbands, attain with the greatest ease the eternal gift of salvation], and "*Saasu sasur gur sevaa karehoo, pati rukh lakhi aayasu anusarehoo*" [Serve the parents of your husband and other elders and do the bidding of your lord according to his pleasure.][38] By the 1980s reliance on such verses was disappearing in the face of a new-found emphasis on the importance of mutual understanding and cooperation between wife and husband. The timing and degree of such transformations simultaneously depended on and reflected the extent and nature of the social, economic and religious transformation occurring within both the Hindu community and the wider society.

However, what really cemented the *Ramayana*'s impact on the Hindu wedding ceremony was the fact that, despite the transformations generated by time, place and circumstance, the core rituals and their basic format corresponded significantly to those contained in the *Ramcharitmanas*. The emphasis placed on operating within the prescribed auspicious times, the ceremonious but celebratory reception and departure of the bridegroom's party, the application of *sindoor*, circumambulation of the ritual fire, the tying together of the bride's and groom's garments, the tying and untying of the sacred thread around the couple's wrists as protection against evil forces, along with the general decor, festivities and forms of entertainment are just some of the points of similarity.[39] The singing of wedding songs at the *matikor* ceremony and on the wedding day itself was another aspect of the *Ramayana* in which women took precedence. Songs such as "Siya Dale Ram Gale Jai Mala" ["Sita has placed the marriage garland around Rama's neck"], which depicted parallel scenes of Rama and Sita's wedding, were often sung by groups of women throughout the wedding ceremony.

In light of the role of the *Ramayana* in the wedding ceremony, the variety in Hindu wedding types provided an interesting paradox. If the *Ramayana* was such an influential factor in this ceremony, what then accounted for the flourishing of other marriage styles? One can point to prevailing socio-economic trends and conditions. During the earliest period of indenture, the "sit-down" relationship, in which a couple quite frequently just started living together, was a common form of union. This was on account of the disparity in the male–female ratio and the uncertainty and general instability of that period. In addition, the high level of both male and female infidelity during this time would have deterred active inclusion of the *Ramayana* into marriage rituals, since it promoted essentially monogamous behaviour. The emergence of Indian villages from the 1880s onwards stimulated a focus on community and family reconstitution and led to reconstruction of fragments of the traditional Hindu wedding ceremony. This facilitated the *Ramayana*'s entrenchment in the Hindu psyche and its incursion into the ceremony and ideology of marriage. Eventually the ceremony depicted in the *Ramayana* became the prime model. This was a result of the intense socio-religious activity of the first three decades after the end of Indian indenture, the markedly higher level of stability in conjugal relationships which was then achieved, and wide subscription to the ideal of monogamy as advocated in the *Ramayana*.

THE *RAMAYANA* TRADITION AS DOCTRINE

The *Ramayana* has always had an undeniable impact on the position and role of women in both the family and the society at large. The essentially patriarchal family system that developed during the early post-indentureship period held Sita – chaste, submissive, faithful and loyal to her husband – as the highest ideal of womanhood. In addition, several incidents in the *Ramayana* highlight the "inherently inferior and potentially dangerous and wicked nature of women",[40] while some verses refer to women in the same breath as animals and untouchables.[41] Verses such as this also served to cement the notion of women as morally, intellectually, spiritually, physically and socially inferior to men: *"Mahaabrishti chali phooti kiaaree, jimi sutantra bhae bigarahi naaree"* [The embankments of the fields have been breached by rains just as women get spoiled by freedom].[42]

The character of Sita and the general *Ramayana* ideology were also used to discourage transformations in the traditional concept of the Hindu woman. This was duly reflected in Seepersad Naipaul's article in the *East Indian Weekly* titled "Dangerous Feminine Evolution", in which he condemned the growing affinity of Indian women for Western fashion: "The advent of bobism in the Trinidad world? What of the inglorious styles . . . and their garments? Cannot these atrocities be helped . . . to clip the hair to enhance the beauty is a wasteful and ridiculous excess." He further supported his position with this quote from the *Ramcharitmanas*: *"Chalat kupanth veda maga chhanday. Kapat kalewara kali-mali bhanday."* [Treading the path of unrighteousness they have forsaken the doctrines of the Vedas; deceit being their food in Kaliyug.][43]

Although exceptions did occur, such perceptions of women persisted until the socio-economic transformations of the 1970s. Since then, and especially since the 1980s, a number of issues have demanded constant reconsideration of both the *Ramcharitmanas'* and some of the reciters' projections of women. Such issues include the changing concept of the ideal Indian wife and woman; the increasing sense of individualism among Hindu women; the changing role of women in rites, rituals and religion; the rapidly increasing numbers of women in almost all occupational fields; and the shifts in priority. The following excerpt from the *Sunday Guardian* (1996) provides an apt example of such reinterpretations. The article analyses Sita "as an individual in her own right" who challenges her husband for not wanting her to accompany him to the forest, confronts and chastises her abductor Ravan, holds herself in very high esteem and marries only he who proves worthy of her. "The woman of the '90s must emulate Tulsidas' Lakshmi by standing on her own, if necessary, to make a positive statement of her own self worth by not following the crowd, by not giving in to circumstances but constantly striving to be true to herself, her Devihood."[44]

It is quite interesting to note, though, that while Sita was idealized for her womanly and wifely virtues, in the local Hindu tradition this figure never attained the prominence of the other, more aggressive and independent female deities such as Lakshmi, Durga and Kali. Until the early twentieth century, the extremely active role of women in the reconstitution of the Indian community and their status as "valuable property" could have accounted for their preference for the more action-oriented, distinctive and even combative representations of womanhood instead of one who complied with all of her husband's wishes and was, in effect, defined by him. It can be argued that, since the 1980s, this tendency was reinforced by the advent of the "independent and modern" Hindu woman. Even during the period from 1930 to the 1970s, which was dominated by patriarchal values, the figure of Sita never attained the status and popularity of the more independent female deities.

From as early as the 1920s there were female *Ramayana* readers in Trinidad. One such young woman, who was admired by her fellow villagers for her "beautiful chanting of the *Ramayana* and other Hindu scriptures", even caught the attention of the Presbyterian missionaries; she was eventually converted to Presbyterianism.[45] Possibly the most blatant (though singular) example of the challenge to male priestly supremacy was the initiation in 1943 of a non-Brahmin woman, Deokie Devi, as a pundit. A notice in the *Trinidad Guardian*, together with her picture, read:

> First Sanatan Woman Pundit in Trinidad, Shrimattee Deokie Devi, 22 year old daughter of pundit Ramlalak of Couva, will appear in public for the first time on February 25 to perform the ceremony of the Sri Satnarine Katha at the San Fernando Hindu Temple. Pundit Shrimattee Devi is trained in Hindu Vedic Philosophy, Hindi and Sanskrit and comes from a family of four pundits. She is the granddaughter of the late Hindu priest, Lal Beharry of India.[46]

The reaction towards female *Ramayana* readers was ambivalent. The intrinsic love and affinity for the *Ramayana* among ordinary people served to suppress outright condemnation of female readers. However, the patriarchal norms and attitudes of the pre-1970s period, enhanced by the many ritual prescriptions that served to socially subjugate women, restricted textual presentation by women in terms of both frequency and scope. Both the idea and the reality of female presence on the sacred *singhasan* (throne) evoked interesting responses which reflected the varying trends of thought within Trinidad Hinduism. The prevalent attitude of the priesthood, both Brahmin and non-Brahmin, was one of grudging resignation to women "preaching Hinduism" and even reading the *Ramayana*, but only in informal settings, and definitely not on the *singhasan* at *yagnas*, a series of religious rites and ceremonial readings spanning five to fourteen days. Their arguments were founded largely upon scriptural prescriptions and the impurities associated with the menstrual cycle. This, however, was tempered by the reality of female socio-economic and intellectual advancement and the enhanced religious position and role of women, especially within many of the rapidly increasing Hindu groups. Attempts to simultaneously retain male and Brahminic monopoly in this sphere and to accommodate the mindset of the contemporary Hindu woman, and society at large, elicited responses such as the following to the issue: "When we look at our scriptural texts we are hard-pressed to find evidence of women holding priestly positions. Women have been assigned a very honorable position, a very high position in that they are the *Devi,* the very Goddess in our homes. . . . It is not to say that women are debarred from elevating themselves spiritually."[47]

It is evident that Hindu women were able either to break out of or to work around the bonds of scriptural and traditional prescriptions in almost all other aspects of their lives. However, notwithstanding the more liberal approach to women of some new organizations such as the Hindu Prachar Kendra and the Trinidad Academy of Hinduism, popular opinion until the 1990s revealed reservations towards (though not as deep-seated or as endemic) or outright non-acceptance of women acting as ritual and textual specialists. Non-acceptance was more marked, especially in the *yagna* setting. This echoed both a characteristic reluctance in the religious sphere to effect such a monumental transformation and the still prevailing, though often denied, patriarchal tendencies of the Hindu community. Nevertheless, the 1990s witnessed the first formal *Ramayana yagnas* conducted by a woman.

The major argument against female involvement in certain rituals and formal textual interpretation was the "impurity" assigned to menstruation. One wonders, given the sometimes erratic nature of the cycle, how feasible it indeed was to schedule discourses around this period of unsuitability. One can surmise that the earlier pundit Deokie Devi, given the fastidious adherence to the taboo at that time, would have had to resort to having another pundit perform her religious duties or have them rescheduled. Interestingly, sometimes the terse yet pregnant excuse "I am not fit to read today" would convey everything.[48] Since the 1980s, however, female readers have displayed a relatively laxer attitude to this issue. While most continue to abstain from readings during their menstrual period, some admit to having participated in the reading but refraining from physically touching the text. This usually occurred when the individual was at odds with the stigma of impurity allotted to menstruation, or, paradoxically, out of sheer embarrassment at having to discuss such a personal matter with the usually elderly and respected male leader of the group. A few, justifying their pragmatic approach to the issue with the notion that the menstrual cycle is "God's work", participate in all aspects of the discourse.

Possibly the major issue that engaged Trinidad Hindus was Rama's treatment and ultimate banishment of his wife, Sita. While great care was exercised not to question Rama's characteristically impeccable judgement and just actions, the apparent injustice inflicted upon that "epitome of wifely devotion" increasingly mandated interpretations that catered to the social, intellectual and cultural dictates of both time and place. Thus the dominant explanation that Rama's status as a king, duty-bound to his subjects, took precedence over his role as a husband seemed to provide the most acceptable resolution of the issue. In what might be termed a direct reflection of patriarchal attitudes, this issue, especially before the 1980s, was downplayed, sidestepped or even ignored, with emphasis being placed instead on Sita's unwavering wifely devotion – "like a Gibraltar Rock"[49] – to her husband. In addition, Rama's "deliberate display of human fallibility" and the strategic highlighting of verses attesting to the "fickle nature" of women (though never aimed directly at Sita) were enough to steer the audience away from any deep reservations about his actions.

Poetic licence was capitalized upon – sometimes to the extreme – leading to explanations of Sita's banishment in her asking to return to the forest alone[50] or in her promise to the sages of the forest that she would return,[51] with the point of ambiguity being the length of her sojourn. By the 1990s many interpreters also chose to focus on her retribution at the end of the epic (where, despite his ardent requests, she refuses to return to her husband and opts instead to descend into the earth with her mother), highlighting her preserved dignity both amid and in spite of the adversities she encounters. Tied to the issue of Sita's banishment was the fact that she was pregnant at the time. While the text does give evidence that Rama was aware of the pregnancy, it was almost the norm to claim that he was not; the social and moral stigma attached to deserting a pregnant wife cut across time in its severity. Thus, having the god/hero desert his wife for the "greater good" is one thing, but doing so while she is pregnant would not have been as easily digested in a society that placed considerable emphasis on the sanctity of family life and considered their offspring as their "riches". Many, even those in positions of socio-religious authority, expressed their "personal difficulty" in reconciling Rama's banishment of his wife. However, the conflict inherent in attempting to reconcile religion and absolute objectivity aborted the few concerted attempts at treating the issue objectively. One pundit claiming such aspirations was promptly cautioned by a "senior learned person in the field" that "if you continue like this people will discredit Rama . . . you are giving them too much of a new concept of Sita which they would not be able to accept".[52]

The validity of the *Ramcharitmanas* as social doctrine is evident in the great influence which the ethics, morals and values of the text have had on Hindus in Trinidad. That the story has a historical base makes the author's instruction more effective, for people can feel that whatever is taught was actually once practised by persons and is not mere precept. These codes of conduct are presented through concrete, convincing characters in crisis situations, rendering them more easily digestible than abstract philosophical and moral expression. Hindu family life in Trinidad has been greatly influenced by the values prevalent in the *Ramcharitmanas*. The text highlights various forms of interpersonal relationships, outlines acceptable tenets of behaviour and provides role models for almost all categories: Rama is the ideal husband and son; Sita is the ideal wife, daughter and daughter-in-law; Bharat and Lakshman are the ideal brothers; Hanuman and Sugriva are the ideal friends. From the time of daily recitals of the *Ramcharitmanas* in the plantation barracks, the text continued to refresh the strong Indian tradition of family life. However, since the 1970s, major changes within the Hindu family in terms of its structure, function and ideology prompted recasting of the text.

The transformation of Hindu family structure – from extended to increasingly nuclear – mandated a grudging de-emphasis of the structure and values of the traditional extended family during textual discourses. This had considerable bearing on the ideology and reality surrounding the lives of Hindu women. Though the extended family was still held up as the ideal, the lived reality, characterized by increasing disagreements among in-laws, arguments over inheritance rights, and the changing dynamics of husband–wife relations, increasingly persuaded reciters of the text to tone down emphasis on this ideal. The decline of the extended family arrangement usually meant that immediate family members no longer lived close to each other, and this often diluted the intensity of emotional bonds. During textual and verbal discourse, this led to attempts to work the values and ideals of the extended family system into the nuclear system. Thus, while Rama's dedication to his father and the love that exists among the four brothers were still accentuated, situations such as the four brothers living together with their respective families in the same home and Sita's unwavering dedication to her in-laws were either reconsidered or downplayed. Consequently, instead of focusing on Sita's unquestioning obedience to her in-laws, as would have been done before the 1970s, now mutual respect, love and admiration were emphasized as the defining and desirable traits of that particular relationship. This was reinforced by verses such as

> *Main puni putrabadhoo priya paaee. Roop raasi guna seel suhaaee. Nayan putari kari preeti bardhaaee. Raakheu praan Jaanakihi laaee.* [Again I have found in her a beloved daughter-in-law, who is amiable and accomplished, and beauty personified. I have treated her as the very apple of my eye and loved her ever more; nay, my very life is centred in Janaki {Sita}.][53]
> *Tumha kahu ban sab bhaati supaasoo. Sang pitu maatu Raamu Siya jaasu.* [You will be happy in every way in the forest since you will have with you your father and mother in Rama and Sita.][54]

Throughout the first half of the twentieth century, the ideal of husband–wife relations was based on loyalty and support of each spouse to the other and sanctioned by the *Ramayana,* wherein both the hero, Rama, and his wife, Sita, observed monogamy. Though monogamy was held as the ideal among Trinidad Hindus, there were digressions on the parts of both spouses. These digressions, viewed against the ideal, impacted directly on the status of the individual within both the family and the larger community. The most glaring aspect of this was the discrepancy in attitude towards males and females. Amid a mixture of pious castigation, grudging admiration and sometimes not-so-secret approval and understanding, the social standing of the adulterous male remained relatively intact, especially when it was suspected that the wife was barren. It may even be said that extramarital relationships were covertly expected of the more prominent men in the community. In the case of those whose status was based on ritual purity, such as the Brahmins and the pundits, there was a more pronounced effect. This involved a combination of largely private ridicule and a decline in the individual's viability as a religious leader, yet, paradoxically, continued faithful following by his disciples.[55]

Women, on the other hand, were still viewed as the "receptacles of the ancestral seed", the sustainers of the lineage, the foundation of family life and honour and those through whose fidelity male sexual prowess was measured. Straying wives were heavily reprimanded, ridiculed, beaten and even ostracized by immediate family members, and often the community as well. As a female interviewee now in her sixties explained, "If as soon as he [husband] leave to go with a next woman I take up with a man, they [society] will say she was just waiting for this man to leave to take up somebody. Then they wouldn't think anything good about me . . . but whatever a man do was well done."[56]

The status of Hindu women during this period was highly conditioned by a desire to control female sexuality through child marriages, glorifying female reproductive powers and preferring sons over daughters. The prevailing attitude was further marked by a lack of sympathy for widows and for widow remarriage and by glorifying women whose husbands were alive, deeming them a source of prosperity and assigning exclusively to them certain rituals and rites. The selective shaping of religious texts and doctrines aided this viewpoint. Verses from the *Ramayana* cemented both the ritually and socially inferior position of women, for example, "*Sahaj apaavanee naaree patin sevat gati lahai*" [A woman is impure by her very birth; but she attains a happy state (hereafter) by serving her lord].[57]

The strong perception of menstruation as "unclean" and not compatible with spirituality also contributed to the inferior position of women on the ritual scale. Menstruating women were forbidden from entering any consecrated space, from having any kind of contact with religious paraphernalia and from cooking for Brahmins; indeed, they possessed an innate feeling of impurity.[58] Western notions concerning this issue would not influence Hindu thought for a very long time. However, local factors did serve to uplift the value of women. These comprised the highly prized position of Indian women during the indenture and immediate post-indenture periods, when they were in scarce supply, and their continued status as breadwinners of the family. Amid the essentially patriarchal values and ideology that characterized Hinduism during this period, "women invariably negotiate[d] within their domestic spaces for changes which [would] improve the conditions of their lives and that of their families".[59]

From 1945 until about the 1960s, the lives of Hindu women were heavily influenced by socio-religious prescriptions which "drew heavily upon sexual imagery transmitted through myths, cultural symbols, artifacts, religious rituals and festivals, which expressed ideas about what constituted male and female characteristics and behavior".[60] Thus, although it was not uncommon for wealthier or more urban Hindu families to consent to their daughters either going abroad to study or engaging in occupations outside the immediate community, even they shared the general consensus that the woman's place was in the home, as daughter, wife and mother. Yet Hindu women had always been able to amicably and astutely navigate patriarchal restrictions while aspiring (though not always successfully) to some sense of self and personal fulfilment. One should remember, though, that during this period even such aspirations were subconsciously defined to a great extent by traditional codes and values and textual prescriptions. Hence the character of Sita in the *Ramcharitmanas,* who demonstrates unwavering loyalty, support and devotion to her husband, was emphasized as the model for Hindu wives. It is not surprising then that, according to oral sources, the acquisition of a moneyed and socially affluent husband who would ensure a secure and promising life for the woman, her offspring and maybe even her relatives could be identified as the highest aspiration of most Hindu women before the 1960s.

However, for the majority of Hindus, the idea of the woman's place being in the home was more socio-religious idealism than lived reality. During the period of Indian indenture, Indian women were working women. After indenture, women continued to work alongside their husbands, families and friends on sugar and cocoa estates and on private garden plots.[61] But by the 1960s the growing number of Hindu women opting for non-agricultural jobs was treated with a mixture of scorn, disapproval, resignation and superficial admiration. This gravitation to non-agricultural jobs was due to the increase in primary and, to a lesser extent, secondary education among Hindu women, enhanced by growing assimilation of non-Indian ideas, values and lifestyles. Since Hindu women had been working outside the physical space of the home and immediate community since the period of indenture, one can surmise that the point of irritation in the 1960s resided in the alien nature of the occupations rather than in the actual idea of working. Also, the physical and social settings of many of the later occupations were often at variance with the established norms of the Indian community, and the absence of male relatives to "protect the virtue" of the women (and, by extension, of the family) in such settings further aggravated the point. However, according to oral sources, unsupervised interaction between Hindu women and men of African descent was probably the cause of the most deep-seated concern.

Such points of aggravation in turn created the foundation of what would eventually become, by the late 1970s, a hotly debated issue within the Hindu community: the "traditional Hindu woman" versus the "modern woman" – dichotomy or compatibility? Although persistence of varying degrees of the traditional idealistic prescriptions for Hindu women could be noted, there was nevertheless a growing awareness (albeit sometimes grudgingly) of the need to redefine their role and position. The Hindu woman's physical and ideological exodus from the confines of the parameters of home and immediate community into the wider Trinidad society was accelerated during the 1980s. This was brought about by the harsh economic conditions of the post-oil-boom period, socio-economic aspirations and women's substantially high levels of academic achievement.

According to Vertovec's survey of the village of Penal Rock Road, in 1960 40 per cent of the employed women worked in agriculture, 43 per cent in manual labour and 15 per cent in non-manual jobs. By 1980 the figures had shifted to 4 per cent, 18 per cent and 76 per cent respectively.[62] The most popular occupations among working women included clerical and sales-related work, service jobs and certain professional and technical positions.[63] However, certain occupations, such as waitressing and working on the US military base, were often regarded with suspicion. Both oral sources and literary works about the Indian community confirmed this attitude. For example, in Seepersad Naipaul's *The Adventures of Gurudeva,* the protagonist's love interest, Daisy, is a young Indian woman who works on the American base. She is totally Westernized in dress, speech and general comportment, openly flaunts her liaisons with American sailors and manages to divert Gurudeva's affections away from his wife and towards herself.[64]

The acknowledgement, if not acceptance, by the major socio-religious organizations of the changing position and function of Hindu women was evident in the number of activities focusing on women organized during the religious ferment of the 1980s. In 1985 the women's arm of the Sanatan Dharma Maha Sabha (SDMS) held a Sangha Shakti Sammelan (Hindu Women's Conference). During that same year, the National Council for Indian Culture

(NCIC) staged the first ever women's singing competition, which was to become a very popular annual event. According to reports in the *Express*, the Caribbean Hindu Centre and the Hindu Swayamsevak Sangh jointly organized an awards distribution ceremony in commemoration of the United Nations Decade of the Woman (1975–85).[65] It should be noted that, notwithstanding their intent, the sporadic and arguably superficial nature and approach of most of these events prevented them from having any substantial impact on the role and position of Hindu women in Trinidad.

Quite predictably, changes in the role of women evoked varied responses reflecting the specific fears, concerns and transformations within the Hindu community. The more traditional yet socially aware, probably in an attempt to defend the traditional role of Hindu women and, by extension, Hinduism itself, expressed concerns such as the following:

> There are social norms which our women folk must not cross . . . but some women do and then society degenerates . . . . Women cannot do certain things that the opposite gender can do, you cannot go certain places that the opposite gender can go because you are the female species; you are the hunted one by the male. The Hindu woman is not a passive woman . . . . She has invented the ideal leadership role: she leads her husband, her family and her community from behind. She is the leader in every community. But to go up to the microphone and make speeches and so on, she leaves that to the others . . . shaking hands, she leaves that to the others . . . this is the culture of the Hindu woman.[66]

Several explanations can be proffered for the exclusion of handshaking from "the culture of the Hindu woman". The social interaction and "assertiveness" that the gesture suggests, especially with members of the opposite sex, contradict the not uncommonly held notion that the Hindu woman should "lead from behind". The physical contact of this essentially non-Hindu gesture both reinforces the contradiction and seems to bring the "hunted" in closer proximity to the "hunter".[67]

According to a report in the *Trinidad Guardian*, at the launching of the Caribbean Hindu Conference in 1987, the main speaker, Anantanand Rambachand, described the position of Hindu women as "still spiritually and socially consigned to an inferior status", notwithstanding considerable advances in several areas.[68] Most interviewees for this study agreed that Hindu women were striking a good balance between their customary and newer roles. However, concern for the preservation of family and religious life remained paramount, as evidenced by the following comments.

> Hindu women are very nicely marrying both traditions and keeping the dharma alive. But the problems occur when the family is under stress – poverty, woman seeking independence from male control.[69]

> Now Hindu women are going out of the homes. There can be temptations and there is potential for disruption in the family life; family may suffer. If they can manage a balance between both, then it can work.[70]

Thus it seems that by the 1990s, the concern resided in whether the Hindu woman could function as effectively in both roles, without detracting from her roles as mother, wife and primary preserver of Hindu religious and cultural traditions, rather than in whether she should be "in the home" or "a working woman". One wonders, though, if this concern for the welfare of the family was totally free of a hidden agenda, namely the preservation of male control. The fear of women being "more susceptible" to committing adultery also persisted. However, it was about more than just succumbing to temptation; the fear seemed to be rooted in uncertainty about how the "new Hindu woman" would react to the shortcomings of her spouse.

CONCLUSION

The foregoing examination of women and the *Ramayana* tradition in Trinidad has yielded a number of salient points. Since their very beginnings in Trinidad, Hindu women have played a vital role in the development and persistence of the *Ramayana* tradition. Their contribution to the various dimensions of the tradition works symbiotically to colour the face of the evolving *Ramayana* tradition in Trinidad, while echoing the changes and developments taking place among both Hindu women and the larger Hindu community. In their role as primary transmitters of culture, Hindu women are substantially responsible for the survival of the *Ramayana* tradition in Trinidad. Thus they have played a key role in the evolution of that tradition as both mirror and metaphor of the Hindu experience in Trinidad.

The endurance and dissemination of the *Ramayana* tradition within

Trinidad's multicultural society and its tight relationship with Hindu women through the periods of indenture, community reconstruction, conflict and affirmation echo the dynamism and flexibility that have enabled the tradition to both flourish and function as a voice for women globally throughout the Indian diaspora. Judging by the endurance and function of the more long-standing *Ramayana* traditions in India, Asia and other countries of the diaspora, one can surmise that the past 160 years has essentially been a period of establishment of the *Ramayana* tradition. During this time it has emerged as an integral dimension of the lives of Hindu women, but one which is still substantially influenced by the values, cultural nuances and systems of the Indian subcontinent.

In the twenty-first century the stage is now fully set to explore whether Hindu women will, like the Southall Black Sisters in Britain, engage in a higher level of dialogue with the *Ramayana* tradition in Trinidad, one that could possibly shed even more of its exclusively Hindu application. Conversely, the nostalgia for the traditional that is constantly being fed by Hinduism's propensity for continuity amid change could work towards deterring the weaning away of the tradition from its ancestral homeland, India. Either way, Hindu women and the *Ramayana* will continue to have a dynamic and profound relationship, not just in Trinidad but throughout the Indian subcontinent and the Indian diaspora.

APPENDIX: A BRIEF SYNOPSIS OF THE *RAMAYANA*

This is Tulsidas's version of the *Ramayana* story. It tells the story of Rama, believed to be a divine incarnation, who has assumed human form in order to rid the earth of social and religious menaces. After many barren years, Dashratha, king of Ayodhya, and his three queens have been blessed with four sons: Rama, by senior queen Kaushalya; Bharat and Lakshmana, by Kaikeyi; and Shatrughana, by Sumitra. The king sends the four young princes with the sage Vishwamitra to rid the sages living in the forest of the atrocities of the *rakshasas* (demons). Mission accomplished, Vishwamitra proceeds with the princes to Mithila, where the king, Janaka, is staging a bow-breaking ceremony for the marriage of his daughter, Sita. Rama succeeds in breaking the bow and marries Sita, while his three brothers are wed to three of her immediate relatives.

Back in Ayodhya, Dashratha prepares to install Rama as prince regent. However, perverted by her personal maid Manthara, Queen Kaikeyi recalls two boons promised to her by the king, demanding that her son Bharat be installed as prince regent and that Rama be banished to the forest for fourteen years. Bound by his word, the king is forced to accede to her demands. Thus Rama, honouring his father's oath, graciously leaves for the forest, accompanied by his wife, Sita, and his brother Lakshmana. The king, overcome by grief, expires, and Bharat, refusing to accept the kingship, proceeds to the forest in search of Rama. Rama, however, citing his duty to fulfil his father's promise, refuses to return. An adamant Bharat returns only after acquiring Rama's sandals, which he enthrones at Ayodhya, only then acquiescing to rule in Rama's name from his austere abode at Nandigrama.

During their sojourn in the forest, Rama and Lakshmana destroy numerous demons and meet with various saints and sages. Incited by his cousin, the demoness Surpanakha, the demon king Ravana abducts Sita. During their search for her, the brothers encounter and form alliances with the monkey king Sugriva and Hanuman. In return for Rama's slaying his brother Vali, King Sugriva and his army of monkeys and bears assist Rama in the search for his wife, who is eventually discovered at Ravana's palace garden in the city of Lanka.

Despite a series of appeals from his kinsmen, Ravana refuses to return Sita. After a raging battle which leads to the destruction of almost all his kinsmen, Ravana is killed by Rama. Rama then crowns Ravana's righteous brother Vibhishana as the new king of Lanka. However, he refuses to accept Sita on account of her having lived at another man's home, thus being defiled. After undergoing a fire test to prove her chastity, Sita is accepted by her husband, and the party returns to Ayodhya, where Rama is installed as king. Marital bliss, however, is sacrificed for the sake of the state: Rama opts to banish his pregnant wife to the forest when a citizen questions her chastity (since she lived at Ravana's home). Sita gives birth to twin sons, Lava and Kusha, at the abode of the sage Valmiki, where they are brought up as ascetics but skilled in the arts of warfare.

Meanwhile, Rama performs the horse sacrifice to acclaim himself supreme ruler. His sons capture the roaming horse and defeat Rama's army and, later, Rama himself. Eventually their identity is revealed and Rama attempts to take his family back to Ayodhya with him. This time, however, Sita refuses and opts instead to take refuge in her mother, the earth. Rama thus returns to his city with his two sons and continues his illustrious reign.

NOTES

1. Bridget Brereton, *A History of Modern Trinidad* (Portsmouth, NH: Heinemann International, 1981), 103.
2. Patricia Mohammed, *Gender Negotiations among Indians in Trinidad, 1917–1947* (Basingstoke, UK: Palgrave, 2002), 37.
3. A detailed description and analysis of the system of indentureship can be found in K.O. Laurence's *A Question of Labour: Indentured Immigration into Trinidad and British Guiana, 1875–1917* (Kingston: Ian Randle, 1994).
4. Steven Vertovec, *Hindu Trinidad: Religion, Ethnicity and Socio-economic Change* (London: Macmillan Education, 1992), 73.
5. Kusha Haraksingh, "Aspects of the Indian Experience in the Caribbean", in *Calcutta to Caroni: The East Indians in Trinidad*, ed. John La Guerre (St Augustine, Trinidad: University of the West Indies Extramural Studies Unit, 1985), 163.
6. Ibid.
7. Vertovec, *Hindu Trinidad*, 106.
8. In Hinduism, the Little Tradition refers to those aspects which have evolved independently of the Great Tradition. These are usually embedded in orality and

are geographically localized and linguistically restrictive. The Great Tradition refers to the essentially Sanskritic/Brahminic strand of Hinduism which is embedded in the Vedas and other Sanskrit literature.

9. V.S. Naipaul, *Reading and Writing: A Personal Account* (New York: New York Review of Books, 2000), 12.

10. S.K. Chatterji, "The Ramayana: Its Character, Genesis, History, Expansion and Exodus", in *The Ramayan Tradition in Asia*, ed. V. Raghavan (New Delhi: Sahitya Akademi, 1980), 242.

11. Paula Richman, *Many Ramayanas: The Diversity of a Narrative Tradition in South Asia* (Berkeley: University of California Press, 1991), 7.

12. Ibid.

13. K.R. Srinivasa Iyengar, *Asian Variations in Ramayana* (New Delhi: Sahitya Akademi, 1983), 7–8.

14. Recitation and interpretation of verses from the *Ramayana* are usually done within a congregational setting.

15. Velcheru Narayana Rao, "The Politics of Telugu Ramayanas: Colonialism, Print Culture, and Literary Movements", in *Questioning Ramayanas: A South Asian Tradition*, ed. Paula Richman (Berkeley: University of California Press, 2001), 159–85.

16. Usha Nilsson, "Grinding Millet but Singing of Sita: Power and Domination in Awadh and Bhojpuri Women's Songs", in *Questioning Ramayanas: A South Asian Tradition*, ed. Paula Richman (Berkeley: University of California Press, 2001), 137–58.

17. Paula Richman, ed., *Questioning Ramayanas: A South Asian Tradition* (Berkeley: University of California Press, 2001), 309–28. The Ramleela is a depiction of the Rama story in dramatic form.

18. Ibid.

19. John Kelly, "Fiji's Fifth Veda: Exile, Sanatan Dharm, and Countercolonial Initiatives in Diaspora", in *Questioning Ramayanas: A South Asian Tradition*, ed. Paula Richman (Berkeley: University of California Press, 2001). In Hinduism there are four Vedas, which are deemed to be the most ancient scriptures in the world and which collectively provide prescriptions and codes of operation for all dimensions of human existence. Thus, assigning the title of "fifth Veda" to the *Ramcharitmanas* would transfer to that text the prestige and religious supremacy of the four Vedas.

20. Ibid., 349.

21. Philip Lutgendorf, *The Life of a Text* (Berkeley: University of California Press, 1991).

22. C. Bulcke, "Ramcaritmanasa and Its Relevance to Modern Age", in *The Ramayan Tradition in Asia*, ed. V. Raghavan (New Delhi: Sahitya Akademi, 1980), 62.

23. Kusha Haraksingh, "The Hindu Experience in Trinidad" (paper presented at the "Beyond Survival" Conference on East Indians in the Caribbean, University of the West Indies, St Augustine, Trinidad, 28 August–5 September 1984), 19.

24. Brereton, *History of Modern Trinidad*, 103.

25. Bulcke, "Ramcaritmanasa", 60.

26. K.P. Bahadur, *Ramcharitmanas: A Study in Perspective* (Delhi: Ess Ess Publications, 1976), 11.

27. Vijay Mishra, *Rama's Banishment: A Centenary Tribute to the Fiji Indians, 1879–1979* (London: Heinemann Educational, 1979).

28. Ramdoorarie Maharajn, *Trinidad Sunday Guardian*, *Divali Supplement*, 14 October 1990.

29. Derek Walcott, *The Antilles: Fragments of Epic Memory. The Nobel Lecture* (New York: Farrar, Straus and Giroux, 1993).

30. *Trinidad Sunday Guardian*, 25 October 1992.

31. Literally, a Divali village. In Trinidad, however, it refers to an annual event observed just prior to the Festival of Lights, showcasing various aspects of Indian culture in Trinidad.

32. This dance-drama tells the story of how Rama's father, King Dashratha, unknowingly killed the only son and support of an old blind couple. The grief-stricken couple consequently cursed the king with the same pain of separation from his offspring that they were enduring.

33. *Trinidad Sunday Guardian*, 14 October 1990.

34. Seepersad Naipaul, *The Adventures of Gurudeva and Other Stories* (London: André Deutsch, 1976), 31.

35. Ibid., 33

36. Lakshmi Persaud, *For the Love of My Name* (Leeds, UK: Peepal Tree, 2000), 299.

37. Harold Sonny Ladoo, *Yesterdays* (Toronto: House of Anansi, 1974), 104.

38. *Sri Ramcharitmanas*, Descent 1, verse 333.2.

39. Ibid., Des. 1, verses 300–361.

40. Ibid., Des. 3, verse 5.

41. Ibid., Des. 5, verse 58.3.

42. Ibid., Des. 4, verse 14.3.

43. Seepersad Naipaul, "Dangerous Feminine Evolution", *East Indian Weekly*, 24 November 1928.

44. Mayavati Maharaj, *Trinidad Sunday Guardian*, 10 November 1996.

45. Brinsley Samaroo, "Women's Work in the Canadian Presbyterian Mission to

Trinidad during the Century after 1868" (paper presented at the Conference on Religions of the New World, University of the West Indies, St Augustine, Trinidad, 6–8 January 2002).

46. *Trinidad Guardian*, 31 January 1945.

47. Pundit Khemraj Vyas, interview by author, 27 November 2002.

48. Bhagwandai Sinanan, interview by author, 17 December 2002.

49. Pundit Hardath Maharaj, interview by author, 24 November 2002.

50. Pundit Doodnath Rampersad, interview by author, 5 October 2002.

51. Pundit Lutchmie Persad, interview by author, 9 February 2002.

52. Pundit Brahmanand Rambachan, interview by author, 22 November 2002.

53. *Ramcharitmanas*, Des. 2, verse 58.1.

54. Ibid., Des. 2, verse 74.2.

55. This occurred even within the Arya Samaj (which, ironically, denounced the system), where a senior pundit and officer, Bhogi Dass, was stripped of both his religious and organizational privileges and duties on account of his appropriation of another man's wife. However, although his immediate *chelas* condoned the action taken by the Samaj, they would not allow anyone to ridicule him. Thus Bhogi Dass still wielded influence based on the *guru–chela* system.

56. Dolly Rampersad, interview by author, 6 January 2002.

57. *Ramcharitmanas*, Des. 3, verse 5.

58. Gaitree Singh, interview by author, 6 January 2002.

59. Mohammed, *Gender Negotiations*, 13–14.

60. Ibid., 136.

61. Shaheeda Hosein, "Rural Indian Women in Trinidad, 1870–1945" (PhD diss., University of the West Indies, 2002).

62. Vertovec, *Hindu Trinidad*, 148.

63. Ibid., 150.

64. S. Naipaul, *Adventures of Gurudeva*.

65. *Express* (Trinidad), 25 February 1986.

66. Satnarayan Maharaj, interview by author, 6 December 2001.

67. The introduction of handshaking into the Hindu repertoire of greetings also served to relegate the more traditional greeting of "Sita Ram" to the religious domain.

68. *Trinidad Guardian*, 17 April 1987.

69. Indrani Rampersad, interview by author, 12 June 2002.

70. Pundit Balram Persad, interview by author, 7 July 2003.

2

Rings, Gifts and Shekels

Marriage and Dowry within the
Indo-Muslim Community in Trinidad,
1930 to the Globalized Present

– HALIMA SA'ADIA KASSIM –

INTRODUCTION

TODAY THE REQUIREMENTS IMPOSED by modern life – namely the emphasis on higher education and the long period needed for education and professional training, as well as the quest for economic empowerment – have contributed to changing cultural and gender dynamics within the Indo-Muslim community. Patterns of marriage behaviour by educational attainment reflect the changing social and economic roles of women in family and society. This has resulted, on one hand, in Muslim women delaying marriage to their early twenties or later, and on the other – and to a lesser extent, provided the space, though not always necessarily enabling – for women to marry non-Muslim men who are their peers and who have converted to Islam in order to marry the women of whom they are enamoured. The corresponding societal changes have implications for Muslim men, who are also delaying marriage to advance professionally and to become economically solvent.

Instead of being a relieving factor, education has created an inverse relationship with timely marriages; that is, the higher the educational attainment, the more likely that marriage and fecundity are delayed. This development can be seen as a proxy indicator for economic resources and thus security. Conversely, ethnic and religious endogamy may be competing against patterns of educational homogamy, with important implications for social and economic mobility and equality. These competing interests also have implications for the social and economic integration of ethnic groups and the weakening influence of parents and extended family in modernizing societies. Nevertheless, given that family is still a fundamental part of life for Muslims, it is not expected that in the present and the immediate future Muslim women who have the choice in terms of economic feasibility will opt out of marriage or that as a population will marry less. Preferences and opportunities for marrying within the same ethnic group should generally remain strong because of shared values and lifestyles, while educational homogamy should be of equal importance. Therefore, exogamy would not be a rejection of the norms and values of the collective, but rather a juxtaposing of traditional and modern roles by a generation of women and men who are willing to challenge Islamic cultural traditions.

The dowry (*mahr*) is integral to the sanctity of Muslim marriages. With the changing age structure of marriages there is also an accompanying change in the value and character of the dowry, shifting from domestic and knowledge-based items, jewellery and shekels (currency) to capital assets such as land, property, vehicles, *halala* (money) and jewellery, as well as support for higher education. This paper frames these issues within globalization, which has not only stimulated new lifestyles and transnational orientations but has also led to renewed emphasis on the "authentic" cultural identity of groups. This resulting revitalization among religious communities is often based on an exclusivist notion of belonging, defined by religious texts and geared to purifying local religion from either foreign or local "stains". Within the Islamic community the rise of fundamentalism provides an umbrella for Islamists who call for a return to original (purist) Islam and repudiation of secular influences, combined with scrupulous rejection of all innovation (*bid'ah*) and perceived anti-Islamic traditions that have infiltrated Islam, or for those with a political agenda. It is the former type of fundamentalist Islam that is present in the Caribbean region.

While these shifts and contestations are taking place in contemporary society, my paper tries to understand how marriages and dowry emerged in post-indentureship Trinidad. This provides insight into the way in which women and girls constructed and reconstructed their (gendered) identities in relation to the processes of social, economic and political change taking place within the Muslim community and in the wider society. It then looks at the cultural and technological changes taking place globally and posits that these will impact upon marriage practices, offering new challenges to Islam.

METHODOLOGY

This chapter begins with a historical perspective on how the Indo-Muslim community negotiated changing age structures, in particular the transition from childhood to marriage after 1917. Statistics and colonial reports paint a stark reality, but a fairly one-dimensional picture. They do not provide a comprehensive insight into how people integrate their culture, religion and factors of mobility into their daily lives, nor do they tell of the resilience, the vitality and the power of a people. This chapter seeks to decipher the nature, continuity and change of those socio-cultural practices that informed the lives of men and women. Conversational narratives therefore add to the storyline and provide another layer to the story of the growth of Indo-Muslim community.

Some of the interviewees were selected based on my previous personal interactions with them within the Muslim community, and others were recommended to me during the course of this study. The majority were between the ages of sixty and eighty-seven, with the exception of four who were younger. The interviewees were from the East–West Corridor, central and urban south Trinidad. Their socio-economic backgrounds were varied. Born into an ethnic group, the men and women interviewed did not flout the traditions of their community, although at times they challenged them. They were not passive actors but were the products of their Indo-Muslim community and the wider society. This led to a separation (sometimes fuzzy) between their secular and cultural-religious lives. Standard of living and the material quality of life were not kept apart from socio-religious and cultural mores as men and women negotiated and renegotiated their reality. Class, education, ethnicity and gender are not static categories, and these had an impact upon the development and progress of Indo-Muslims as well as their life choices and patterns.

DEMOGRAPHICS

As generally posited in the recounting of historical circumstances surrounding the migration of Indian labourers to the Caribbean from 1845, Muslims were in the minority. One historian estimated that 80 per cent of the migrants were Hindus, 15 per cent were Muslims and the rest were tribal, Christians, Sikhs and others.[1]

As the East Indian[2] population expanded, issues of demographic security[3] surfaced, externally and internally. In the context of this chapter, the issue of internal demographic security takes precedence, as it has implications not only for demographic conditions but also for interactions within marked spaces. The age and sex distribution of the population are of particular significance in the retention of cultural and religious norms and their mani-festations. Equally important is how the community negotiated its accommo-dation within a Western Christian society.

A review of the age structure of the Indian population shows that there were slightly more males than females under fifteen years, while for persons forty-five years and over there were appreciably more males than females. This pattern reflects the effect of large-scale immigration and its particular sex characteristics and replacement stock by way of fertility within the com-

Table 2.1: Representation of Muslim Population as Numerical Value of Indian Population

Year	Total Population	Total Indian Population	Muslim Population
1891	218,381	70,218	8,638
1901	273,899	86,383	11,478
1911	333,552	110,911	14,957
1921	365,913	121,420	17,698
1932	412,783	138,667	20,992
1946	557,970	195,747	32,615
1960	827,957	301,946	49,736

Source: Jack Harewood, The Population of Trinidad and Tobago, CICRED Series, 1975, 91, 95, 97 and 108.

Table 2.2: Age and Sex Distribution on Indian Population

Year	Age Group	Indian	Sex Ratio
1946	0–4	34,211	1 994
	5–14	50,544	1,022
	15–44	83,967	1,047
	45–64	20,483	1,404
	65+	6,542	1,153
	Total	261,485	–
1960	0–4	51,290	1,017
	5–14	88,934	1,001
	15–44	123,387	996
	45–64	29,602	1,264
	65+	8,732	1,110
	Total	301,945	–

Source: Jack Harewood, The Population of Trinidad and Tobago, CICRED Series, 1975, 100.

munity. This demographic bodes well for the social and economic development of the community, as there is the requisite social capital. The sex ratios (males per 1,000 females) for the Indians were high in 1891 but declined thereafter. Available data from 1946 and 1960 representing the age and sex ratios is captured in table 2.2.

SOCIO-ECONOMIC OVERVIEW OF THE COMMUNITY

Throughout the indentureship period and thereafter, the majority of Indians were low-paid manual labourers on the estates, while those who migrated to the towns from circa 1884 worked as scavengers or porters. Indians accounted for 70 per cent of agricultural labourers in 1917; by 1921 only 187 were classified as "officials and professionals",[4] with the majority holding agricultural or mercantile jobs.[5] Clearly many of the Indians remained employed in the agricultural sector, although some were small shopkeepers or moneylenders and some sought employment in towns as scavengers, porters and skilled labourers. Poverty, poor diet and ill health were rampant within the Indian community.

By the late nineteenth century the Indo-Muslim community as part of the wider Indian community had reconstituted itself through religion and culture. Social mobility was important. Improvement of their condition was one of the major reasons for the immigrants' coming to this part of the world, and purchases of land and acquisition of education were pursued for social mobility. From 1882 the development of cane farming allowed individuals to rent or purchase land from sugar estates and share in the risks of cultivation. The establishment of the land commutation scheme and the opening up of Crown lands to small purchasers in 1869 marked the development of the Indian peasantry, the establishment of village settlements and the reconstitution of religious and certain socio-cultural practices. There evolved a set of ideas that guided and explained the actions and decisions of the community, which became entities in their own way.

By 1927 the employment practices of the Indians were gradually beginning to change. The protector of immigrants, Lieutenant-Colonel A. de Boissiere, recorded them thus:

> Many were merchants of great wealth, and others are shop keepers. Many of their descendants are professional men – doctors, barristers, schoolmasters &c. Many are employed as clerks at remunerative salaries in Government service and throughout the Mercantile Community. About nine-tenths of the Dairies in the Island are run by them, especially those who originally emigrated from India. They own and run approximately nine-tenths of the Motor-Buses in the Island. A large sector comprise proprietors, agriculturists and otherwise.[6]

Except for the "professional" men, occupational practices within the Indo-Muslim community generally reflect this assessment, and by 1940 there had been little change in occupational status. Muslim women engaged in income-generating activities and in reproductive care that contributed to social and economic development of the family and the community, but no mention is made of them.

In 1868 the Canadian Mission began to establish schools for Indian children; it was more successful than the ward schools in attracting Indian atten-

Table 2.3: Number of Indian Children on the Register of Government and Assisted Primary Schools, 1916–1939

Year	GS: On Register	GS: DAA	AS: On Register	AS: DAA
1916	1,199	611	13,624	7,250
1922	1,410	764	12,022	6,475
1926	1,769	932	13,119	7,029
1931	2,137	1,378	16,326	9,277
1936	3,184	2,141	19,809	12,092
1939	3,758	2,471	22,536	14,958

GS: government schools; AS: assisted schools; DAA: daily average attendance

Source: Administrative Reports of the Protector of Immigrants, 1917–40.

dance.[7] While land acquisition remained the primary factor of social mobility in the remaining years of the nineteenth century and in the first half of the succeeding century, the twentieth century witnessed the growing worth of education to some Indians, particularly among the Christian urban merchant subgroup. Whatever the nature of the Indians' occupational status, an increasing number sent their children to primary school. Table 2.3 shows the number of Indian children on the register of government and assisted primary schools during the period 1916 to 1939.

It can be observed that the attendance of children improved at both government and assisted schools. The reports of the protector of immigrants ceased in 1940, but the census of 1946 shows that there were 50,544 Indian children among the colony's total of 122,286 children of school age (five to fourteen), and of those 68.6 per cent were illiterate.[8] The correlation between the increased attendance of Indian children in school and marriage would manifest itself in the changing age structure of marriages.

RECONSTITUTION OF ISLAM

Islam is an ideology which influences much more than the ritual life of a people. It equally affects their social, political, economic, psychological and aesthetic lives and includes a wide spectrum of practices and ideas which affect
almost every aspect of the daily life of the Muslim individual. Islam and
Islamic traditions, therefore, are seen by many Muslims as the main source
of cohesiveness for nurturing an identity and providing stability to confront
intruding influences, and as the premise for building the cooperation needed
to sustain the community.

It is important to note that there were two waves of Muslim immigrants to
Trinidad. The enslaved African peoples were the first to bring Islam to the
Caribbean, although by the time of emancipation there was no significant
African Muslim presence. However, from the 1960s, global linkages sparked
a level of consciousness about black roots and identity in which conversion/
reversion to Islam was one of the outcomes. A black Muslim community has
since come into existence, but generally not as part of the established Indian
Muslim community.

The Indo-Muslim migrants – the indentured labourers – arrived in Trinidad
from India from 1845 to 1917. These immigrants were hardly drawn from the
middle to upper castes, or *varnas*.[9] Islam did not recognize the Hindu caste
system, but the Indo-Muslims who came to Trinidad had little or no wealth
or property in the form of land. The leadership of community rested on the
few educated or learned men who, through intergenerational learning or
attendance at *madrasahs/maktabs* (Islamic schools), had the knowledge to nurture a community. This knowledge was based upon memory and the Qur'an
(Holy Book), which formed part of the migrants' assets from India. These men
were the leaders of unlettered adherents of Islam who depended on them to
nurture their faith on the estates and in the villages. With the commencement
of *masjid* (mosque) building in the 1860s, religion became more and more
institutionalized and the role of the *imama* (priests) and other learned religious
men increased. Hence the development of Islam and interpretation of the
texts and rituals were firmly in the hands of certain men. In setting themselves
up to interpret gender roles, these men sought to deny women the right of
ijtihad (independent judgement) which Islam accords its believers.

ISLAM AND FEMINISM

Internal developments such as the particular history and dynamism of the society, particularly the social praxis of women, have influenced the course of women's movements and feminism in Muslim and non-Muslim societies. Concomitantly, external factors such as colonialism, post-colonialism and globalization have also had their impact. The history and heritage of Muslim peoples are radically different from those of the people of western Europe and America. The legal rights which Western women sought in the reform of English common law had already been granted to Muslim women in the seventh century; the feminism relevant to Muslim women and society must be correspondingly different. Islam provides a core set of rights and entitlements for women (and men) sourced directly from the Qur'an and strengthened by the Sunnah (the way of life of the Prophet Muhammad). Among these are socio-economic rights such as the rights to own and inherit wealth and property independently, to negotiate a consensual contract of marriage and the sum and timing of the *mahr*, and to be completely supported financially; in addition, women may choose to work or not to work within or outside the home and to be paid for this work, including that of cooking and child care. In relation to God, no difference whatever is made between the sexes in the Qur'an, which speaks to piety and charity *inter alia*.[10]

Nevertheless, the way Islam is understood and applied in daily life indicates the extent to which patriarchy uses and subverts religion. For men, moral imperatives are outlined in general terms; for women, they are conveyed in specific terms and keyed to submission to male authority. Subsequently the role of woman as wife and mother is extolled. Both women and men perpetuate the belief that women cannot live up to the moral code, thus necessitating their submission to male authority. The Islamic fundamentalists would argue that women must seek liberation within the Islamic community, but it is a community in which men draft definitions of women's roles yet claim that these roles are divinely (not culturally) constructed. In setting themselves up to interpret women's roles, these men seek to deny women the right of *ijtihad*.

If, as is often accepted by Islamic feminist reformers, the reassertion of patriarchy and traditional social conventions has impacted social justice and gender equity, it would appear that the contestation is between modernity and traditionalism, not between religious values and feminism. In this regard, Islamic feminism must be developed, advocated and experienced in the context of Islam as an ideology with prescriptions found in the Qur'an and the Hadith (the recorded sayings and actions of the Prophet Muhammad), with systematic alleviation of the disadvantageous factors and working with and to the benefit of both women and men.

The economic imperatives of growing urbanization and educational attainment among women are forcing changes within the global Muslim community. Hence Muslims are provided with opportunities to interrogate the model of Muslim womanhood that is generally given prominence – the traditional patriarchal gender regime emphasizing sex differences and a sex-based division of labour. Concurrently it provides a space for the entry of other models of Muslim womanhood in Islamic feminist discourse that existed during the early period of Islamic history.[11]

Islamic feminism calls for equal rights in the public sphere and complementary rights in the private sphere. So, Islamic feminists argue, women can be heads of state and *imama*. In the private sphere, Islamic feminists are challenging the conventional notion of male authority over and protection of females in marriage and the family, calling on Muslims to live by the egalitarianism of Islam. Thus Islamic feminism has taken on the twofold task of exposing and eradicating patriarchal ideas and practices glossed as Islamic (in the words of Margot Badran, "naturalised" and perpetuated in that guise) and recovering Islam's core idea of gender equality as indivisible from human equality.

Conceptually feminism, Islamic or otherwise, did not pervade the reconstitution of Indo-Caribbean communities, in which an underlying premise of identity was religion and culture. The contestation lay between the forces of modernity and traditional values and customs; these provided a framework in which the community could function as a subset of the culture and was capable of being influenced by non-religious factors. Even now the concept of feminism is not typically used to interrogate Islamic practices and Muslim culture in the Caribbean. This could be because transplanted Islam is still new and there is a lack of critical intellectual Islamic activism or *ijtihad* that encourages the probing of alternative truths or perspectives. At the same time, one is reminded of the Indian's vision of him- or herself and the world. For Indians there was no separation between church and state. Muslims were

equally proud of their rich cultural heritage; they found it impossible to
separate the secular from the religious, being accustomed to the "idea that
the real basis of all knowledge is a faith in the values which are inculcated by
religion".[12]

The concerns of women around the world therefore have to be addressed
in the historicized particularity of their relationship to multiple systems of
subordination and oppression: patriarchy and/or male supremacy at local levels (family, community, nation) and international sexism and economic hegemony at the global level.[13] Thus it is not surprising that feminist scholars and
activists in the quest for social justice and equality in the Middle East have
rooted the search in history and indigenous practices and in understanding,
defining and interpreting the religious frameworks.

Any development of Caribbean Islamic feminism, like Middle Eastern and
African Islamic feminism, must have as its starting point the religious laws –
that is, the moral framework duly combined with the systemic inequalities
that permeate the wider society and thus the group. Change must come from
within if it is to be taken seriously by the Islamist male elite and their female
allies. It is this type of feminism that can claim an authentic space within
and as part of Islam, and provide for Islam a place within the now polycentric
global feminist discourse. It is also likely that, in the Caribbean as in other
parts of the Islamic world and in diasporic or niche Muslim communities,
the interest would be in promoting gender respect and justice rather than in
gender equity. Hence, to the extent that it supports women's agency within a
family or community, feminism acts to legitimize women's choices.

FAMILY AND COMMUNITY LIFE WITHIN THE
CONTEXT OF ISLAM

Family is seen as the basic unit of civilization and also as the basis for a harmonious social order. "Residentially extended families" are not uncommon,
and even when the residential version of the extended family is not possible
or adhered to, family connections reaching far beyond the nuclear unit are
evident in strong psychological, social, economic and even political ties.
Mutual supports and responsibilities affecting these larger consanguineous
groups are not just considered desirable but are made incumbent on members
of the society by Islamic law.[14] The Qur'an itself exhorts family solidarity; it

specifies the extent of such responsibilities and contains prescriptive measures for inheritance, support and other close interdependencies within the extended family. Islamic traditions also prescribe very strong family participation in the contracting and preservation of marriages, and so reinforce social responsibility to the group. The importance of community life to Muslims is underscored by a doctrine that defines behaviour codes in which there is individual accountability to community standards. Equally important in the Caribbean is the fact that Islam was also the unifying force around which a group of people converged to retain the purity and piety of their faith in a society that was intolerant, if not hostile, to them. Islam provided the means to withstand the proselytizing of the Christians; it became not only an ethnic/religious demarcation but also a weapon in the struggle for political, economic and social space in a heterogeneous society. Thus the concept of the *umma* (Islamic community), as negotiated ties of interdependency among a people that hold them together, provides the key to the process of building social capital.

MARRIAGE, HORSE AND CARRIAGE

GOVERNANCE

As the Muslim community was re-established, arranged marriages were reinstituted. In the traditional arranged Hindu marriage, "it is geared around the assumption that ideally the girl and the boy are strangers to each other and that it is their obligation to their parents that makes them sometimes reluctant, but consenting parties to the marriage".[15] Conversely, in Islam, marriages arranged by suggestion and recommendation are more the practice, as long as both parties are agreeable. This is based upon the understanding that marriage is a voluntary union and on the precept that for it to be valid there must be consent by the two participants, who would take into consideration family opinion, social standing and similarity of interests, background and personality. Islam places importance on the durability of the relationship between man and woman rather than on romantic love. An Arabic proverb says, "The mirror of love is blind; it turns zucchini into okra."

While Islam did not recognize the Hindu caste system, Indian Muslims were influenced by caste rules; in particular the system of gender relations resonated in the Caribbean. Mohammed notes that "a system of hypergamy was developed; in which a woman had to marry into her own class or any class above, though a man was permitted to marry a woman of any class to whom he had access".[16] This was similar to the concept of *anuloma*, in which marriage between an upper-caste boy and a lower-caste girl met with approval; *pratiloma,* marriage of a woman to a man of a lower caste, was seen as offensive.

Marriage is often an indicator of the transition from childhood to adulthood, and this was no different within the Indian/Muslim community. Marriage ensured security for the female, allowing her to fulfil her role as child-bearer and nurturer and offering her financial security, but it also gave men heavy responsibilities for girls they scarcely knew. Through the lens of Western feminism, arranged marriages are seen as negative because of their apparent restriction of individual freedom and responsibility. Arranged marriages in the case of girls demonstrated the "acceptance of patriarchy and latent matriarchy, of moving from the control and protection of her father, to that of her husband, and furthermore to that of her father-in-law in her husband's household and from her mother to her mother-in-law".[17]

Thus one form of social control is exchanged for another, sometimes even harsher than what the young girl experienced within the walls of her own home. Early arranged marriages, a feature of Indian (Hindu and Muslim) culture replicating institutionalized inequalities, also curtailed the educational opportunities of both boys and girls attending school. Simultaneously they satisfied the plantocracy's need to secure a labour supply for the estates and the patriarchy's to secure ongoing labour for households and family-owned businesses. However, within the typology of arranged marriages (fully arranged or semi- and consensual), generational as well as gendered (dis)-empowerment operated for younger women. For example, the domains where relative power existed were manifest in the domestic sphere. Daughters-in-law were expected to do the socially reproductive work under the watchful eye of their mother-in-law. Despite the indices of power leveraged within the household, women through enterprising ways found agency to ensure that their children (boys and girls) were educated, and to save money or supplement the family income to improve the quality of their or their family's lives, immediately or in the long term. For the Indo-Muslim community, the pursuit of happiness lay in incremental building blocks towards generational improvement in the quality of life.

During the late nineteenth and early twentieth century it was not uncommon for girls as young as nine to be betrothed to men five years their senior or older; after the girl's first menstrual cycle the couple would be married. Such early marriages were a well-established tradition in India. A respondent noted that the rationale for early and arranged marriages was, "Yuh cayn't leave dem to make *chokha*",[18] thus emphasizing the valuation of marriage and the taboos that surround sex and sexuality. It was a general assumption that a female was incapable of resisting sexual advances; however, at all cost she was expected to be a virgin (both physically and intellectually sexually ignorant) on her wedding day, which made her sexually vulnerable to her husband. The context for marriage was one of mistrust of the young bride by the husband and his family. Mastery over the sexuality of women was anchored to the fact that an unmarried daughter who was not a virgin would bring dishonour on her father, and in turn, the daughter would be toppled from the pedestal on which she had been placed.

This need to protect females from their own libidinous instincts is also present in patriarchal Islamic philosophy. After all, the Muslim woman is seen to be "Fitna, the epitome of the uncontrollable, a living representative of the dangers of sexuality and its rampant destructive potential . . . . Women [are seen as] the embodiment of destruction, the symbol of disorder."[19]

Respect for family and community, therefore, underpinned the community's codes of conduct, as seen in this quotation: "While in theory codes of honour and shame refer to the behaviour codes of men and women, honour is seen more as men's responsibility and shame as women's. This division of honour and shame is related to the fact that honour is seen as actively achieved while shame is seen as passively defended, resulting in different expectations of behaviour for men and women."[20]

Under the Ordinance to Make Provision for the Marriage and Divorces of Indian Immigrants, the minimum age stipulated for marriage was "sixteen years for the man and thirteen years for the woman", which Stephanie Daly says was higher than under English common law.[21] In 1916 an amendment to the 1881 ordinance reduced the minimum age for marriage from thirteen to twelve. The 1935 Muslim Marriage and Divorce Ordinance did not alter the marital ages: "the age at which a person, being a member of the Muslim community, is capable of contracting a marriage shall be sixteen in the case of males and twelve in the case of females".[22]

Under the marriage ordinance of 1881 and its amendments in 1916, the majority of Hindus and Muslims did not register their nuptials. This prompted the protector of immigrants, A. de Boissiere, to state in his 1928 report: "Many more [marriages] of course were effected according to their rites, but not registered. I would again urge the East Indians to register their marriage, not only in their own interest, but in the interest of the community in general."[23] In 1931 the protector of immigrants, G.E. Lechmere Guppy, writing on the failure of East Indians to register their marriages, stated: "These people [do] not register [their marriages] for many reasons to be deplored. Generally, because children of such unions are counted as illegitimate and consequently, do not inherit property in the event of their parents dying intestate."[24]

The lobbying for the recognition of Muslim marriages which began in the late nineteenth century was seen as important for purposes of inheritance. The majority were still agricultural labourers who had little to pass on to their progeny, so initially most of the Indian population in Trinidad were generally apathetic to the marriage issue. J.C. Jha questioned its significance at this time, when the majority of Indians felt an inherent distrust of the wider society, which had expressed hostility to them, their religion and their culture.[25] It was an issue for the nationalists, however, as a mark of recognition and distinctiveness, as well as for the wealthy few. By the turn of the twentieth century, when Indians began to acquire property – some in lieu of their return passage to India – the problem of a "rightful inheritor" became important. As they began to aspire to higher positions in society, the status of illegitimacy for children of unrecognized marriages became a concern. Group validation of nuptials sanctioned by the imam (priest) was perhaps seen as more important, and it remains so well into the twenty-first century.

Within three years there was a shift in concern by the protector of immigrants from consideration of the general community to the effects of illegitimate children on the Indian community. In connection with the latter, the 1931 *Report of the Protector of Immigrants* noted that a committee had been appointed by the governor, "To enquire and report to the Governor whether any system can be devised to bring about the more effectual registration of marriages celebrated under Hindu and Muslim rites, so as to secure the status of children of such marriage, with particular reference to the inheritance of property under the local law."[26] The Muslim Marriage and Divorce Ordinance, which came into law in 1936, permitted *imama* to serve as marriage officers, thereby ensuring automatic registration as part of the religious ceremonies. Although there was an increase in nuptials registered under the ordinance, a significant number still did not register their marriages with the registrar general or at the warden's office. During 1936 and 1937, 298 nuptials were registered under the newly passed ordinance, while in 1939 there were 267 registered marriages.[27] Among these were couples who had remarried under Muslim rites in order to have their marriages registered. Such was the case with Daniel Sahadat and Edan of the Guaico-Tamana district, who were first married under Muslim rites in 1906.[28]

As noted earlier, family for the Indian community was not only mother, father and children but comprised an extended family that embraced three or more generations and could also include individuals who did not share blood ties. The extended family not only ensured shared resources (land) and protection but also provided a potential supply of brides and grooms for alliances with other families. The reconstitution of family life which emerged when villages were formed around 1870 centred on patriarchal control and reintroduced the concept of chastity of young girls. The termination of indentureship (re)emphasized the importance of the extended family, which featured patriarchal authority, strict control of female sexuality, and arranged marriages, and in which husband–wife relations were less important than the man's relationship with his family. As such, it was not uncommon for extended and step-families to play a role in the prospective marriage of young females, which would ensure purity and strengthening of the family line.

The stigma of age in terms of marriage is universal but is significantly influenced by cultural values. In the Indo-Muslim community, within a century – two to three generations – the marital age for girls increased from nine years old to the early twenties. Niehoff and Niehoff note that "the majority of Indian females are married before the age of 19 and with well over a third being married before the age of 14".[29] While the marital ages of males and females gradually increased, factors of mobility coalesced with religious endogamy, skin colour, good character and reputation in the contracting of marriages. Mohammed affirms that the conditions for negotiation of love, marriage and family revolved around three key elements: (1) the reconstitution of conditions which would reinforce responsibility to the group and family, (2) the entry of the state into this negotiation, and (3) altered conditions for both sexes, along with changing circumstances that challenged traditional rules of religion and community.[30] Hence there was a gradual exercising of free will within the context and limits set by the requirements for social cohesion.

The customary way of creating marital matches was through the medium of *fakirs,* travelling mendicants who carried news from one village to the next of families who had sons or daughters of marriageable age.[31] Parents (particularly mothers), members of the extended family and *imama* were the principal brokers or facilitators in marital negotiations between families. This informal system was reliable and effective. Negotiation started after initiation through intermediaries, and when concurrence was achieved, a day was fixed for the marriage. Generally it was the bridegroom's party that took the initiative and made the proposal of marriage. El-Solh and Mabro, using Soraya Altorki's concept of differentiation of power in Saudi Arabia, note that "men's power may in specific situations be predicated on the support of women, however invisible the female role may be to outsiders. Such dependency is reflected in the women's role as brokers in marital negotiations, which provide them with the opportunity of enlarging the domain of their autonomy vis-à-vis their men."[32]

Similarly within the Indo-Muslim Trinidadian society, females acted as marriage brokers or facilitators, generally in collusion with their male counterparts, including the imam, in negotiating or advising on marital contracts for their daughters and sons. Social standing and a family's good character and reputation were of grave importance, as was social compatibility. Regardless of who brokered the marriage, the issue of credibility was important, and communities provided the credibility factor. Frequent interaction among and between community members ensured that a system of checks and balances was in place to maintain honour.

CONTEXTUALIZATION

Intra-family Marriages

For migrant communities in the period of transition, consanguineous unions were not uncommon. Extrapolating from what presently occurs in western

Europe, Australasia and North America among sub-populations from south, east and middle-eastern Asia, the evidence suggests that the prevalence of consanguineous unions is increasing, in many cases from an already high level.[33] This is because of a desire to find a marital partner from within the community, which may be numerically small and composed of a restricted number of kindred, and the wish to maintain community traditions in a new and unfamiliar environment. These reasons hold true for community endogamy as much as for family endogamy. The increase in the numbers of persons of marriageable age within these communities would generally facilitate the growth of community endogamy while decreasing family endogamy.

Within the Muslim community in the period under discussion, marriage among kin was not unusual. It ensured maintenance of the family structure and concentrated wealth and property within the family group while simultaneously strengthening familial ties. Such was the case with A.B. She, her two sisters and her elder brother married their first cousins, while her remaining siblings married other "respectable" Indo-Muslims. She says, "You may have met other boys at school, but you could not marry them; you simply could not."[34] A.B. was twenty-two when she married, while her mother and grandmother were married immediately after their first menstrual cycle. She describes how a marriage arrangement would take place in her mother's family:

> If a boy was interested in a girl from the family, he and his parents would visit the girl's home and discuss the matter with the girl's parents. If the families agree, the marriage would be arranged. Things like the habits, likes of the parties [the boy and girl], living arrangements would be discussed, the occupation of the boy and so on would be discussed. The girl did not choose; the boy did. This was what happened to my mother.[35]

A.B.'s mother's situation deviated from the classic arranged marriage, where neither partner had a choice about whom they could marry; their partners were chosen for them by their parents. The classic type eventually gave way to a semi-arranged form in which some element of choice or knowledge on the part of the couple entered into the negotiations. The statement "The girl did not choose; the boy did" is consequently very revealing. Although in Islam the girl's consent is necessary and crucial for the validity of the marriage,[36] within a patriarchal society a girl's consent is not seen as necessary.

In the case of the former, a lack of such knowledge, fear and intimidation may prevent the female from voicing objections to marriage or the prospective spouse, while in the latter the female's wishes are subordinate to the good of the family. Niehoff and Niehoff rightly note then that "it is uncommon for Indian parents to ignore the wishes of their children entirely, although they may apply considerable pressure to get them to accept a mate they selected".[37]

Family Influences on Marriage

Z.K., age seventeen, was sent to her aunt in Maraval for a short stay. There she received her first offer of marriage. In this instance, the boy took the initiative, not the parents. Z.K. recalls the incident:

> A boy livin not far from meh *chachee* [father's sister-in-law] saw me. He was a Muslim an he come to see *chachee* an tell her he interested in me. *Chachee* told him that I was her niece an if he interested he had to talk to meh parents in St James. He agree to meet dem an a meeting was set up. I was told to stay inside, but ah want to hear what goin on, what dey sayin. I hear he say he live with he father an two brothers, but one of dem gettin married soon an he would move out. He tell meh parents if dey give their blessings he would build a house on the property before we get married. Pa tell him dey would have to think 'bout it an dey'd get back to him . . . . I was never asked my opinion; dat was the way things were done back then. If you had an opinion you keep it to yourself.[38]

Parents were always on the lookout for a more lucrative offer to ensure that their daughter would be well provided for during her life. In this case the first marital proposal was not accepted, even though the suitor intimated that he had the means to provide house and property. Another marital offer soon came Z.K.'s way. Her stepsister's husband told his father-in-law that he had a boy in mind for Z.K. to marry. When Z.K. heard about it, she used the mother–daughter network to express her opinion on the matter, as she felt her safety was being threatened. In contriving to control the direction of her life, she exercised her veto rights and told her mother, "My father don't drink. But he, he does drink plenty rum. When he drink he does get on bad. I ain't go marry he."[39]

Meanwhile a neighbour had hired a young man to do some work at her place. Z.K. and the young labourer would see each other.

There was no fence. It was jus one big, open yard. When I see him, I like him right away and he, he seemed to like me too. We use to see each other every day. My mother sees him too. She saw me watching him. Soon he sends he sister an sister-in-laws to visit my parents. I was told to stay out of sight again. But my mother know I really like de boy. I knew dey come to talk 'bout marriage. I try to hear what going on outside, but dey talking really low.⁴⁰

At that first meeting, arrangements were made for the *nikah* (marriage contract), and within four months the marriage took place. Marriage theoretically offered protection and status for young girls. Further, in a community where power and hierarchy were clearly defined, young girls were not often in a position to refuse; they understood their role vis-à-vis their family and their familial duty and honour. The mother–daughter network was often an important mechanism in finalizing the choice of marital partner for some – "bargaining with patriarchy", as conceptualized by Kandiyoti. This is one of the myriad ways in which females negotiated power within a patriarchal setting, one open door for female agency at this particular point in their lives. It was this method which Z.K. used to intimate her interest in and consent to marriage.

Sugar-Estate Love

The sugar estates or peasant farms also provided the "space" for males and females to meet. F.A.'s family owned a substantial plot of land adjacent to the Aranguez sugar estate in 1916. As he worked he could see the sugar-estate workers, and one particular female worker caught his attention. Sometimes when he was returning by donkey cart from selling produce at the George Street market in Port of Spain, he would see her as he passed by the estate. He says, "But I never I talk to she. The family knew I like she." The two sets of parents eventually arranged a wedding, "and so I marry Jawaharlal's daughter, Zohora". When they got married, "She was sixteen and I was twenty. It was a night wedding. Small. We were married under Muslim rites. Yes, she and the family was Muslims."⁴¹

Role of the Community

While Qur'an *khawanni* (prayers) and *maulood shareef* (programmes of devotional songs and praises) served as a meeting place for betrothed couples to socialize, weddings provided more fertile ground for parents to find spouses for their children. S.M.S. was eighteen when she went with her mother to a Penal wedding. Her father was at another wedding, also in Penal. S.M.S. recalls that she was in the bride's room, helping her dress, when she felt someone's eyes on her: "I turned around and saw this old woman watching me. She continued to watch me as I move about the room helping the bride dress. Whatever I do, wherever I go, she watching me. I started to feel uncomfortable. I began to think I did something wrong. But she did not say a word, she just watching."[42]

It turned out that the old woman's son and relatives were in attendance at the other wedding in Penal that S.M.S.'s father had gone to. The relatives approached him and engaged in conversation. When he returned to their San Fernando home, her father called S.M.S. and asked if she was interested in getting married. She said yes, and he told her that a boy and his mother would visit their home the next Sunday. The next weekend the boy, M.S., and his mother visited her parents. After their departure, S.M.S. was lounging in the family room when her father called her.

> "Fina, you ain't like the boy? You ain't wanting him to come back and visit? If so, tell me. I would write a letter telling him we ain't interested."
> "If you like, Pa," I said.
> "Well, he is coming back next Sunday to visit. You would make up your mind then."
> He came back next Sunday with his mother and uncle. My family was there, parents, brothers and aunt from across the road. It was overwhelming, so many people. I wondered if I would do something wrong. Everybody liked M.S. It was important for them to like him. When I see that they did, I was happy. So I said yes to the marriage.[43]

This is one of the shifts seen in marital arrangements: the boy and girl had an opportunity to meet each other, though chaperoned. In earlier times, the first time the groom and bride saw each other was on the wedding day following the *nikah* (marriage ceremony). However, familial approval and contingencies take precedence over individual choice. S.M.S. recalls: "It took one year, one month and one day for us to be married. I was nineteen and he was twenty-six when the *nikah* took place. He checked the time it took for us to be married. My mother was pregnant when M.S. and I met. This caused the delay because I had to help with the housework."[44]

Community Influence to Marry

Marriage was not only an important socio-cultural obligation but also an indicator of social standing within the community. The marital act or the contrived meeting became both a family affair and a community concern, particularly if the male was a public figure. N.N.M.A. recalls that her aunt arranged for her to meet a suitable marriage partner.

> My aunt's husband knew the *moulvi* from the *masjid*. My aunt asked her husband to invite the *moulvi* to their home in Curepe. During the course of the visit, she asked the *moulvi* about marriage. He said in time. My aunt then asked him to meet me. He agreed. She organized a meeting. We liked each other right away. We continued to meet at my aunt's for a short time. He asked me to marry him and said that we won't be rich or comfortable, but we'd be happy. I said, "Yes, I accept that. Happiness is more important."[45]

Here again there is the opportunity for chaperoned meetings. The aunt took the initiative but it was the man who asked the girl to marry him, thereby establishing the terms of the marriage. Furthermore, a man who was religiously educated and prominent in society, and wanted to retain such stature, had to be married. This man was already in his thirties, and unmarried status would have been offensive to the matriarchs of the Muslim community. Perhaps a more important consideration is that Islam prohibits celibacy.

Role of the Imam

Imama as leaders of the community also played the role of marriage negotiators. J.M.A.'s marriage was co-arranged by the imam of Caroni and her father. J.M.A. recalls: "My father came home and said to my mother an me dat he hav a boy for me to marry. When parents see someone an dey like dem for you an say you hav to marry dem, yuh do so. He an I see each other a few times before we marry, but we never talk."[46] The marriage took one year to arrange. J.M.A. was fourteen and N.A. was twenty-one when the ceremony took place.

O.G.'s marriage was co-arranged by his parents, the imam of San Juan and uncles of his wife-to-be in 1943. The bride, like the groom, was from the district of Aranguez. Both families were engaged in the same occupation, agri-

culture. "We would see each other when I pass by Boundary Street. I sometimes see she when I go to *masjid*."[47] The family and the imam arranged for
them to meet with a chaperone present, and they were soon engaged. O.G.
was eighteen and his bride-to-be was sixteen. They were engaged for three
years. When engagements similar to the Western type of marital arrangement
entered the Indo-Muslim marital system, they may have provided the groom
with an opportunity to accumulate wealth. Until they married in 1946, the
engaged couple continued to meet at the home of the prospective groom's
family. This allowed the woman a chance to get acquainted with the family
and learn their habits and practices. O.G. recalls that his wife's family told
him when they got engaged, "Meena not accustomed to working hard and
she must not work hard when she get married."[48]

R.A.'s marriage was essentially arranged by his parents, although the district imam played a part, visiting R.A.'s home and in the presence of his parents offering his niece's hand in marriage. The girl, like R.A.'s mother, was
from Rail Street, San Juan. A meeting was set up; R.A. says, "I found her
acceptable and within three weeks we were married."[49]

Intra-village and Community Connections

In the quest to re-establish ties with family and community, children were
sometimes left with relatives in Trinidad while their parents returned to India.
R.A.R. relates how her maternal grandfather went to India in 1904 and left
his daughter, S.A., who was four, in the care of her uncle, giving him ten
shillings to care for his daughter.

> In 1904 Nana [R.A.R.'s maternal grandfather] went back to India. Mama was
> four. So Nana leave Mama with he Mamoo [his mother's brother] and give him
> ten shillings. He tell his Mamoo to engage S.A. to a good boy, but wait for him
> to come back to marry she. Nana didn't want Mama to marry anyone from St
> James or Tacarigua. Mama didn't live her with father's Mamoo but by an aunt
> in Port of Spain.[50]

Nevertheless, S.A.'s great-uncle arranged her marriage to S.A.B. of Peru
Village (St James) before his nephew returned. The context of care can extend
to brokering a marriage, as it takes into consideration fears about a young girl's
sexuality, responsibility for and protection of which are handed to the husband
and his family at marriage. S.A. was nine years old when she was betrothed.

After her father returned and heard that his daughter was married to someone from Peru Village, he never contacted her. R.A.R. believes that because "Nana used to drink and gamble, he heard stories 'bout people from St James and Tacarigua, and so he didn't want Mama marrying someone from there".[51]

Marriages among the children of family acquaintances in the same district were common, especially if they were in the same trade. S.A.'s daughter, R.A.R., was twenty when she married in 1941. In the span of one generation the marital age had increased from nine to twenty. R.A.R.'s spouse was H.R., whose family owned a provision and vegetable stall on St James Main Road. R.A.R., whose family were agriculturalists, recalls that from her young child-hood there was commercial and community interaction between the two fam-ilies. In fact, as a child and a young female, she had heard from her future aunt-in-law that she would marry into the family. R.A.R. acknowledges that H.R., her future husband, seemed nice and that she was interested, but she was quick to note, "In dem days it was unheard of for girls to visit a man's house or go out with him before dey married. But he could visit, though, when there was a chaperone. For Qur'an *khawani* and *maulood shareef* we'd meet and talk, as the family was there and people around." Despite the planting of the idea about whom she should marry when she became of age, R.A.R. says the family never forced the decision. "It just happened. We used to talk and they see we like each other and believe we suit, so they marry we."[52]

In the 1950s "bamboo-shed marriages" underwent a change. Registration of marriages performed under Muslim rites was becoming the norm rather than the exception, a result of education, acculturation and legislation specific to the Muslim community. Additionally, the marital age was on the rise. There was some shifting in the arrangement of marriages. Parents were still the prin-cipal negotiators but the parties had some interaction with each other from childhood or adolescence. They also had a similar educational background. Talking about her husband, M.K.S. recalls:

> We use to pass each other on our way to school and from school nearly every day. He was going Naparima Boys' College and I was at Naparima Girls' High School. We would never talk to the other, though. My marriage was arranged but my consent was sought. His parents met with mine. It would seem that the parents felt we were suitable for each other, as a date was arranged for us to meet in the presence of our respective parents. When we met, I exclaimed, "But I know him!" A date was set for us to marry.[53]

In 1958 H.M.M. was married to S.M. at eighteen. It was a friendship from schooldays, and they lived only a few streets apart. When the couple were teenagers, H.M.M. would visit the home of her future in-laws, with her mother's permission.[54] H.M.M. and S.M. both had secondary-level education. However, she had only Cambridge ordinary levels while he had Cambridge advanced levels. Although it was becoming important for females to attain a secondary education, her education level did not exceed that of her husband's, thereby reinforcing male supremacy.

PRESENTS AND *HALALA*

The Muslim dowry, or *mahr*, which is determined by class and occupation, is an actual gift or an undertaking the groom gives to the bride, and it is her exclusive property once received. This is different from the Western understanding of dowry as the gifts and treasures ("trousseau") the bride brings to the marriage. It is unequivocally not payment for the bride. In Islam the dowry is legally necessary, an integral condition for the validation of the marital contract. It is a symbolic expression of the groom's cognizance of the economic responsibilities of marriage and of his readiness to assume all such responsibilities after the ceremony. Generally the dowry is fixed by taking into consideration the groom's financial position, and it can be handed over at the time of the marriage or given at a later date fixed by the man and agreed to by the woman. Thus a woman's access to property can theoretically come at various stages of life, most notably through her "rights" to inheritance and, in particular, her dowry and maintenance.

Within the Indo-Muslim community these ideals were not always met. Some men never paid the dowry; others paid the dowry and then they or their families reclaimed it after the marriage was consummated. This may have been a result of financial difficulty or belief that the dowry was unimportant, thus reflecting the regard the husband had for his wife as person in her own right. Niehoff and Niehoff note that "the Moslems [*sic*] do not give dowries and, in contrast to Hindus, the bride receives a sum which averages $25–$75, though the range is from a few sweetmeats for poor families to hundreds of dollars for the rich".[55]

There were instances when wives returned the dowry to their husbands.

Jewellery was pawned or sold and the funds given to the husband to assist
him in developing a business enterprise or purchasing land. Gold was also
melted down to produce other of pieces jewellery that could be sold in the
husband's goldsmith shop. These acts should be viewed as proactive; the
women were attempting to improve the quality of their joint lives by selling
or giving away their dowry. While the setting of the *mahr* formed part of marital negotiations and was yet another example of "patriarchy and latent matriarchy" in the Indo-Muslim home, it was also one of the few opportunities for
females to escape from the cycle of patriarchy and matriarchy that informed
their lives. The *mahr* was ideally theirs, and they could dispose of it as they
deemed fit.

N.N.M.A., who was married in 1932, received a Singer sewing machine, a
copy of the Qur'an and a book on the life of Prophet Muhammad.[56] The latter
two gifts are not surprising, since the husband was a religious scholar. H.A.'s
mother, M.A., who was married in 1927, also received a Singer sewing
machine, plus a short sewing course from the Singer Company.[57] Such gifts
would ensure and preserve the role of female domestication, but they also
provided a means by which women could supplement the family income by
contracting out their services to others in the community.

When the dowry payment was in gold, *beras* (wrist bangles) or *churias* (connected bracelets worn from elbow to wrist) were usually given. In 1958
H.M.M. received a "gold watch from Y. de Lima" for her dowry.[58] The giving
of money was also not uncommon. In 1916 F.A. gave his bride thirty dollars
for her *mahr*. R.A., a tailor, gave his bride seventy-five dollars in 1942, while
O.G., a labourer at the Botanical Gardens, gave thirty dollars to his bride in
1946.[60] H.M.M.'s husband was a teacher, while F.A. was an agricultural
labourer on his parent's land. Clearly occupation informed the generosity of
the *mahr*.

Z.M., whose husband worked as a tailor at a commercial enterprise, gave
her fifty dollars' worth of gold jewellery.[61] Afrose Hydal, one of the women
who mounted the lecture podium of the Tackveeyatul Islamia Association
(TIA) during the 1930s, accepted as her dower a payment of forty dollars from
her tailor husband-to-be in 1924.[62] However, the dowry was not paid until forty
years later, in 1964, when the Hydals' children were adults and the dowry payment no longer represented an economic strain.

Z.K., who was married in 1938, received a *mala* (a necklace of gold flowers) for her *mahr*, which she says was "taken back by he family after we live together for a while. I believed it was wrong, as yuh doh take back things when you give it to someone."[63] Neither was it unusual for the dowry to be a part of the mother-in-law's jewellery collection. S.M.S. received as her dowry a pair of *churias* made from her mother-in-law's melted *pan-ka-haikul* (a thick necklace with a leaf-shaped pendant).[64] F.K., daughter of Al Haj Moulvi Fateh Dad Khan, a British Guianese missionary, says that her mother received in 1943 a gold band for her dowry,[65] which is very different from the gifts N.N.M.A. received from her religious scholar–missionary husband.

J.M.A. was supposed to receive forty dollars for her dowry, but it was never paid. Not until six or seven years later did her husband seek to recompense her, as a result of a bet. He gave her a pair of *churia* from Y. de Lima's that were worth a hundred dollars.

> He bring home dis gif for me. When he gave me it, I ask him, "What is this?" He tell me, "Open it, girl." Well, I open it and I see is a pair of *churia*. I ask him where he get it from. He tell me, he and his friends went to Port of Spain an dey pass by Y. de Lima's. Dey began bettin each other on who go buy it for deir wife. Niamath, he stupid. He bet with dem an decide to buy it to win a bet.[66]

It must be kept in mind that among Indians, jewellery was a signifier of status and wealth. The dowry gave the women an opportunity to engage in an act of self-determination about her immediate future and improve the quality of her life. As Shameen Ali observes, "Young women no longer needed to come to marriage with a dowry [bridal price] to equalize the asymmetry in the relationship. Whereas formerly the groom was the centre of attention and a wedding was an opportunity to show respect to him (and his family), the focus of attention was now shifting to the bride."[67]

Whatever the transformation taking place within the Hindu community, the Muslim community continued to focus on "protecting" the female by way of the *mahr*. As with the changing age structure of marriages, the value and character of the dowry have undergone many modifications. Today it can include gifts to the bride of capital assets such as land, property, vehicles, money and jewellery, as well as support for higher education (as in recent weddings within my own family).

HOUSEHOLD DYNAMICS

New income opportunities for women facilitate the process of renegotiating gender identities; not only is the concept of a good woman challenged but also that of the male as provider of the family. This has implications for the age of marriage and dowry in terms of form, value and content. In the post-indentureship period most women lived with their in-laws in extended family households. There evolved nuanced and complex power dynamics between and among the various members of the household and the daughter-in-law. The household is often imbued with rituals and norms of the wider Indian society, which ascribes, and sometimes obligates, roles for members. In essence, the household dynamics represent multiple functions of patriarchy and culture related to gender, age and class. While Muslim women also worked in the fields or the family business, they were responsible for the domestic sphere. Daughters-in-law were expected to be compliant, respectful, modest and diligent, and above all to perform the household chores in the context of an omnipresent and omnipotent mother-in-law. The gradual shift from the extended family – which Shameen Ali notes began a steady decline from the 1940s and 1950s – to a nuclear family altered the gender politics in the household.

Some females, like S.A., J.A. and J.M.A., endured physical abuse from their husbands. Others, like Z.K., received verbal denunciations from their in-laws. When R.A.R.'s husband returned home drunk, she bore the brunt of his ravings. N.N.M.A. stood by her husband's side and accepted religious disparagement. Some women worked to supplement the family's income. Some were barely literate and others had a primary-level education. Just as their mothers had endured hardship, these women also lived it. For a number of women and girls today – regardless of ethnicity and religion – intergenerational poverty, violence and violation of fundamental human rights prevent them from attaining the best quality of life available. For others their quality of life is the result of choices and sacrifices made by their forebears that redounded to their benefit. Separation and divorce were generally not options that these women pursued (nor did some men), even after 1936, with the promulgation of the Muslim Marriage and Divorce Ordinance. Rather, economic reality, coupled with traditions of female shame and family honour, led women to negotiate amity within the household.

MARRIAGES WITHIN AN INCREASINGLY GLOBALIZED SOCIETY

Factors such as increased education, participation in the labour market, industrialization and urbanization, the effects of the Trinidad oil boom, and the influence of American culture impacted the revitalization and reconstruction of traditional cultural forms to incorporate Western Christian elements into the Indo-Muslim world view. This has led to increasing accommodation of Western-style dating and love marriages. Furthermore, prolonging the period between puberty and marriage has had an impact on courtship patterns, as young people today have many more opportunities to meet and interact with members of the opposite sex on their own, independent of direct parental oversight. In the early twentieth century Seepersad Naipaul captured the fears of the time in *The Adventures of Gurudeva and Other Stories*. The protagonist comments, "in the first place they learned to write love-letters, then again, they wore knee-length frocks, and – the most shameful thing of all – many of them choose their own husbands".[69] Now those concerns have been realized.

In recent weddings in my own family, the marriage ceremony was a hybrid of Islamic and Western traditions. This is a reflection of identity as defined by the individuals' and the couple's world view – of themselves, of family and community and of marriage. It opens an exciting area for exploration of how men and women see themselves pre- and post-marriage, their relations to each other, the relationship within wider familial networks and community, and how they see themselves in relation to the roles defined by secular Westernized images of the nuclear family and romantic love and by new forms of Islam.

In my own relatives' weddings within the past five years, my highly educated professional male and female cousins have married either Muslims or converts to Islam in either traditional marriage ceremonies or table marriages. In articulating their agreement to the marriage during the ceremony, the female converts usually gave their consent by saying "I do" three times, whereas the non-converts tended to signal their agreement by saying "yes" three times. By and large the women wore modest traditional white wedding dresses, and occasionally the *ghagra choli* (a long, flowing skirt and snug cropped blouse, often accompanied by a *dupatta* or *orhni*, or headscarf). The grooms tended to wear *kurta salwaar* (a loose jacket worn with traditional loose trousers). Painting of the bride's hands and feet with *mehendi* (a red paste made of dried leaves, also known as henna) has reasserted itself. Music, if present, tends to be Indian film music or Arabic music. On some occasions there was a live band, also playing Indian film music (which would morph into chutney later in the evening), or a *tassa* group. The other festive parts of a Western-style wedding, such as cake-cutting, the first dance and such, were not generally part of the proceedings, although if they were, it was later in the evening, with the couple's contemporaries.

While Islamic fundamentalism has led to retention of arranged and semi-arranged marriages, marriage by personal choice, preferably with parental approval, is not uncommon. These developments can be seen as contradistinctions to the greater incidence of veiling and modest clothing styles among some females, and to Islamist appeals *inter alia* for premarital chastity and *purdah* (segregation by sex).

For young Muslim girls there is collusion between the Western and Islamic practices in forging the path they traverse, which they negotiate by choice. H.B., eighteen years old, was married in July 1993.[70] Marriage, she notes, affected her life; she has more responsibility, as she has to balance her life among multiple demands: her husband and his family, her family, Islamic activities, social activities and education. Their meeting was an arranged one orchestrated by one of her sisters two years before, but she adds that once she and her sisters had attained puberty their father provided opportunities for them to meet suitable Muslim boys. She says that she and her beau wanted to strengthen their relationship.

H.B. notes that, despite the new emphasis on education, female autonomy and self-sufficiency, women are still expected to maintain their chastity prior to marriage. During the course of her relationship with her intended they were consistently chaperoned. Once they had agreed to marriage, the *nikah* (marriage ceremony) and *walima* (marriage banquet) took place one week after, reinforcing the moral and social authority of marriage. Both she and her husband were enrolled in university programmes and thus were financially dependent on their parents. H.B. is adamant that, in accord with her verbal prenuptial agreement, she would not accept violence from her husband against her or her children, nor would she accept his taking another wife; those actions, she believes, are grounds for divorce. The importance of honour and adherence to the tenets of religion competes with the practical realities associated with marriage, including economic autonomy.

While H.B. insists that participating in a polygamous marriage would be unacceptable, some women do, despite the Muslim Marriage and Divorce Act. Of women interviewed in 1994, two were involved in a polygamous marriage and neither felt that she had been cheated or violated.[71] For instance, A.A.B. says that in this, her third marriage she did not want any more children; she already had two from her previous marriages. That is why her husband approached her and she agreed to his taking another wife, one who was younger, healthier and desirable to him. She indicates that she harbours no feelings of betrayal, anger, jealousy or animosity to her husband's co-partner. She says there exists a level of cordiality in their relationships, acknowledging that they all have separate residences, which allows for that cordiality. She notes that while equality is the essential prescription for polygamy in Islam, it would be unfair of her to expect the same level of maintenance. She, unlike the second wife (who does not work), is highly educated and works, receiving a relatively high remuneration.

The third wife in this polygamous marriage (F.A.) notes that she was welcomed by her co-wives and that she views the situation as akin to an extended family. She says that if she feels her faith waning she can depend on her husband or co-partners to "pull her up". F.A. also declares that being a part of a polygamous relationship has strengthened both her as an individual and her faith as she learned to cope with the negative emotions. She further notes that her husband is not the type of man to openly show his affection or preference for one wife over the other; she likes to think that he treats them all fairly. F.A. is particularly steadfast in her view that Islam is a way of life that allows for the practice of polygamy; she sees herself as legally married, with the right to refer to herself by her husband's name.

Issues such as jealousy, violence, dominance and unequal treatment were not identified by the interviewees; in fact, the relationships were portrayed as harmonious. What was observed during the interviews was the issue of power vis-à-vis the husband – referred to as "the imam" – highlighted by the fact that both respondents sought permission from him for the interview, which may have tempered their responses to the interview questions. The Muslim Marriage and Divorce Act states: "nothing in this Act shall authorise or validate the contracting or registration of a polygamous marriage". The Muslim community therefore must identify ways through its moral framework to come to terms with the issue of polygamy, especially as it places women, regardless of age, in very vulnerable position vis-à-vis powerful and wealthy men.

Despite the impact of modernity, which provides a space for intense moral and political contestation – not least of all regarding ideals of self and sexuality, femininity, family and religion – marriage continues to be seen as pivotal to the protection of a daughter's sexuality and the family's status and reputation. In south Trinidad in the 1990s, an eighteen-year-old Muslim woman (Mrs A.) from a wealthy traditional Indian family was married to a distant cousin, a man twenty years her senior. She indicates that she has no strong emotional attachment to the man she married but will remain "true" to the marriage, as to do otherwise would shame not only her but her family. She also says she would not consider divorce, despite the fact that it is permitted in Islam and under the Muslim Marriage and Divorce Act, because another man and his family would consider her "experienced and impure". She acknowledges that she has no way of eking out an independent existence; her education does not extend beyond secondary school, and all she has been trained for is to be a "good wife".

Mrs A.'s marriage was consummated and eventually she became pregnant. She recognized that all sources of escape would be barred to her, as having a child further consolidates a marriage. Consequently she made a decision to have an abortion, although abortion is by and large illegal in Trinidad and generally *haram* (forbidden) in Islam.[72] At the time of the interview her husband had no knowledge that a pregnancy had resulted from their sexual activity.[73] Thus Mrs A. chose a solution which, as long as knowledge of it remained hidden, allowed for a temporary solution and assured her respect within the community. Subsequent to this interview it was learned that she had divorced her husband under the Muslim Marriage and Divorce Act, which suggests that either her circumstances or her perspectives had changed.

CULTURAL AND GENDER NEGOTIATIONS IN MODERN SOCIETY

History and historical evidence provide crucial insight into a people's sense of identity; they illuminate the challenges of the present and suggest potentials for the future through understanding of the past. In this regard the narrative provided here validates the agency of the Indo-Muslim community, which has developed an internal logic and dynamism in its reconstitution of a cosmology, political system and family structure, including gender systems. What does this narrative of the past suggest for the present and immediate future in the context of the economic imperatives of globalization? Caribbean societies are concerned about the benefits and impacts of regional integration, expanding market access, high public debt, growing joblessness, crime and violence, social infrastructure, homogenization of diverse populations and social exclusion of some groups. The paradoxes of modernity hold both opportunities and constraints for disadvantaged groups or "Others" in terms of the intersections provided by race/ethnicity, class and culture/religion. As Reddock explains, the politics of the late twentieth century saw a shift from emphasis solely on economic and political justice for oppressed groups to a focus on (multi)cultural citizenship. Hence there is growing recognition of the need for the culture of the mainstream to be more inclusive and representative of the diversity of all constituents, thereby resulting in meaningful citizenship.[74]

The history of colonial and post-colonial multi-ethnic Trinidad and Tobago in the late nineteenth and twentieth centuries can be characterized by a demand for respect, acceptance and inclusion, manifested in part through demands for recognition of Muslim marriages (*nikah*) and realized through the Muslim Marriage and Divorce Act of 1935 (last amended in 1980). But the problematic of culture and identity, which historiography contributes to identifying and defining, does not always reflect the dynamism, fluidity and diversity within the collective. Thus a greater appreciation for nuances within cultures is required.

Reddock argues that the struggle for recognition of this cultural/religious difference revealed the codification of male privilege within private and public familial space. During the debates and discussions leading up to the Muslim Marriage and Divorce Ordinance, on only one recorded occasion was there a female advocate. In October 1934 the Young Muslim Women's Association hosted a meeting where Afrose Hydal was the principal speaker; her topic was "Problems of Women in Islam". She advocated education for women, urging them to form clubs for their social and educational advancement that would raise them to the same status as men. In the conclusion of her speech, she said that Muslims should unanimously support the Muslim Marriage and

Divorce bill. F.H. Aziz, an attendee at the lecture, suggested that Muslim women should hold a mass meeting to get a deputation headed by Hydal to approach the governor about the bill.[75] This provides a cogent example of women who are members of religious and ethnic collectivities recognizing at the same time the need for individual interventions to sway others.

While the historical and cultural experiences of the Muslim community must be seen through the lens of its own conditions, the Indo-Muslim community of Trinidad illustrates the complexities of modernity, gender relations and cultural recognition and inclusion. The paradox of modernity includes "the struggle for the realisation of the potential – not only individual rights but also the self-actualisation of the individual and their desires, accompanied by a presumed emancipation from some of the constraints of community".[76] Time and space, coupled with disembedding mechanisms such as education, erode established precepts and practices developed during the period of reconstitution. Instead they provide an opportunity for modification (adaptation or innovation) of marital arrangements in a spectrum ranging from arranged to Western-influenced marital negotiations and ceremonies. Bauer's explanations provide insights into the constructions of masculinity and its role in the reconstitution of communities, and hence insight into the relations of gender power and how it is normalized. What remains important is the notion of clinging to a particular construction of religion and culture as the arbiter of social norms in transplanted communities over time. Hence there is increasing pressure for feminism to focus on the diversity of selves, performativity and desires, individual agency and increasingly self-conscious subjects.[77]

Despite various pieces of legislation in Trinidad and Tobago that give recognition to diverse ethnic, cultural and religious demands and the incremental gains made towards achievement of gender equity – particularly since the first United Nations Decade for Women Conference – in the areas of legislation and policy, labour market participation and increased access to public resources such as tertiary education and health care, there is still cause for concern. The continued existence of provisions within the Muslim Marriage Act which conflict with new provisions in recently enacted legislation has been a source of concern for the UN committees on the Convention on the Rights of the Child and the Convention on the Elimination of All Forms of

Discrimination against Women. Achieving consensus on the disparity in the age of marriage under the Muslim Marriage Act has not been realized. Reddock notes:

> The continued existence of provisions within the marriage acts which actually conflict with new legislation suggests that they continue to be of great symbolic importance. This was evident, as noted above, in the resistance to changing the age of marriage for women in the Muslim and Hindu Marriage Acts. These acts serve to maintain distinct axes of patriarchal power and recognition along religious and ethnic lines hence the reason religious leaders (mainly male) have resisted efforts to bring them in line with other legislative changes and new thinking on women's human rights.[78]

Reddock's sentiments are echoed in the 2005 shadow report to the UN Commission on the Rights of the Child:

> due consideration must be given to "who" the parties to the decision making process are. In a society where positions of power within political, religious, cultural and social organizations are still largely held by men and patriarchal views and positions are articulated and maintained the human rights of women and girls continue to be marginalized.[79]

The statement by H.B. that she will not tolerate domestic violence is recalled here. Shelters for victims of domestic violence are also run by a Muslim body. Hence multiculturalism – as argued by several scholars, including Nira Yuval-Davis, and supported by Reddock – while providing recognition can also increase the predicaments and vulnerability of women and other disadvantaged groups. Religion is part of modernization, even though it does not necessarily liberate women. Islam is no different. What is required now is more nuanced understanding of the intersections of Islam, capitalism, modernity, gender and generation in Trinidad, and how all of this is structured in the context of design and circumstance.

IMMEDIATE FUTURE CONCERNS

Today the Muslim community, like many other sub-populations, confronts the impact of persistent and acute poverty and socio-economic inequalities, social and religious fundamentalism, and varying levels of educational attainment. This community is also forced to consider the impact of these social injustices, fundamentalism and changing social conditions on marriage and fertility, and by extension the community's demographic security. Though they are not very common, it also has to concern itself with inter-religious marriage and what that means for the next generation. But equally important is the fact that the community has to come to terms with issues such as sexually transmitted infections (STIs), including HIV and AIDS; domestic violence, including cyber-violence; homosexuality; in vitro fertilization (IVF); and polygamy, which is not condoned by the Muslim Marriage and Divorce Act. The Muslim community needs to consider taking a look at its moral framework, including personal laws, to bring it more in line with the challenges that modern society poses (such as foreign online marriage sites) and ensure the protection of its members.

Online marriage and matrimonial sites, paid or free, in developed and developing countries, provide a platform for online dating and matrimonial cyber-courtship. This provides a new twist to arranged marriages – self-directed but mediated through the Internet. The services are either free or charge a modest membership fee.[80] A Reuters article from May 2007 notes, "on some sites, more than half the registered users are professional women with above-average incomes who use the service to save time and broaden the scope of their search. They are direct and demanding about what they are looking for."[81] Visiting a few of these websites reveals their similar approaches.

> These are great places to meet other Muslims. If faith is important to you – and will be an important part of your relationship – then this site will make it easy to find the right person for you. . . . You can use our site to meet Muslim singles, *Muslim ladies* seeking marriage, Muslim chat, *Muslim friends* or *Muslim penpals.*
>
> Our site is one of the largest Muslim matrimonials and *personals* sites with *single Muslim women* and men from all over the world. *Sign up free today!*
>
> Single Muslim is a closely monitored and cost effective matrimonial service for single Muslims, making it a safe, secure and economical choice for your search for an ideal marriage partner. Our goal is to use technology to provide the best possible help for single Muslim members to increase their chances of finding an ideal Muslim marriage partner.[82]

BestMuslim.com is another free Muslim online dating/matrimonial/ marriage service. Membership is free, though one has to register to contact any person registered. A perusal of this website in late August 2009 indicated that thirty-four Trinidadians had registered since February 2008. Presently eighteen males and thirteen females are registered. Other sites, such as singlemuslim.com, muslimmuslima.com and muslimfriends.com, provide searchable databases of Trinidadian Muslims seeking friendship and/or marriage. These sites provide photo galleries, video introductions, live chat rooms and voice messaging. They are seen as providing a safe (and *halal*, or acceptable) space in which Muslims can meet and socialize.

An arranged marriage was the norm in the past, but dating/matrimonial and social networking websites have created a compromise between traditional and contemporary attitudes. While the tenets of Islam prohibit premarital relationships of any kind between members of the opposite sex, the Web provides a space where women and men can interact with each other. The Internet is thus replacing the family and marriage bureaus as the intermediary in arranging marriages. These online facilities indicate the globalized nature of Islam and the Muslim world and suggest that there are postscripts to be considered, such as forging new identities or manipulating old ones, cross-border and transnational marriages, and the impact of new immigration laws/policies/dialogue. What may seem like a shift in the concept of arranged marriages (or even dating) is in fact a movement along the continuum of negotiated marriages involving bride and groom, families and communities.

According to the 2000 Population and Housing Census (PHC), the Muslim community constituted about 6 percent of the total population, with a lower proportion of children under fifteen and an increasing proportion of working-age population (fifteen to sixty-four years). This meant that more young people would be exploring productive opportunities and making decisions about their reproductive future. To respond to this need, the Islamic Ladies Social and Cultural Association (ILSCA) of the Islamic Academy, formed in 1970, set up a programme that provides marriage counselling, premarital advice and guidance and a "forum for youths (males and females) to meet and discuss their problems regarding life as it relates to religion, social needs and family life".[83] The ILSCA hosted a social and cultural evening for youths during the 1990s that was very similar to the Islamic Society of North America's "matrimonial banquet" in 2006, where young males and females chaperoned by parents met in a *halal* environment. The banquet was followed by an hour-long social hour that gave participants time to collect e-mail addresses and telephone numbers over a pasta dinner with sodas.

Nevertheless, the new spaces provided and enabled by technology provide youths with a space – as exciting as it is risky – in which to shape and affirm their identity, negotiate their sexuality and meet a potential dating partner. Modern technology has raised new questions and created new challenges as to which personal laws should incorporate these contemporary means of communication. Since 2003 attention has been drawn to the use of SMS (short message service) and e-mail in the matter of divorce proceedings. Digital divorces have taken place in the United Arab Emirates and in Malaysia: cell phones were used to end marriages by SMS messaging *"Talaq, talaq, talaq"* ("I divorce thee" three times in succession).[84]

"Afsana Mushtaq" of Delhi became the first Indian woman to be digitally divorced when her husband e-mailed her the triple *talaq*. This provides a clear example of how Islamic authorities need to adapt their rules to new technology or risk losing relevance to today's Muslims, who are living in a world in which information and communications technology is pervasive. *Shar'iah* (Islamic law) treats technology as a medium of communication, and once the message is communicated and authenticated, under *shar'iah* it becomes legal. The issue is abuse of the privilege and reinforcement of the privilege and power. The Muslim community of Trinidad needs to recognize the new influences, threats and risks that are likely to impact upon the community and to advocate for changes to the existing Muslim marriage and divorce acts.

For young people growing up in this world, the Internet offers a place for cultural consumption and production, a venue for information exchange and engagement. Until a survey is conducted on the purposes for which the Internet is used in the Caribbean, its reach will remain shrouded in mystery. In Iran there have been examples of Internet use for unregulated meeting, mating and cheating with online partners.[85] In the courtship of H.B., it will be recalled that their encounters were chaperoned, a practice which was guided by the Islamic precepts of heterosociality. Heterosexuality in Iran is similarly heavily regulated, so Internet meetings and mating take on a new significance. Within a regime that legislates on people's bodies, sexualities and intimacy there is now a forum for women and men to exercise their sexuality in which reputations, respect and honour are important. Cyberspace provides for interaction in the form of courtship that could lead to meeting and, possibly, to cybersex or cyber-cheating.

So the question remains: how do young Muslim men and women exist in the dual space in Trinidad – modern/secular and religious/traditional – and exercise their sexual identity? And to what extent is redefinition of Muslim identity, as distinct from ethnic and national identity, (re)defining masculinity and femininity? For young people, social networking sites have proven popular. In 2007 more than 105 million Muslims were online globally.[86] To what extent are Muslim Trinidadian men and women (and girls and boys) using social utility sites such as Facebook, MySpace, Friendster, Twitter and YouTube? Or are they using Muslim social media sites, such as Naseeb, Muxlim, Muslimica, MuslimSocial.com and Mecca.com, that cater to a specific public within their cultural space? Are they traversing between the global and local sites? We have seen that some Trinidadians use Muslim matrimonial/dating sites and that these sites are aware that there is niche market for Trinidadian Muslims. A more detailed content analysis of social networking and online matrimonial sites and a targeted survey are required to elicit further information on uses and influences of the Internet among young Muslim men and women.

This issue touches on Islamic discourses. An acculturated form of Islam draws from the cultural resources of the environs; being Muslim, Indian and Trinidadian are not mutually exclusive. In this regard three positions are posited: (1) to turn away from Islam, assimilate entirely into society and become a "secular" or "cultural" Muslim; (2) to subscribe to a culturally transcendental form of Islam by arguing that just as South Asian (or Middle Eastern or East African) cultural accretions have got in the way of a "pure" Islam, all non-Islamic cultural outputs are alien and threatening to Islam and must be rejected; and (3) to accept that Islam is practised differently in various contexts, and that Trinidadian Muslims must understand their religion in light of their context.

CONCLUSION

In the early days, class and occupation influenced marital patterns among Indo-Muslims but generally religious endogamy prevailed. During the course of the twentieth century, marital forms in the Indo-Muslim community were in transition, moving from the classical arranged type to the semi-arranged form to adopting characteristics of the Western type. The education system and the mobility that it brought was perhaps the most significant motivation for change; the process of education does not exist independently of other structures, communities, culture and class. Just as education patterns changed, so too did marriage patterns. Marriage and dowry were among the significant features of cultural retention, while marital age increased over time. The Muslim community now faces the impact of contemporary technologies and needs to respond to those developments. But as ethnic (religious) identity formation evolved and continues to do so, through objectification and commodification of ethnicity and also in the context of Other, certain aspects of shared practices based upon ethnic/class lines remain.[87] Globalization, therefore, has maintained, even reinforced, the fractured and fragmented identities – ethnic and religious – and thus the ways in which mating, marriage, *mahr* and separation/divorce are coded will depend on opportunity and preference within the collective.

NOTES

1. Brij Lal, "The Odyssey of Indenture: Fragmentation and Reconstitution in the Indian Diaspora", *Diaspora* 5, no. 2 (1996): 9.
2. In this chapter "East Indian" is used to mark ancestry; while "Indo-Muslim" is used, it privileges the Indian (ancestry) first and then the religious identity. This contestation about privileging of identities continues to be a mantra in the discourse today. Nevertheless, "Indo-Muslim" is used in this chapter to signal being part of a wider Indian community but with a particular religious belief system that influences or guides action.
3. Demographic security addresses *inter alia* changes in these demographic conditions and interactions among them, including migration, population growth, shifts in age structure and the changing location and proportion of ethnic and religious groups. See Richard P. Cincotta, "Demographic Security Comes of Age", *ECSP Report* 10 (2004): 24, http://www.wilsoncenter.org/topics/pubs/ecspr10-C-cincotta.pdf (accessed 15 January 2007).
4. Bridget Brereton, *A History of Modern Trinidad, 1783–1962* (Kingston: Heinemann, 1981), 110.
5. *Census of Trinidad and Tobago, 1921.*

6. *Administrative Report of the Protector of Immigrants for the Year 1927*, Council Paper 45 (1928).

7. The system of ward schools was established in Trinidad by the Education Ordinance of 1851. Ward schools were free and run by a board of education and a salaried inspector. Instruction was to be entirely secular, but each week at stated times the clergyman of the majority faith in the ward would undertake to teach religion; parents were free to withdraw their children if they wished. However, the challenges faced by the ward schools led to enunciation of a new Education Ordinance in 1870, which led to establishment of a dual system of state-aided schools co-existing with Christian denominational schools. See Brereton, *History of Modern Trinidad*, 123–24.

8. *Census of Trinidad and Tobago, 1946.*

9. The caste system is an organization of social life that ranks individuals by an ascribed social status. In India the caste system was made up of Brahmins (priests), Kshatriyas (warriors), Vaishyas (tradesmen), Shudras (workers) and Chamar ("untouchables"). The Brahmins, Kshatriyas and Vaishyas occupied the highest positions in society. The system of caste categorization and hierarchy, or *varna*, was retained and corresponded to occupational groups.

10. Holy Qur'an, 33:35, 16:97 and 2:195; 4:124, 32; and 9:71–72.

11. These include women from the early Muslim community who lived alongside the Prophet and in the succeeding communities of the Salaf and Khalaf. These role models include the Prophet's wife, Khadija bint Khuwaylid, the first convert to Islam and a powerful, savvy businesswoman; Sumayyah bint Khabbab, the first martyr of Islam; women who excelled in scholarship such as Aiysha, whose interest in politics is also famous; Fatima the Prophet's daughter and Nafisa bint Hassan, treasured for their spirituality and wisdom; and fearsome fighters such as Nusaybah bint Ka'b.

12. Ishtiaq H. Qureshi, *The Muslim Community of the Indo-Pakistan Continent, 610–1947: A Brief Historical Analysis* (Delhi: Renaissance, 1985), 253.

13. An influential local/global element in effecting feminism in the Muslim world (that is, the Middle East and Africa) is the role of exiles and migrant women in diaspora communities in the West. Despite the steady outward migration of Caribbean nationals, including Muslims, to Britain or North America, there are no known links between Caribbean and diasporic Muslim associations that make contributions at the political, informational, theoretical, technical and organizational levels to spur awareness of Islamic feminism or to address women's issues both theologically and theoretically. This gap can be bridged by facilitating connections through exchanges between women's activist groups and sharing liter-

ature via the Internet – what Fatima Mernissi calls the "digital Islamic galaxy". See N. Tohidi, "The Global–Local Intersection of Feminism in Muslim Societies: The Cases of Iran and Azerbaijan", *Social Research* (2002), http://goliath.ecnext. com/coms2-0199-22114859/The-global-local-intersection-of.html (accessed 5 March 2007).

14. Lois Lamya' al Faruqi, "Islamic Traditions and the Feminist Movement: Confrontation or Cooperation?", http://www.jannah.org/sisters/feminism.html (accessed 15 January 2007).

15. Michiel Baas, "Arranged Love: Marriage in a Transnational Work Environment", *IIAS Newsletter* 45 (Autumn 2007): 9.

16. Patricia Mohammed, *Gender Negotiations among Indians in Trinidad, 1917–1947* (Basingstoke, UK: Palgrave, 2002), 23.

17. Patricia Mohammed, "Internal Affairs: Arranged Marriages among Indians in Trinidad between 1917 and 1947" (paper presented at the Lunchtime Seminar Series, Women and Development Studies, University of the West Indies, St Augustine, Trinidad, 1991), 10.

18. R.A.R., interview by author, St James, Trinidad, 22 March 1996.

19. Fatima Mernissi, *Beyond the Veil: Male–Female Relations in a Modern Muslim Society* (London: Al Saqui, 1975), 44.

20. Camille Fawzi El-Solh and Judy Mabro, eds., *Muslim Women's Choices, Religious Belief and Social Reality: Cross Cultural Perspectives on Women*, vol. 12 (Oxford: Berg, 1994), 8.

21. Stephanie Daly, "The Development of Law Affecting East Indians in Trinidad and Tobago" (paper presented at the Conference on East Indians, University of the West Indies, St Augustine, Trinidad, 1984), 13.

22. Muslim Marriage and Divorce Ordinance, 1935.

23. *Administrative Report of the Protector of Immigrants, 1928.*

24. *Administrative Report of the Protector of Immigrants, 1931.*

25. J.C. Jha, "The Background to the Legalization of Non-Christian Marriage in Trinidad and Tobago", in *East Indians in the Caribbean: Colonialism and the Struggle for Identity*, edited by Bridget Brereton and Winston Dookeran (New York: Kraus International, 1982).

26. *Administrative Report of the Protector of Immigrants, 1931.*

27. See the reports of the protector of immigrants, 1936–39.

28. D. Sahadat and Edan were remarried by Subhan Ali, the Muslim Marriage Officer of the Eastern counties. Their marriage was reregistered at the Sangre Grande warden's office, 19 December 1938. "1906 Marriage Legalised", *Sunday Guardian*, 25 December 1938, 26.

29. Arthur Niehoff and Juanita Niehoff, *East Indians in the West Indies*, Milwaukee Public Museum Publications in Anthropology 6 (Milwaukee, Wis.: Olsen, 1961), 102.

30. Mohammed, *Gender Negotiations*, 217.

31. Ibid., 259.

32. El-Solh and Mabro, *Muslim Women's Choices*, 14.

33. A.H. Bittles, "A Background Summary of Consanguineous Union" (Perth, Australia: Centre for Human Genetics, Edith Cowan University, 2001), 3, http://www.consang.net/images/d/dd/01AHBWeb3.pdf (accessed 5 March 2007).

34. A.B., interview by author, St James, Trinidad, 21 March 1996.

35. Ibid.

36. Bukhari and Muslim, two authoritative transmitters of *hadith* (record of the words and deeds of the Prophet), report that the Prophet Muhammad said, "a virgin's consent must be asked about herself, her consent being her silence". See Yusuf Qaradawi, *The Lawful and Prohibited in Islam* (Malaysia: Islamic Book Trust, 1995), 176–77.

37. Niehoff and Niehoff, *East Indians*, 102.

38. Z.K., interview by author, St James, Trinidad, 31 July 1996.

39. Ibid.

40. Ibid.

41. F.A., interview by author, Aranguez, Trinidad, 26 February 1998.

42. S.M.S., interview by author, Valsayn, Trinidad, 19 February 1998.

43. Ibid.

44. Ibid.

45. N.N.M.A., interview by author, St Joseph, Trinidad, 6 July 1996.

46. J.M.A., interview by author, Caroni, Trinidad, 26 March 1998.

47. O.G., interview by author, Aranguez, Trinidad, 26 February 1998.

48. Ibid.

49. R.A., interview by author, San Juan, Trinidad, 16 February 1998.

50. R.A.R., interview by author, St James, Trinidad, 22 March 1996.

51. Ibid.

52. Ibid.

53. M.K.S., interview by author, San Fernando, Trinidad, 25 October 1996.

54. H.M.M., interview by author, San Juan, Trinidad, 20 June 1996.

55. Niehoff and Niehoff, *East Indians*, 105.

56. N.N.M.A., interview by author, St Joseph, Trinidad, 11 October 1996.

57. H.A., interview by author, Warrenville, Trinidad, 11 December 1996.

58. H.M.M. interview.

59. F.A. interview.
60. R.A. interview; O.G. interview.
61. Z.M., interview by author, Barataria, Trinidad, 23 April 1997.
62. Maulana M.K. Hydal (son of Afrose Hydal), interview by author, St Augustine, Trinidad, 2 November 1997.
63. Z.K. interview.
64. S.M.S. interview.
65. F.K., interview by author, Arima, Trinidad, 24 January 1998.
66. J.M.A. interview.
67. Shameen Ali, "A Social History of East Indian Women in Trinidad Since 1870" (PhD diss., University of the West Indies, St Augustine, Trinidad, 1993), 65.
68. Ibid.
69. Seepersad Naipaul, *The Adventures of Gurudeva and Other Stories* (London: André Deutsch, 1964), 146.
70. Halima-Sa'adia Kassim, "The Muslim Woman in Trinidad and Tobago: Myth vs Reality, 1960–1993" (Caribbean Studies project, University of the West Indies, St Augustine, Trinidad, 1994), 44–45.
71. Ibid., 36–43.
72. Muslims generally regard abortion as wrong and *haram*, but many accept that it may be permitted if continuing the pregnancy would put the mother's life in real danger. This permission is based on the principle of the lesser of two evils, known in Islamic legal terminology as *al-ahamm wa 'l-muhimm* (the more important and the less important). Performing abortions is generally illegal in Trinidad and Tobago under the Offences Against the Person Act of 3 April 1925, as amended. Nonetheless, under general criminal law principles of necessity, an abortion can be legally performed to save the life of a pregnant woman. Moreover, Trinidad and Tobago, like a number of Commonwealth countries whose legal systems are based on English common law, follows the holding of the English *Rex v. Bourne* decision (1938) in determining whether an abortion performed for health reasons is lawful. See Ibrahim B. Syed, "Abortion in Islam", http://www.islamawareness.net/FamilyPlanning/Abortion/abortion3.h tml, and United Nations Department of Economic and Social Affairs, "Trinidad and Tobago Abortion Policy", http://www.un.org/esa/population/publications/abortion/doc/trinidad.doc 30:08:2009.
73. Kassim, "Muslim Woman", 31–32.
74. Rhoda Reddock, "Gender, Nation and the Dilemmas of Citizenship: The Case of the Marriage Acts of Trinidad and Tobago", in *The Global Empowerment of Women*, edited by Carolyn M. Elliott (New York: Routledge, 2008). I would like

to express my appreciation to Rhoda Reddock for sharing with me this article prior to the release of the collection in which it appeared.

75. Ibid., 26.

76. Janet Bauer, "'Accented Feminisms': The Misrecognition of Iranian Gender and Modernity in Western (Feminist) Theory", in *Gender Relations and Modernity in Iran*, edited by Golnaz Amin (Proceedings of the Fifteenth International Conference of the Iranian Women's Studies Foundation, Massachusetts, Summer 2004).

77. Ibid.

78. Reddock, "Gender, Nation".

79. Trinidad and Tobago Coalition on the Rights of the Child, "NGO Comments on Trinidad and Tobago Second Periodic Report under the Convention on the Rights of the Child", CRC-NGO Alternative Report, April 2005, http://www.crin. org/docs/resources/treaties/crc.40/Trinidad ngo report.doc/resources/treaties/ crc.40/Trinidad-ngo-report.pdf (accessed 20 August 2008).

80. The fees range from $30 (€23) for three months' membership in muslimwed ding.org to £25 (€37) for muslim-marriages.co.uk.

81. Luke Baker, "Muslim, Traditional, but Finding Love on the Web", Reuters, 1 May 2007, http://www.ioltechnology.co.za/article_page.php?iSectionId=2891&i ArticleId=3808376 (accessed 19 March 2008).

82. The quotations are from, respectively, MuslimSingles, http://www.lookbetter online.com/onlinedatingsites/Muslim_Singles.html; Muslima.com http://www. muslima.com/; and SingleMuslims.com, http://uk.singlemuslim.com/about_us. php. Italicized text represents hyperlinks.

83. Kassim, "Muslim Woman", 13.

84. A Malaysian *shar'iah* court allowed a husband to begin divorce proceedings by sending a text message on his cell phone to his wife. This ruling generated intense debate throughout the country, and initially the Malaysian government rejected the ruling outright. But later it accepted the decision, and in the future divorces through the short message system (SMS) of cell phones will be permitted. While there are concerns regarding the sender's identity and sincerity, SMS can be seen as another form of writing. See Eric Taylor, "Cellular Phone Divorces: Malaysia Permits Husbands to Divorce Their Wives via Text Message", http://www.lawandreligion.com/new_devs/RJLR_ND_75.pdf. 20:06:2007. SMS divorces are valid in the UAE.

85. Pardis Mahdavi, "Meeting, Mating and Cheating Online in Iran", *ISIM Review* 19 (Spring 2007), 18.

86. Zahed Amanullah, "For Muslims, Social Networks Bring New Challenges", 26

July 2007, http://www.altmuslim.com/a/a/print/2509 (accessed 9 September 2009).

87. Kevin Yelvington, ed., *Trinidad Ethnicity* (Warwick, UK: Warwick University Caribbean Series, 1993), 10–11.

Constructing Self

3

Unlikely Matriarchs

Rural Indo-Trinidadian Women in the Domestic Sphere

– SHAHEEDA HOSEIN –

THIS CHAPTER EXAMINES THE domestic lives of rural Indo-Trinidadian women in the first forty years of the twentieth century. It grew out of research that I undertook for my doctoral thesis in 1996–98 when it became apparent that there was an almost absolute absence and invisibility for this group. Much of what these women did in the domestic sphere, and their own interpretations, has been left out of the official written records of Caribbean and Trinidadian history. Rather, they appear only as statistics in Colonial Office documents and other materials about labour, immigration and related social problems. Their lived reality remained invisible within the discourse of traditional historiography, influenced as it was by a conventional patriarchal methodology.

I saw oral narratives as crucial in providing a more complete picture of the Indian female in the historical process that witnessed the emergence and consolidation of the Indian community in Trinidad. Interviewees were selected on criteria of age, residence and previous occupation. All the women interviewed were more than eighty years old at the time of the interviews in 1997–98, and therefore they came of age in the 1920s. Since the intention was to analyse the lives of rural Indo-Trinidadian women, all the interviewees lived in rural areas where, until recently, agriculture was the economic mainstay. To achieve regional diversity I drew from Siparia in the south; Tacarigua, Maracas/St Joseph, Guaico, Tamana and Manzanilla in the east; and Cunupia in the central part of the island. Because of the intimate nature of some of these conversations, which divulged personal information that would not ordinarily be given to strangers, it is necessary to maintain anonymity.

Through the use of oral narratives I was able to analyse the historical experiences of the women through their eyes and in their sphere: the private domain. This gave the clearest picture of the power of the Indian female, her ingenuity, her creativity and her resourcefulness – all factors which were previously either taken for granted or marginalized as not the stuff of which history is made. This project makes a valuable contribution to the theorizing of Caribbean feminism, drawing on the actual words of women who did not know the term *feminism* but who developed strengths and strategies to forge viable lives for themselves in an ethnic community that was patriarchal, and in a wider colonial context that was patriarchal as well as racially hierarchical.

Undoubtedly over the past two decades there has been increased visibility of women in Caribbean historiography. Hilary Beckles and Mary Chamberlain have examined the peasantry in Barbados. Veront Satchell and Verene Shepherd did the same for Jamaica, where Shepherd has done extensive work on Indo-Jamaican women in both the indentureship and post-indentureship periods. Their work has legitimized the use of the oral in building a picture of the lived reality of Caribbean women. Amid the body of historical writings emerging out of Trinidad, much work has been done on Indo-Trinidadian females, beginning in the 1980s with Rhoda Reddock's extensive paper, "Freedom Denied: Indian Women and Indentureship in Trinidad". It was the forerunner of several important works dealing exclusively with Indo-Trinidadian women. Perhaps the most definitive historian on Indo-Trinidadian women has been Patricia Mohammed. Her book *Gender Negotiations among Indians in Trinidad, 1917–1947* assesses the changing relationship between Indo-Trinidadian females and males in the post-indentureship period from a gendered perspective. The strength of her work is that it developed a theoretical framework of analysis that posits gender as a process of continuous negotiation between females and males. Other valuable work has been done by Shameen Ali and Bridget Brereton. Historically important, their works have, in the main, placed emphasis on the role of education and business in the mobility of Indian women and disregarded those who remained in rural peasant agriculture long after they had withdrawn from plantation labour. This chapter examines the way of life for these women, which to a large extent was determined by the fact that they dwelt in rural areas.

These women's ability to own arable land contributed in no small way to their mobility. Private ownership of arable land meant that they had a means of production that assisted their economic independence and gave them leverage in negotiating with the existing patriarchal family. Property became the fulcrum on which the autonomy of the Indian woman rested. For example, land ownership relieved many a widow in her otherwise onerous situation – her physical strength declining and without a domestic partner. However, even while these women found empowerment in land ownership, there were demands on them that were part of the rural life.

HOUSEHOLD CHORES AND MAINTENANCE OF THE HOUSE

Household chores and maintenance of the home were crucial factors in the daily rounds of the Indian female. In many ways the very survival of the Indian family depended on the efficiency with which the woman performed her household duties. The concept of "eating out" was alien to rural Indian households, as were convenience foods. The family was dependent on the female's ability to prepare nutritious meals from limited resources. Typically the woman's day began at three in the morning. Her first task was lighting the *chulha* on which she would cook the family's meals. As one informant describes, this could sometimes be quite difficult, especially in the rainy season: "Sometime so early when we get up is trouble to light the fire. The wood damp and only smoking. We blowing and no fire ent coming. And so your eyes burning and watering out. We had *pookanie* to blow the fire."[1] All the women interviewed said that the morning cooking was a long process, as both breakfast and lunch had to be prepared. Meat did not generally form part of the daily diet; breakfast and lunch would typically consist of *saada roti* and one or more vegetables, either curried or fried. Rice would be eaten at dinner when the workers returned from their labours and had a longer time to eat.

With limited available resources, the woman's culinary creativity was put to great test in an effort to provide tasty, wholesome food for those who depended on her.

Cooking was the first skill a young girl learned, with a certain harshness in the tutelage that reflected the harshness of the living conditions of rural Indians at this time. It was not unusual for the young girl to be beaten by her mother, mother-in-law or, in the case of this informant, her grandmother, while being taught to cook.

> I get plenty licks with me grandmother to cook, to make bake and *roti* and thing nah. I making it but it a kinda way and she beating me with a piece of wood. I was a little child then – about seven or eight. They want me to cook in proper way. We didn't have no stove and thing. We use to cook on *chulha*, fireside, nah. We use to cook *roti*, *dhal*, *bhat*, *talkari*, *dosti*, *dhalpuri* – all kinda thing on the *chulha*.[2]

The novice soon became adept at preparing many different dishes that added variety to what would otherwise have been a mundane diet. All preparations started from scratch, and even the most rudimentary of dishes entailed the use of certain skills which, while not difficult to acquire, required a level of proficiency: "Every time you cook, you use to have to grind *massala* and *hardi*. The first thing they teach me is how to grind on the *sil* and *lorha* . . . . We sit down on the ground and we dey grinding *massala*. And is every day we have to do this because is every day we eating *massala*."[3]

In the skills that a young girl acquired could be discerned a certain ingenuity and resourcefulness that was tantamount to an expression of love. So much of the culture of rural Indians revolved around food that the care and attention which the woman displayed in her cooking became an extension of her love and affection for her family. In a culture that allowed very few public displays of affection, the cooking and offering of food became a symbolic offering of the woman's love. Much of the life of the home revolved around the kitchen, where the hearth became the heart of the home and where vital links developed between the young girl and her mother or mother-in-law. Moreover, in the sharing and passing on of culinary skills, there was a site of preservation of a culture and the formation of a culinary legacy that connected future generations with the past in a tangible and lasting way. This created a sense of belonging in the individual, connecting her to something bigger and giving her a sense of rootedness, so necessary in a society that in many other senses marginalized her.

The link between Indo-Trinidadian culture and the culinary skills of a young woman was the sense of virtue associated with culinary creativity. Ethnic pride saw the ability to produce complex meals as evidence that the girl had been exposed to a good upbringing, so there was a moral aspect to it as well. It was understood within the community that there was a connection between doing good housework and being a virtuous woman. The true measure of a woman's worth lay in her ability to keep and maintain a good household, with homemade meals and a well-kept house. The mother, in training her daughter in these skills, undertook the social, moral and spiritual upbringing of the girl. The daughter's skill and competence were a direct reflection of the mother's tutelage.

In the absence of refrigeration or other means of keeping leftover food safe, Indians in the rural areas were not in the habit of eating leftovers, so there was a practical need to cook every meal. Firewood had to be collected; often on Sunday, their "rest" day, the entire family would go out and collect firewood to be used for the week. The tasks involved were gender-identified but collaborative: "When Sunday we have to go and bring wood. That entire woman, we had to go and cut wood and tote and bring for the whole week you know. . . . Men use to cut and women toting the wood back."[4] Women who lived on or near cocoa estates found that getting wood for fuel was not so difficult. For those who lived in the sugar areas, however, finding sufficient firewood could be problematic.

Another time-consuming task was the collection of water for household use. During the rainy season women could collect water in barrels. In the dry season, however, the collection of water became a daily chore which the women found irksome.

> We want water every day for everything – washing and cooking. And we have to tote water from the river with pitchoil pan . . . . The water was the worse trouble. We had to walk so far through high wood to the river. And this is every morning before you go to work. When you done you make two trip of water before you go. That is before we have to reach on the estate for seven o'clock.[5]

From this hard work, and the resentment that they obviously felt, came these women's determination to educate their daughters so that the next generation would escape the drudgery and relative hardship of their lives. They were determined that their daughters would enjoy a materially easier life. These women would eventually measure their success by the achievements of their children, both female and male. Self-sacrifice for the next generation was clearly their motivation and their success.

While cooking and fetching water occupied a large portion of the Indian woman's day, the bulk of the washing of the family's clothes and other household articles was done on the weekend, particularly if the woman worked during the week. The clothes washed at the river were the everyday clothes of the family, including the husband's, this being done in a very public setting. There were clothes, however, which were washed privately; these were the pieces of cloth used during menstruation. The washing of menses cloths was done in great secrecy. The woman would wash and rinse in buckets of water in her backyard, making sure that the blood flowed through the drains. The cloths were then hung out to dry well away from any other clothes. All of this was in keeping with the notion among Indians that at the time of menses, the woman became "unclean", and also vulnerable. Also underlying this secrecy was the very private nature of things pertaining to female fertility, which concerned only the woman. In a real sense the ritual underscored the feelings of self-worth that the woman preserved, even in the degenerate conditions of the immediate post-indentureship period. In this very personal matter, she protected her privacy and held on to her dignity.

The irksome and the onerous were turned into fulfilling experiences through a capacity to make the best of life. For women who accessed water from rivers, washdays meant an entire morning spent at the riverside. It was a time when they exchanged news with each other, when children were bathed at leisure, and when the network which held women of the village together was strengthened. Work and fun were conjoined in a uniquely female space. Washday liberated women from the immediate house and yard and became a close connection with nature that was an almost spiritual experience.

> We use to start out early in the morning – a big group of we, ladies with their children. The children glad too bad because is whole morning to play in the water. And we done cook in the morning so we on we own time. We make a tray with clothes to wash and we put it on top [of the head]. And we dey scrubbing the clothes in your hand, and you rubbing it quick. We ent know nothing 'bout scrubbing and thing [on a washboard] . . . . When we go in the river, it have a

big stone. We use to beat the clothes on the stone dey. And then they had them
"bound flowers". You taking and rubbing that on the stone, rubbing, the clothes
coming clean, clean.[6]

Of course there were women for whom doing the laundry was just another
chore. Some had access to pipe-borne water or lived on estates where water
was more easily available and could be brought home in large quantities for
washing.

Most of the women interviewed, whether barrack dwellers or those who
lived in their own houses, said that to keep their "going-out" clothes, there
was a line hung over the bed called an *alganee* on which they hung their "good
clothes". Here again we see how the Indian female maintained her dignity in
conditions of deprivation, and how clearly she had an internal sense of beauty
that expressed itself in the many ways in which she claimed her own space.

The system of housing provided for indentured labourers on the estate was
known as the barrack system; it was, for all intents and purposes, barely util-
itarian. Only the most basic amenities were provided and conditions were
generally unsanitary. Each barrack room was provided with a gallery which
generally served as the kitchen. Partitions were made within the main room
by hanging cotton sheets from lines drawn across the room. In such a manner
"private" quarters were created within the single dwelling room. The absolute
lack of privacy was harder on the females than on the males. A defining feature of womanhood was the need for respectability, and barrack life exacer-
bated this quest.

Even within these confined living quarters, the Indian woman placed her
individual mark. If she had little choice as to where she lived when resident
on the estates, she made that space her own. Not only did she create a sem-
blance of privacy within the one room, she also created a kitchen out of the
gallery. After all, if her domain was the house, then she would logically have
the ability to decide on her own terms – albeit within the limits of the space
given to her – how her space should be arranged. And she found dignity and
beauty, oftentimes a beauty that was of her own making.

Within the Indian villages that started to be established as early as the
1880s, the inhabitants were able to build their own houses. These were typically small, usually two rooms, with a semi-open gallery. The walls of the house
were adobe: a mixture of tapia grass, mud, cow dung and whitewash. Roofs

were made mainly of leaves of the carat palm or timit palm, which were intertwined between rods and rafters. Carat and timit palm leaves were used mainly
in the cocoa-growing areas of Trinidad. In the sugarcane-growing areas the
houses were sometimes covered with palm leaves but more commonly with
what was known locally as "house grass" – a tall grass which was dried and
tied into bundles; these bundles were fastened to the rafters with lianas or
strips of bark from the palmiste. The floors of these houses were generally
earthen. As the twentieth century progressed, thatched roofs were gradually
replaced by zinc sheeting, and the adobe houses were increasingly built on
stilts about four feet above ground level, with wooden floors. The major house
building was usually done by the men, although it was not unusual for the
women to participate.

The women were responsible for the general maintenance of the house
structure. They patched holes which periodically appeared in the walls, using
a mixture of mud and tapia grass or mud and cow dung. They also white-
washed the walls with a carbide paste – a thick white limestone runoff. To
get a different colours, ochre powders were added to the paste. All the women
interviewed said that such major maintenance generally took place once a
year, just before major festivals such as the Hindu festival of Divali. Some of
the women said that it would also take place in preparation for Christmas
(even though these women were not Christians, they all took part in Christmas festivities, showing that very early on they were at least partly engaged in
the creole culture). The walls of the houses were often decorated with the
women's handprints in various colours. There was a belief that the handprints
would ward off evil spirits. More important, these handprints became their
signatures – tangible proof that they had made these houses beautiful – and
symbols of the pride they felt in the space they were carving out for themselves and their families.

The earthen floor, common in these mud dwellings, was maintained on a
more regular basis. Once a week the woman would go to the river and dig a
quantity of white clay, which she would then mix with cow dung and water
into a paste. This mixture would then be smoothed over the entire floor by
hand in a process known as *leepay*. As one respondent described, "We house
had a ground dirt floor so we had to *leepay* the floor every week. I learn to
leepay floor as a small girl. We had to stoop down and do it till the floor
smooth."[7] In the same way the fireside, or *chulha*, on which the woman

cooked was cleaned at the end of the day by rubbing a mixture of white clay and water over the structure with a cloth to remove accumulated soot and ash and repair daily wear and tear. The woman was constantly cleaning and rebuilding; it was her art, her love and her pride. All the women interviewed agreed that the general condition of their home was a direct reflection on them – like culinary skills, another tangible display of the virtuous woman.

EXPECTATIONS AND GUIDANCE IN GENDER, GENDER ROLES AND SEXUALITY

The presence of children within the family was regarded with great joy and their arrival into the family was greeted with much celebration. What is clear from the oral testimonies is that it is only with the birth of the first child that the young wife achieved status within her husband's family. Her position within the extended family became secure because she had proved her worth as a woman. She could now make a bid for her nuclear family – that is, her husband, her baby and herself – to strike out on their own, away from her husband's extended family. Certainly the value of the woman was linked to her fertility. Even though she would also contribute to the income of the home, her main importance lay in her ability to reproduce. This endowed her with a matriarchal power since, in a literal sense, she was producing the next generation. Said one woman,

> When I did get the first child, well, is then you was considered a woman. It mean I not barren, and so the husband feel more better. Is from then you could start to make you life for yourself. After you go and have the baby, then you have your own life. If is boy it better, but boy or girl, is good to have children. That is what make you a woman.[8]

While there was indeed gender discrimination in the preference for male children, great value was attached to all children. Indians in Trinidad were still in the process of consolidating themselves into a community within the larger society, and reproducing the family unit was not taken for granted. Also, many Indians were rural dwellers and agriculture continued to be the main-stay of their economic activities. Particularly for those engaged in independent economic activities such as cane farming or rice growing, children became an invaluable source of unpaid labour. Everywhere that Indians were engaged in agriculture, entire families were to be seen working in the fields. Therefore the woman's fertility was directly linked to the income-earning capacity of the family. Having children, particularly boys, also meant that inheritances, particularly land, could be passed from one generation to the next without the danger of being passed out of the family. As the twentieth century progressed, education became an important goal for the Indian family; parents took great pride in the educational achievements of their children, especially their sons, who were selected, as it were, for the gift of higher education.

For a number of reasons, therefore, children were an integral part of the family, and much care was given to their upbringing and socialization. The overriding principle in the socialization of the child was that of duty to parents. There were very clear codes of conduct, which were passed from parents to children and which children were expected to accept without question. Although these codes were applicable to both girls and boys, they seemed more emphasized for the girls. Typically boys were given greater freedom than girls to break the rules. The irony here is that, although the mother was the matriarch of the family, she was operating within the constructs of a patriarchal society that imposed stricter behaviour codes on females. The obvious conflict that arose from this situation would, over time, be broken by the increasing access of Indian females to education. As education became more accessible to females, particularly in the post-independence period from the early 1960s, when education became free up to the secondary level, girls started to outstrip boys in performance; this trend that has continued until the present.

The mother was entrusted with bringing up the child as part of her domestic duties and her role as wife and mother. Thus she had responsibility for moral guidance of the children. As one respondent remembers, "Not me father much bring we up, is me mother. Mother do everything. She work outside, she work home, she do a lot. And is she what teach we right from wrong."[9] The mother-in-law also played a vital role in the socialization of the young girl (the role of the mother-in-law will be discussed in more detail later in this chapter).

One of the major concerns of a community where early, arranged marriages were the norm was contact between boys and girls. Often Indian girls were prohibited from attending school for fear that they would come in contact

with boys and something might happen – such as premarital sexual activity.
One respondent remembers,

> I never go school. Those days they didn't use to send we . . . . They send the
> boys . . . they say they wouldn't send the girl children, only the boy children
> . . . Indian people don't like to send they daughter to school. Some people say
> if you send you daughter to school, they will meet boys and they going to write
> letter . . . . It have a story about Saranga and Tharabhij – a king's daughter and
> a king's son, and two of them go to school. So they write letter [to each other].
> And the teacher send and tell the fathers, the two kings, "You children done
> learn."[10]

Instead, girls' education focused on socialization in the expected role
of wife and mother. Girls were taught what was expected and accepted
behaviour.

> You mother and father don't like it [talking to boys], you mustn't do wrong things.
> They don't like you to go on this road – this friend not good, you know, don't fol-
> low this friend. You have to dress to suit your mother and father. And when you
> go by you husband house, then you will dress to suit them, how they want you
> to dress. . . . If they [husband] want you to have an *orhni* on your head, you have
> to put it. You mother-in-law tell you put it on you head, your father-in-law telling
> you, your husband telling you. Anybody come, you must have your *orhni*.[11]

The instructions went further than acceptable dress. There was an entire
prescribed pattern of behaviour regarding interactions with strangers. Since
the main aim of bringing up girls was to make them into ideal wives, much of
the socialization process of the young girl revolved around this. From very
early on she was taught how to treat her husband.

> When you husband go to work, when he come home, you have to talk nice with
> him. Don't tell him that this thing happen there and that thing happen there
> and this thing what-not. When he now come and he hot and sweaty, he get vex
> when you tell him everything as he reach. What happen in the house, you have
> to control that. When he come, you ask him, "How was your day? You hungry,
> you thirsty, you want something to drink, you want something to eat?" You have
> to see the house go good – your house. You not working nowhere, you cleaning
> your house, you fix up everything, have he clothes in order, have he food in order,
> have all these things right.[12]

From this testimony it is clear that the Indian female was aware of her duty towards her husband. Her only option was to subvert domesticity by making it a position of power.

PURVEYORS OF CULTURE, HEALERS AND GUIDES IN MORAL AND SPIRITUAL MATTERS

One important role of the mother was her guidance of the child in the performance of religious practices within the home. This was particularly true of the Hindu family.

> I learn from me mother . . . I was always there behind she. She gone to "throw water", I go with she and do that all the time . . . . But we didn't know what to say, what to do . . . she use to say for we to say, "Rama, Rama", and I use to feel that so funny. My mother use to do *puja* every year, and then on Saturdays, me father use to go and do Hanuman thing with sugar and *ghee* and *tulsi* leaf. And when he bathe and he finish and put it in the fire and he come, he use to share that sugar and *ghee* and *tulsi* . . . like *parsad* for all of we . . . But is really we mother what teach we the little bit she did know.[13]

What is apparent from this disclosure is that the young girl did not always understand the prayers and acts of worship, but she trusted and followed her mother, who taught her "the little bit she did know". The father's actions, certainly combining religion and family love, were more distant.

For Muslim children as well, religious instruction was very important. However, the Muslim girl was usually permitted to attend a *maqtab* – informal classes where both the Urdu language and the tenets of Islam were taught. Religious practices influenced every aspect of the life of the individual, and the instruction which the young child received within the home was crucial in socializing her into an acceptable pattern of behaviour within the group. Religion was fundamental in holding the Indian community together, in giving it a sense of continuity and cohesiveness. The individual first came into contact with religion within the family, and it was almost obligatory for the Indian woman to carry on the religious practices and pass them along.

The birth of a child into the Indian family was an occasion for much celebration. For the Hindu mother and child, an elaborate and prolonged ceremony, the *chatkee*, was performed. In its playing out is revealed all the mystery and joy of birthing.

> When I have children, I have to stay inside for a whole two weeks before I could do anything. They does bathe after six days. They use to have a *chatkee* on the sixth-day bath. They make a little *peerha* and they cook *halwa*. Only women does attend. In the evening they make a little food and offer it to the Hindu saints. Everybody there, they put a little *sindhoor* in they head, beat they drum and sing song and thing. After the sixth day, then the mother bathe again on the twelfth day and on the twenty-first day. Is only then you could cross a river, only then to go anywhere. After the sixth day, the woman could do light work because she still sick. But she could go in the kitchen and do little things. To protect the baby is important. You put a knife or a scissors open under the pillow of the baby like a protection from evil. They put it whilst the baby small, until the baby have a month or two months and thing as a protection for the baby. Only women sing and dance on the *chatkee*, at the ceremony at night.[14]

What the ceremony surrounding the birth of a child reveals is that it was very much a celebration of female fertility. The woman's ability to give birth made her almost a goddess. Part of the health and welfare of the mother and new-born was protection from evil forces. The ritual bath on the sixth day was also observed by Muslims in Trinidad, as this was an Indian custom. However, it was not accompanied by the elaborate rituals of the Hindu ceremony. What Muslims had was a *hakeeka*, technically a naming ceremony.

> Here we make a sacrifice of goats for the children – two goats for a boy and one goat for a girl. You have to invite everybody. And then the imam will come and recite from the Qur'an Sharif. Then you have to cook and feed everybody. Now the hair of the animal, you have to shave it and weigh the hair and then give its weight in money to the poor. You should really do it when the child small yet, a baby, but he could be at any age when the *hakeeka* is done, when the parents could afford.[15]

Whether Hindu or Muslim, what is clear is that the birth of a child was sacred, to be marked by religious ritual and observances. These rituals were female-centric as well as communal; the pattern of building matriarchal power thus begins. Often superstition and religion were intertwined, particularly in rural communities; many such cultural traditions were left behind with urbanization and Western medical practices, with some loss of women's centrality.

Marriage was necessary for retention and continuance of the Indian family in Trinidad, and so the wedding ceremony was of great importance. Here again the female was central. Up to the 1940s Indian weddings took place at night and were spread over three nights, each night with its own significance.

> On the first night was the saffron [turmeric] night. It had plenty singing, dancing and cooking and feeding people. You put saffron on the bride that night. On the saffron night the pundit would put the *khangan* on the girl's hand and you make your prayers. They have six little girls come and they put saffron for you, they touch you all over with saffron. This first night was also the *matikor*. Only women take part in this. A group only of ladies and young girls have to go to collect dirt by the river, or some water place. . . . And they singing and drumming. They use to do some rude dance too what show what happen with a man and he wife. So that is why is only ladies use to go. This thing is the woman business. . . . The second night now was the *bhatuan* night. This night it have plenty more singing and dancing but no ceremony. That was what we call the cooking night because you cooking and thing for the next night. . . . Then on the third night, well, that is the wedding night, when you actually getting married. . . . It have women who use to sing right through the ceremony.[16]

As the testimony reveals, the wedding was women's business, from beginning to end. The entire celebration was a time of female bonding, of merriment and strengthening of female communal and spiritual ties. *Matikor*, in particular, included earth-based fertility rites that symbolically worshipped female fertility.[17]

A Muslim wedding was far less ritualistic than the Hindu wedding, and took place over a two-night period. On the night before the wedding night all the cooking would be done, and then on the actual wedding night the ceremony took place. The Muslim wedding ceremony was relatively short and straightforward, and much was conducted by proxy. Typically the bride and her attendants remained inside her family house, secluded from everyone. The bridegroom would sit outside in the area where the guests had assembled. The three witnesses, two for the groom and one for the bride, would speak to the groom and listen as he repeated his offer of the dowry and his willingness to marry the girl. The three witnesses would then go into the house and repeat the dowry offer to the bride. If she accepted and also stated her willingness to marry the boy, only then would the wedding proceed. There was sex segregation in the seating and feeding of guests, as gender separation had to be maintained in the public sphere. Men were obviously given precedence, but women had leeway to use their "private" power to shape their families and, by extension, their communities. This was the innocuous way in which an Indo-Trinidadian matriarchy was being shaped.

Death, too, was treated as a rite of passage. Elaborate rituals were associated with the funeral rites of the Hindus, for whom cremation of the dead was incumbent. But perhaps one of the most final rites was that performed by the wife to signify her becoming a widow: "When your husband die, then is like you life done. You take his hand and put *sindhoor* for you in your hair and wash it out. Then you put coals [ashes]. The coals is put there so you could never have *sindhoor* again. It mean you couldn't remarry."[18] In the context where for the Hindu woman marriage and having a husband were almost her *raison d'être*, there was a certain finality to this act; it symbolized the ignominious nature of the widow. This ideology was inherited from India, but the Indo-Trinidadian woman was able to transform the pariah stigma of widowhood: "But although you couldn't remarried, that don't mean you didn't have somebody else. Plenty women went to live with other men. They take up other men, but the men usually had to be married before."[19] Whereas Islam allowed remarriage, and consequently quite frequently Muslim women did remarry, Hindus circumvented the prohibition by simply living together. In the new environment, and particularly with access to and ownership of land, widowhood was less ignominious. Not only could the woman remarry or engage in a common-law relationship, she ensured that her children would take care of her in her old age, since it was understood that whoever took care of her stood to inherit.

In the absence of public health care, it was necessary for the rural Indian family to be able to take care of itself in times of illness. The Indian woman became the repository of folk medical knowledge. She was responsible for taking care of her family in times of illness and she therefore needed to know what local herbs and bushes were used for specific illnesses. But perhaps her most important knowledge lay in birth deliveries, and indeed in all aspects of women's illnesses.

> My grandmother was a boss in seeing about women what sick, in rubbing *narah* and thing. Nanee use to rub you if you fall, and anywhere "unrange", she use to

fix it. . . . If you have any kind of bad *narah*, if anything happen to you, she will see about you and you will feel good. People use to come or send for she. She had a lot of respect from the community because she use to do this. She use to use the *lotah* and glass for cupping to move the *narah*. That would pull it and put the muscles back in place. Women from all over use to come by she to consult she. . . . As it didn't have health centre and thing so, then she use to have plenty sick to see about.[20]

When asked where her grandmother had acquired this particular knowledge, the respondent said simply that it was a gift from God. In the author's personal experience, her maternal grandmother had the same knowledge. Such knowledge was passed from one generation of women to another, each succeeding generation becoming the repositories and exponents of these particular skills. Some of these practices were actually rooted in science but were handed down through tradition, within the framework of religion and spirituality. Such practices went hand in hand with prayers and other religious practices, and therefore a link was made with this knowledge as a gift from God.

A woman who possessed knowledge of healing and herbal medicine usually had enhanced status in the community. Her importance changed from that of child-bearer to healer. She became the centre of spirituality, vested as she was with the ability to "lay hands" as masseuse, chiropractor and healer. Age and wisdom were important levers in the bargaining process between Indian men and women and in the construction of a practical matriarchy. Since females generally outlived males, the older woman eventually became the head of the family. She also became an important force in keeping the community together, often acting as mediator in family and community conflicts, becoming the "mother of all" as she nurtured the entire community with practical, spiritual and medicinal knowledge. It was quite usual for these elderly women to be called "Ma" or "Agee" by everyone in the community, as a sign of respect.

THE MOTHER-IN-LAW

The mother-in-law was such an integral part of the extended Indian family that she needs to be examined on her own. No other figure has been more maligned. An enigmatic presence, whether kind or cruel, she had a central role within the family. That she sometimes became a second mother to her young daughter-in-law is undoubtedly true.

> My mother-in-law replaced my mother in my life. She use to quarrel with me and tell me, "When you don't know, you don't know, eh?" She was teaching me like a mother. I learn to cook by me mother-in-law. My mother use to show me from small too, so I learn little by me mother. Most of the time I spend by me mother-in-law, so is she what really teach me.[21]

Some females married as children and grew into womanhood under the guidance of their mother-in-law rather than the biological mother.

> When I married and come by me mother-in-law, I did have nine and a half years. I had was to stay with me mother-in-law as a child and I use to cook a little food, whatever I could cook, wash up the wares and go for water in the river. I was so small, is she what teach me everything. My mother-in-law had cocoa land. So when I married and go there, they use to pick cocoa and I use to go and pick up. She use to pay me. She what make me and me husband live together. And she keep we there . . . . When me mother-in-law dead, I couldn't live there again. Me husband brother tell we now we have to see for weself.[22]

Not only did the mother-in-law teach the young girl the womanly skills of cooking and keeping house, she also protected the young bride, maintained peace among the brothers and assured that all had a roof over their heads. She would sometimes take care of the grandchildren while the young mother went out to work in the fields. One thing was clear, and that was that the young woman had a multiplicity of roles, one of which was as part of the income-earning activities of the extended family.

> When I use to go in the cocoa land with me husband, we use to go to pick cocoa and heap it and thing, me mother-in-law use to help me out with the children. She was old and kind of sickly, so she use mainly to stay home. But she always use to see about my children, make sure they eat and bathe and thing, when I gone to work. That was a real ease-up. We use to get along really good. I was living so far from me own mother and she was just like one to me.[23]

Here there emerges a picture of a caring mother-in-law, intent on helping her daughter-in-law adjust to a new life, and essentially mothering her. However, some women painted pictures of mothers-in-law whose characters ranged from difficult to incredibly sinister. The major complaint against their mothers-in-law was that they expected the woman to do everything in the home – all the housework – whether the mother-in-law worked outside the home or remained at home. They transformed the new bride into a household drudge.

> At his mother's house it wasn't so nice . . . she wasn't no bed of roses. . . . At his house I had was to take care of his brothers and sisters, my mother-in-law and father-in-law. I had to take care of all of them – like cook for them, wash for them, go in the field and work with them and come back home and do the housework. The tradition was when a daughter-in-law come in the house she had was to do everything. . . . She never work anywhere. She use to be home, but I still had to do everything.[24]

This situation was common to many of the women interviewed. The daughter-in-law resents her role as a servant catering to the whims of her mother-in-law, who appears to be effectively her employer.

Clearly the mother-in-law could and sometimes did abuse her matriarchal powers. What were the reasons behind this somewhat contradictory behaviour? A likely explanation is that some mothers-in-law were still young enough to be of child-bearing age, and perhaps the entry of a younger woman into her extended family was viewed as an intrusion by a potential rival – a rival certainly for the affection of her son, the bride's husband, and perhaps even a potential source of temptation for the older woman's husband. It was not uncommon for a young daughter-in-law to be accused by the older woman of being sexually involved with her father-in-law, or at least being a sexual temptation: "Me father-in-law was a nice man. He use to feel sorry for me when she treating me so. Plenty time when she quarrel, she shouting at him, 'You living with she.' Just because he use to tell she she treating me bad."[25]

The older woman could possibly have felt that such harsh measures against her daughter-in-law were all part of the disciplinary process which any mother would use when training her young daughters. There was also the likelihood that the mother-in-law felt that no woman would be good enough for her son, no matter how obedient or patient or malleable the young bride might be. Eventually the daughter-in-law would become a mother-in-law, and perhaps she would exhibit the same behaviour as her mother-in-law. Therefore, to some extent, this was learned behaviour. But the harshness of the mother-in-law could also have reflected the harshness of their lives in general.

Whatever the reasons for her behaviour, whether saint or sinner, the epitome of benevolence or the essence of malevolence, undeniably the role of the mother-in-law was central to the Indian family and an essential element in the life of the young daughter-in-law. All the women interviewed spoke of going to their husband's home for the first time as going to their mother-in-law's house. Even if the father-in-law was the legal head of the household, even if social tradition designated him as such and even if he was the major breadwinner in the home, she was the de facto head of the household, controlling what took place within what was effectively her domain. The domestic power of the Indian woman is nowhere more clearly seen than in the role of the mother-in-law within the extended family. She became the matriarch who ruled her household without opposition, and who often held the family purse-strings.

CONCLUSION

In the early twentieth century the Indian family was the bulwark against outside forces hostile towards them, and the woman played a pivotal role in the preservation and continuance of this family. Women made the home their private domain and a place of strength and stability that was vital to improving the standards of living of the community as a whole. In contemporary times, Indian women have done exceedingly well, gaining economic and social mobility through high levels of education, and success in the professions, in politics, as writers and journalists and as entrepreneurs. The labours of our mothers, mothers-in-law and grandmothers laid the foundation so that succeeding generations could grasp and build on the opportunities that became available in later years. The sacrifices of the mothers have given voice to the daughters. I personally have always felt a great pride in my grandmothers, both of whose lives are reflected in this chapter, and it was a desire to tell their stories that drew me to this research. It has been the stereotypical view for a long time that these women were subservient and backward. Yet what I know from my grandmothers, and from my research with a cross-section of rural Indian women, is that their lives embodied qualities for which feminists strive nowadays. Through their hard work and spiritual depth, this present generation of Indo-Trinidadian women has been given the strength to walk and speak.

NOTES

1. Mrs P., interview by author, Guaico, Tamana, Trinidad, 7 February 1997.
2. Ibid.
3. Ibid.
4. Mrs G.M., interview by author, Maracas, St Joseph, Trinidad, 4 February 1997.
5. Ibid.
6. Mrs P. interview.
7. Mrs M., interview by author, Five Rivers, Arouca, Trinidad, 27 April 1997.
8. Mrs S.R., interview by author, Guaico, Tamana, Trinidad, 7 February 1997.
9. Mrs P., interview by author, Guaico, Tamana, Trinidad, 14 February 1997.
10. Mrs R., interview by author, Guaico, Tamana, Trinidad, 19 December 1997.
11. Mrs B.M., interview by author, El Dorado, Trinidad, 19 December 1997.
12. Mrs B.M., interview by author, El Dorado, Trinidad, 13 December 1997.
13. Mrs B.M. interview, 19 December 1997.
14. Mrs C.S., interview by author, Guaico, Tamana, Trinidad, 7 February 1997.
15. Ibid.
16. Mrs S.O., interview by author, Cunupia, Trinidad, 27 November 1997.
17. Rosanne Kanhai, Introduction to *Matikor: The Politics of Identity for Indo-Caribbean Women* (St Augustine, Trinidad: University of the West Indies School of Continuing Studies, 1999).
18. Mrs S.D., interview by author, Cunupia, Trinidad, 27 November 1997.
19. Ibid.
20. Ibid.
21. Mrs Z.B., interview by author, Siparia, Trinidad, 27 June 1998.
22. Mrs P., interview, 7 February 1997.
23. Ibid.
24. Mrs R., interview by author, Guaico, Tamana, Trinidad, 7 February 1997.
25. Mrs J.M., interview by author, Manzanilla, Trinidad, 13 February 1997.

4

Finding Self in the
Transition from East to West

– VALERIE YOUSSEF –

INTRODUCTION

THIS CHAPTER FOCUSES ON the ways in which some young women of Indian
descent in Trinidad and Tobago perceive their gender and ethnic identity. It
was originally a paper prepared for the Ninth International Interdisciplinary
Congress on Women, held in Seoul, South Korea, in 2005, which gathered
two thousand women activists. One of the themes of the conference, to which
this chapter responds, was the effects of current and past migration and settlement upon women's development.

The chapter considers how much Indo-Trinidadian women's identity owes
to their tradition and history in the Indian subcontinent, their religious belief
systems, and their life experience as Trinidadians. The information presented
is gleaned from personal interviews with three young Indian women in their
twenties, students at the University of the West Indies, St Augustine,
Trinidad, at the time of the interviews. They were selected as belonging to
different religious backgrounds – one was Muslim, one Pentecostal Christian
and one Hindu – since it was recognized that their belief systems influenced
their sense of identity. The study was concerned with finding out how much
they perceived themselves as Trinidadian and how much they perceived themselves as Indo-Trinidadian at this point in their lives, and it considered

whether their identity was in any sense conflictual. The interviews were analysed for content but they were also considered discursively to assess how far their form of expression indicated positioning, as assessed from the precise framing of the utterances themselves.

BACKGROUND

Trinidad and Tobago is a twin-island state at the base of the Caribbean Sea, eight miles from the northern coast of Latin America (specifically, Venezuela). Its population is made up predominantly of persons of African and Indian descent, with an increasing mixed population. There are relatively small numbers of Chinese, Syrians, Lebanese, Europeans and other races. Trinidad and Tobago is prosperous because of its oil and natural gas reserves; it enjoys a high standard of living, industrialization and development. At the present time it has a large diasporic community resident in both the United States and Canada, and, to a lesser extent, in the United Kingdom. Citizens travel frequently to these metropolitan countries and some stay on to work.

Historically the African population came as slaves in the seventeenth and eighteenth centuries, while the Indian population came as indentured labourers between 1849 and 1917. The latter were brought to work the plantations that had been emptied of Africans by emancipation in 1848, and they were promised their own land in Trinidad or passage back to India, neither of which promises were met. A rift was established between the African population that had moved off the land and the Indians, who chose to separate themselves from the Africans to preserve their own identity. This separation was a matter of culture, race and caste. Overall, mutual tolerance has characterized the interracial relationship down to the present, but necessarily there is a measure of suspicion and distrust also. Despite this context, however, a *dougla* or mixed race has developed, and the current divisions may be as much the product of political and media hype as of outright animosity.

The early indentured woman who migrated as an indentee, rather than as a wife, came from the margins of nineteenth-century Indian society; the marginal status of these women gave them both the need and the space to volunteer as indentees. She enjoyed relative autonomy from the traditional patriarchal strictures when she first arrived in Trinidad in 1849, since she had come alone and had thereby achieved wage-earning status. Many women who came to Trinidad and Guyana (which has a similar history) were expressly seeking their freedom. Pivotal to the subsequent male attempt at Indian cultural reconstruction was the task of harnessing these women back into the perceived role of subservient wives; violence was a major plank of this process.

The threatened patriarchy combined with colonial dictates, the strong forces of traditional Islam and Hinduism and the work of early Christian missionaries to bring women into subjugation.[1] The traditional image of the Indian woman as dutiful and subservient was subsequently re-established, despite the fierce resistance of many. The man was reinstated as both overlord and master. Endurance of poverty and violence became a key feature of the Indian woman's existence, precipitated by the very high level of alcoholism in the society generally and in the male Hindu population in particular.[2] Brereton provides us with some telling facts:

> Between 1872 and 1880, 22 Indians were murdered by Indians, and all the victims were women; between 1901 and 1910, 62 Indians were murdered by Indians, with 20 of the victims women. Between 1872 and 1900, there were 87 murders of Indian women, of which 65 were wife-murders. The tragic "*Coolie wife-murders*" reflected the skewed sex ratio on the plantations during the period of indentured immigration, the abnormal living conditions in the estate barracks, the disruption of traditional gender relations and patterns of marriage, and the concentration of young single males competing for the small number of Indian girls and women of marriageable age.[3]

The woman's acceptance of her position, and the fact that she could find honour and purpose within the role assigned to her, caused her to become reconciled in some cases to a positioning that might otherwise have been untenable.[4] As Mohammed noted in relation to Trinidad, Indian women in the early twentieth century "took pride in carrying out what they saw as their responsibility . . . at times making a virtue of necessity, at others determining their own goals".[5]

As time has elapsed, however, this reconciliation of their subservient circumstances to their gender rights in a modern world, struggling to get beyond specific ethnic boundaries, has created sometimes untenable conflict.[6] Indian women generally are seeking emancipation through education and occupational status, as well as through art forms such as "chutney" (an Indian adaptation of the local calypso song form), dance, and full participation in the annual Carnival. Female chutney singers such as Drupatee Ramgoonai have radically challenged the traditional established strictures and have openly explored their sexuality. The less educated – as well as some educated Indian males – continue to resist this emancipation. There is considerable violence in male-female relations, and a patriarchal justice system which continues implicitly, if not explicitly, to support male atrocities in this regard.[7]

Recent studies such as Hosein's have noted that young Indian girls now look to the United States for role models. Hosein has cited singers such as Madonna, Britney Spears and Beyoncé as modern images of womanhood to which Indo-Trinidadian teenagers aspire as much as they aim for education and careers as lawyers or doctors. Educational level as well as age will make a significant difference to the nature of ambition in this regard. Erickson, while noting a strong Carnival-type influence on traditional religious forms such as the Muslim festival of Hosay, also indicates that rock music has emerged as a symbol of modernity, and specifically non-blackness: "The cult around rock music enables young Indians to communicate modernity and non-blackness (their taste generally goes in the direction of heavy rock, which is emphatically non-black within the wider Anglo-American reference system)."[9] Erickson also points to development of a self-conscious Indianness which simultaneously rejects over-creolization while distancing itself from India, which is recognized as having been impoverished at the time of their migration and as having less to offer materially than their ultimate homeland.

For the majority, to be female and Indo-Trinidadian today entails a duality of being which balances a desire for education and a strong career path with vital roles as wife, mother and transmitter of values to the next generation. Emancipation is working itself out through music and other art forms and a certain tendency to aspire to Western standards. Indo-Trinidadian culture has stood the test of time, though, and has indeed transcended the loss, as a native language, of a distinct language of expression rooted in the Indian subcontinent. It has proven that a separate language is not necessary for the preservation of culture. It has obliterated the strongest notions of caste while developing a preference for prevailingly foreign and white role models and music forms. Despite the spread of Christianity historically – through Canadian Presbyterian missionaries in the early twentieth century – the customary religions of Hinduism and Islam continue to exert profound influence as well as provide a broad cultural framework. Indian value systems also encompass strong family ties which have transcended space and time, notwithstanding a strong trend towards nuclear family living patterns as opposed to the traditional extended family units. This study explores the distinctive nature of Indo-Trinidadianness as it is expressed by three young women of diverse religious beliefs.

METHODOLOGY

Three young women were interviewed for this study and asked to speak informally on their sense of identity; their national, cultural and ethnic loyalties; and their gender roles and ambitions. They were all acquainted with the interviewer as her students at either the undergraduate or postgraduate level, and seemed to feel no constraint in the conduct of the exercise. Their self-perceptions and their own perceived conflicts are drawn from the content of their personal narratives. The interviews were of a minimum thirty minutes' duration and were fully transcribed using the conventions of conversational analysis. This raw information was supplemented by using the analytical framework of critical linguistics, which focuses on specific discursive frames and devices used by individuals in interactions and taken as indicators of their attitudes and positionings.

As Johnstone has put it, "There are no truly synonymous grammatical transformations: if the grammatical conventions . . . allow alternative ways of formulating a phrase or sentence, these alternatives must serve different functions."[10] In other words, the way we speak, as well as what we say, unmasks our positioning. Without their realizing it, all speakers select ways of expressing meaning which relate to how they express that meaning – what they would highlight, what they would confirm, what they are doubtful of. The means of expression then becomes a tool to our understanding the full meaning, over and above the content value of the words themselves. Conversational structuring, such as that of the data in this study, allows more leeway for ongoing modification than the written word, and for this reason gives manifold cues to positioning that would not be discerned in writing.

The three analyses are set out below. False names are used to maintain the privacy of the women concerned. Salient utterances are extracted from the larger discourse according to key themes and words which pertain most specifically to the areas of concern. The detail which can be gained from this form of discourse analysis necessitates interrogation of a relatively small number of interviewees. It yields insights, however, which may act as cues in typifying larger subsets of Indo-Trinidadian women and which may be further explored though more focused questionnaires. The richness of this data set, however, should not be underestimated. Conversational analysis has become a powerful research tool, since it has been recognized that it can bring to light much fuller explication of personal experience than mere content analysis. It is significant that these women speak for themselves without fear of judgement, even at an intellectual level. The reader for his or her part must guard against any judgement in assessment. For example, if the young women watch Indian films and regard this activity as a mark of their Indianness, it is not for us to denounce this interest as superficial. Their contacts with tradition are maintained in diverse and not necessarily intellectual ways. The interviewer herself drew her determinations strictly from the words of the young women themselves and avoided extrapolating beyond these words as far as possible.

THE INTERVIEWS

JAMEELA

At the time of the interview, Jameela was twenty-two and had been married for one year. She was following a strict Muslim lifestyle but argued strongly that she was Trinidadian and that she loved the Trinidadian way of life, only excluding those elements which conflicted with her religion. She felt that some local Muslims were too strict, seeing only the negative in the laid-back lifestyle of the island; she also stressed that extreme Muslims in the country, particularly those of Afro-Trinidadian descent, had a bad public image through their association with Yasin Abu Bakr, who had led an abortive coup attempt in 1990, and that for the most part they were good people seeking the best for their country.

The salient features of Jameela's identity base are identified below as developed in her own discourse, which reveals strong proclivities. She tends to depart from a normative sentence style to achieve emphasis through pauses, non-normative focusing of phrases, repetition of ideas and the use of tag questions and hedging devices such as "you know" and "right?" She frequently enumerates a series of items which she identifies with a particular positioning. She argues first for a strong "Trinidadian" base in her life because her father, who was from a racially mixed home, "loves a lot of things that are not specific to Indian culture". Her discourse indicates that she is close to her father and has inherited his love of Trinidad culture. The early part of the interview focuses on their relationship and its influence on her. She develops her argument as follows.

> *I would call myself Trinidadian* because my dad is not from a strict Indian home. His mother – she's a *dougla*, right? And my dad loves a lot of things that are not specific to Indian culture – like, you know, pan and calypso *and things like that.* And I have come to love pan through him. And cricket is a kind of related thing, and you know, *things like that* which are not specific to Indian culture that I find myself very much involved in and I like, so *I think I would really call myself Trinidadian* – dress, weather, beaches, certain games: all fours and cards. I enjoy all these things. *So I think I would call myself Trinidadian.*

This extract draws heavily on conversational features which have been identified as establishing shared understanding.[11] The tag "right?" seeks a shared understanding of cultural reality with the hearer/interviewer in reference to her father's mixed race. She inserts examples of the cultural elements her father loves, such as "pan and calypso" and "cricket", and she twice repeats the generalizer "things like that", drawing on examples familiar to the hearer and claiming shared understanding to strengthen her point with the use of "you know". Three times in this extract she repeats her declaration of Trinidadianness – "I would call myself Trinidadian" – evidencing her considered concern to put across this positioning. Twice she prefaces the statement by the words "I think", which, so placed, would indicate that she is not absolutely definitive about it but still holding the matter in consideration.

As the discourse continues, she also indicates that her grandmother, who would have been the main Indian influence in her life, had not had substantial influence because of her age relative to Jameela's at the time when she was growing up.

> *I don't know* – because of age – because she was in her eighties *and stuff like that*, there wasn't really much for her to pass on to me . . . the most would be external things like dress and speech, because we still use a lot of Indian terms.

She initially seems uncertain as to the reason for the lack of influence through her initial use of "I don't know" and through the generalizer "and stuff like that".

When asked about her current way of life and Muslim dress style, she declares this to be "strictly religion". She continues:

> At the end of the day something will mean more to you. And as far as religion goes, if God says for a woman to dress in a particular way, I will dress in a particular way. There is a greater obligation for me to God than to country.

It is noteworthy that the above extract is devoid of the kinds of hesitation or hedging phenomena which characterize other extracts. She argues firmly that her religion is not something she has acquired from tradition but rather that she has come to it "on my own", though paradoxically she links it to her husband and friends.

> Because of the company I keep now [pause] – that really influenced me, and I came to it on my own after decisions, confrontations, opposition too from my mum, who is Muslim, right? I decided this is what I have to do because I really am God-conscious.

There is clear self-contradiction here in the expression of an independent choice which is nonetheless influenced by the "company" she keeps. She focuses on "opposition from my mum" as if to stress the ambivalence in her mother's positioning, since she herself is of the Muslim faith. She seeks confirmation of the interviewer's recognition of that ambivalence in her use of the tag "right?" Finally she reasserts an independent choice made in spite of parental opposition.

Subsequently Jameela takes pains to identify herself as a woman aware of her rights, who has studied the Qur'an. She argues that she needed to do this to establish exactly what her rights were, as well as to answer those within her native Trinidadian society who would question her choices as detrimental to womanhood. She separates herself from women in places like Saudi Arabia, whom she believes are unfairly oppressed.

And I am very happy to be Trinidadian – people who understand, women who stand up for their rights. And it's amazing in that respect. And to that extent, perspectives would be different. A woman growing up in Saudi Arabia wouldn't know better but in a secular society like Trinidad you would know about your rights.

In this utterance she juxtaposes phrases which, first, define Trinidadians positively and progressively and, second, contrast with the limited knowledge of the Saudi Arabian woman. These observations are personal but they evidence a strong cultural bias towards her homeland. It is Trinidadians who are "people who understand", whereas "a woman growing up in Saudi Arabia" doesn't "know better".

In response to a question as to whether she would want to travel to her ancestral home, Jameela says that she looks forward to making the *haj* rather than visiting her land of origin. This is clearly a novel idea, not one she has contemplated, for in the stream of discourse she pauses to consider it.

The first place I would like to visit is Mecca, obviously for the *haj* . . . After that, yes, I wouldn't mind travelling to those places, you know [lengthy pause] – yes, it would be very interesting. See what they have to offer [laughs].

This last statement is decisive in the first sentence and reflective in the second. The structuring actually clues in the hearer to the first position as requiring no reflection. She explicates for her interviewer her reason for visiting Mecca, lest it should appear unclear, by insertion of a defining final phrase: "obviously for the *haj*". She pauses several times in the following statement as if thinking, considering and perhaps even dismissing, for "See what they have to offer" suggests no fixed notion of there being anything on offer or of her having come to any determination on the matter.

Politically Jameela sees it as important to be "encouraging Trinidadianness". She declares that she will bring her children up as Muslims but will also want them to appreciate all positive aspects of Trinidad's culture, and indeed the world.

I could see the negatives too . . . but I'm not narrow. With my husband, his friends are varied and they're not bad boys . . . You have responsibility to your neighbours to help better society whether they are Muslims or non-Muslims.

She proceeds to give an example of the Muslim group joining together with Catholics on the university campus to lobby for the non-sale of alcohol. She points out that superficially this activity may appear to be motivated by a religious purpose, but it is in fact concerned with a better campus environment.

Summary

Identity for Jameela seems to hinge on an Islamic faith base worked out in the context of modern Trinidad culture. She has acquired this faith, rather than inherited it, and embraced it from a discovery base in the Qur'an rather than from the mixed religious traditions out of which she has emerged. She is concerned for her own gender rights within this context but sees them as protected by the Qur'an itself and by the wider contextualization of the faith in a liberal national context. While she expresses the independence of her position, it becomes clear that both her father and her husband have had strong influences on it, the former as an upholder of national cultural practices and the latter as spiritual partner. She is firm in her sense of being Trinidadian, of the importance of the nation's culture, not merely that associated with her own ethnic group or religion. She is public-spirited and embracing of all in her outlook and takes pains to distance herself from stereotypical attitudes towards her faith.

SHALINI

The second young woman, Shalini, was twenty-five at the time of the interview. She is dependent on the interview structure, making sure to answer questions fairly briefly and diverting less than the other young women. There is an uncertainty in her positioning also; it is brought out through her language use, in particular of a variety of hedging devices. She makes use of front-focusing of key subjects, repetition and the piling of parallel phrases as she develops and expands thoughts. Her word choice is sometimes childlike in form.

She too has made her own religious choice, in this case Pentecostal Christianity, and like Jameela, she distinguishes her decision-making from her mother's ambivalence.

> I am a Pentecostal. My mum, I don't know what she is. Sometimes she says she
> is a Hindu but she is not practising, she does not do any Hindu stuff. . . . We
> grew up getting to know about the Hindu religion and the Christian religion.
> . . . I liked the style of preaching and stuff, so eventually I became a Pentecostal.
> . . . I don't know where she is, really and truly I don't know where she is, but a
> lot of her sisters are Hindu. There is always the tension between them.

Her mother apparently does not practise Hinduism, which the daughter rede-
fines as not "doing any Hindu stuff". Three times in this short extract, Shalini
repeats that she does not know "where [my mum] is" with respect to religion
but that there is a distance between her and her Hindu sisters. For emphasis
she selects the childlike expression "really and truly". She front-focuses her
"mum" early, at the start of the second sentence, and this together with her
reiteration of the utterance suggests that she is concerned deeply about her
mother's positioning or lack of it, that her mother should know but she does
not. While she describes an early life which exposed her to two religions,
there is no perceived value in this; rather, confusion has caused her to espouse
Christianity, apparently because she liked "the preaching and stuff" rather
than from any profound spiritual basis.

Shalini expresses a strong family loyalty but distances herself from the traditional ways of her forebears, making connection in terms of character traits
rather than history. She sees herself as a combination of herself and her grandmother, but she expresses negative feelings about her propensity for becoming
like her mother, speaking far more positively about her grandmother.

> Actually I used to think that my mum and I were so different. There was a time
> when I wouldn't be able to speak to her for months. But as I get older I think I
> am growing into her, and it's so scary. It's like I would hear her voice in my head
> all the time now and at one point I would just want to separate from her.

Here she defines figuratively an emotional reaction against her affinity with
her mother: "I think I am growing into her, and it's so scary. It's like I would
hear her voice in my head all the time." The use of the adjective "scary" and
the simple figurative introduction "It's like" is almost childlike; it evidences
at the same time a strong emotional reaction against becoming her mother.
Her words reflect a reaction common among those who closely interrogate
their parental relationships and who, in so doing, recognize a subconsciously

evolved similitude of development in the very presence of their rejecting this development at a surface level.

> My grandmother, she has a strong will. She has eight kids. All of them are edu-cated. She educated all of them. All of them went to university . . . they became engineers and what not. My grandmother may have been a stronger personality than my mum . . . somehow I always saw my grandmother as being stronger – the way she handled situations, her thinking process, so different from my mum. She is a stronger personality and I guess I am a mixture of both.

In contrast, she defines her grandmother in terms of the education and professional achievement of her children, for which Shalini clearly holds her responsible. In fact, she rephrases an initial statement about her grand-mother's children's advancement; first presenting them as having been edu-cated, using the passive voice, she shifts to the active: "She educated all of them", focusing on the pivotal role her grandmother played. As with her mother earlier in the interview, she front-focuses her grandmother – "My grandmother, she has a strong will" – and repeats this statement of her strength as compared to her mother's, elaborating through parallel nominal phrases – "the way she handled situations", "her thinking process" – areas in which she sees her grandmother as stronger.

It is interesting to note that a desire for the fullest education is Shalini's primary motivating goal. She may have adopted this concern from her grand-mother as she is described in the example above. She admits to pressure from her family to marry and, at one stage, a conscious decision not to. She has made a choice of education before marriage, despite family pressure to marry young, thus separating herself from the more traditional value systems of her community.

> Sometimes I look at Janet – she's already married, she has children – maybe I could have done it that way. But not now. I just want to do my education first . . . I don't want to follow the teaching path like my parents . . . I am not going in my mother's footsteps to be a teacher.

Again we see Shalini's distancing from her mother in terms of both career goals and the traditional demands upon her. A string of short sentences defines her position in contrast to an earlier string related to a married fellow student. She rejects both early marriage and her parents' chosen occupation of teaching. She speaks figuratively in two consecutive sentences with parallel semantic intent, declaring that she will not follow the "teaching path" nor will she "go in [her] mother's footsteps to be a teacher".

Shalini embraces the multiculturalism of present-day Trinidad but does define herself as Indo-Trinidadian, with an affinity for Indian films and dress. She has no special desire to visit India, however. In response to whether she sees herself as Trinidadian or Indo-Trinidadian, she is ambivalent.

> Once you're born a Trinidadian, automatically you become involved in all these cultures, no matter what race or religion you belong to . . . But maybe I am Indo, because I love Indian movies with subtitles, not as much as my mother . . . I would be inclined to say Indo because of my name . . . because of my parents.

It is superficial features of her Indianness that she enumerates: "movies", "my name" and the physical reality, "my parents". She qualifies her speaking with hedging adverbs and phrases – "maybe" as well as "I would be inclined to say" – and subsequently mentions that she has no desire to go back to India to discover her roots.

Shalini sees her goals as liberation and empowerment in a modern context, but even these notions are epitomized by education and a "good salary". To the issue of twenty-first-century womanhood, she responds:

> It is something that has been on my mind. It is constantly on my mind but I haven't had any answers. I guess the twenty-first-century woman would represent freedom, to a large extent, empowerment. When I think about empowerment I think about being educated, earning a good salary, being financially independent.

Here Shalini displays features that we are coming to associate with her – repetition of her first statement, "It is . . . on my mind"; markers of uncertainty ("I guess", "I haven't had any answers"); and a string of phrases denoting her indecision. She does elaborate on the way in which she perceives empowerment – "being educated, earning a good salary, being financially independent" – unlinked by conjunctions but linked rather by a parallelism of structure.

She always comes back to her family base as a strong factor determining her choices. However, she has rejected marriage partly because it would involve leaving the country and being away from home. In the same way, she

does not want to live away from home even for her career; she wants liberation, but not at the expense of living far from home and not returning there
at the weekend.

> Women are now liberated even if they're married . . . I prefer home . . . I guess
> a lot of my friends, they don't go home on weekends; some of them don't go
> home for, like, three months. I can't ever see myself doing that. So I don't know
> if maybe that is East Indian.

Once again we note the recourse to "I guess" and "I don't know if maybe".
Shalini appears to muse about the capacity of her friends for not regularly
returning home, reiterating the idea twice before rejecting it for herself. This
love of home is another area of uncertainty for her: she is unsure whether it
has arisen as a feature of her Indian family background and culture.

Summary

There are clearly certain contradictions in Shalini's positioning, as we
observed with Jameela, but Shalini appears more uncertain of her views. Discourse markers of uncertainty characterize her speech, as well as childlike
images and phrases. When she considers her Indianness it is superficialities
that she focuses on, and she evinces little interest in the real India of the
present day. As for contradiction, there is a pulling away from demands for
marriage and traditional strictures but at the same time a cleaving to her
Indian family base; there is a stated appreciation of multiculturalism with an
ultimate positioning in an Indian familial context. A focus on education and
career is key to her working out of a liberated identity, but when we consider
her background, we can see that these foci as much reflect her grandmother's
ideals as they do the modern twenty-first-century woman.

JANINE

Finally there is Janine, also twenty-five, a graduate student in social sciences
who is deeply enmeshed intellectually through her research work on a postmodern positioning, of which the interviewer is aware and which therefore
stands as background rather than as part of this interview. Indeed, her current

intellectual position, as discussed in an academic context with the researcher on a previous occasion, seems at odds with her positioning in this interview. She is cleaving more strongly to her Hindu roots as time passes but claims briefly to be capable of reconciling the traditional and the postmodern in her thinking. Her speech style relies heavily on repetition of salient points, with constant self-examination and responsiveness brought out through very frequent use of the personal pronouns "I" and "me". She charts a course of development from early rejection of her cultural background to a more recent and increasing cleaving to it.

Janine recounts that as a schoolgirl she felt "very strongly Trinidadian", resenting the Indian names her mother would give to household items. She saw herself as moving forward, "becoming more knowledgeable, more intelligent", but recounts how her attitudes changed when her younger brother was born and she increasingly adopted the familial role marked out for her as his older sister in the context of the Hindu faith.

> But there [at school] I was becoming strongly Trinidadian. *I did not like my mother*, who would call all the different names, you know, like *chowki* and *bilna* – *I didn't like that kind of thing* because I felt like I was becoming more knowledgeable, more intelligent. I was gaining abstract concepts. I was gaining recognition in those things. I went to the extreme . . . But those things changed for me . . . before A levels, when my little brother was born. That was the turning point for me. My father introduced us and said, "Okay, he has to call you *bibi*", and I liked that. And because of that I started reading the *Gita*. . . . There was this whole new person that I wanted to be. *I didn't fight against tradition anymore.* I took a year off from A levels. *Tradition became very important to me.*

Here principally we see repetition of responsive negative emotions to traditional terms: "I did not like" repeated twice. This contrasts with "I liked that" in response to the relationship culturally established at the time of her brother's birth, and then the further double focus on cultural aspects. She declares that she no longer fought tradition and that it became "very important to me". Her account is replete with references to "I" and "me"; she is at pains to express her emotional responses to different situations and events far more than the other interviewees.

Janine expresses a strong interest in tracing her lineage but describes her resistance to the dependency on her own brothers prescribed for her.

Daddy talked about being able to trace our roots and I said, "Yeah" – to me that was a real good project. *Let's go to the archives, where do we have to go to the archives, where do we have to do this* . . . But I ended up reading more of the *Gita*. But then I read a particular line that the father and the brothers have to support the girls *and I close that Gita one time*. That the girls have to depend on the brother. *I close that Gita for months*. And I quarrelled because how I had to support them. I am the big sister. I'm supporting all of them. *How come they have to support me just because I'm a woman?* And I really had difficulty accepting that. It took me a long time to get used to that.

The repetition of questions associated with the discovery process on the theme "Where do we have to go to the archives?" defines Janine's excitement about the investigation of her lineage. In contrast there is her repeated negative reaction to what she reads in the *Bhagavad-Gita* on male support systems: "I close the *Gita* one time. . . . I close that *Gita* for months." We notice her break into local creole dialect with the use of the verb form "close" – as distinct from Standard English "closed" – signifying both immediacy and emotional involvement. The rhetorical question which follows – "How come they have to support me just because I'm a woman?" – shows the clash of ideology between her traditional loyalties and her status as an educated twenty-first-century woman. Every utterance expresses a conflict in its working out, feelings that are first positive being quickly superseded by ones that are equally negative.

Janine subsequently reconciles to tradition, however, because of the "beautiful, beautiful bond between the three of us" (herself and her two brothers). She speaks of the Trinidadian and Hindu dimensions of their relationship and depicts herself as cleaving more and more sharply to her Indianness.

You could be Indian and Trinidadian but, you know, for me it's a moral sense. You understand the link between brothers and sisters . . . It is a whole mesh – Indian mesh – that I will not negate: the Indian part of me. Though I may not have this fanciful thing of flying back to India and finding my roots.

Once more repetition supports her focus in the stream of speech, and she nominalizes and focuses on what she cannot negate: "the Indian part of me". Thus she clarifies precisely what she cannot act against.

Ultimately, however, Janine declares that her children will follow their father's religion, even if it be Catholicism, the religion of her boyfriend. She accepts the ascendancy of the male positioning on this count while explaining that she will share her own faith and give the children space to ultimately choose for themselves. She also mentions the mixing and possible syncretism of the different faiths in her own mind.

> I have made up my mind [that my] children will follow their father's religion, because I understand the importance of the male line. It doesn't mean to say I won't teach them about my faith, and if they want to change later, they could. I would have no problem teaching my children Christianity too. You see, Mummy's family were Christian too. And I had an immense respect for my grandfather, who was Baptist . . . He was a priest. But people don't know how there are a lot of commonalties between the Baptist and Hindu faith.

Her decision with regard to her children's faith respects a male ascendancy characteristic of the system which she has grown up in and renders her ready to give way to the religious systems of her husband at the very time of finding satisfaction in her own. Her capacity to adapt to a mixed religious system characterizes many Trinidadians today, since marital ties have crossed religious lines in numerous cases. Ironically it is the patriarchal dimension of her Hindu belief system that is causing her to consider bringing her children up as Christians.

Summary

In Janine too we see complex contradictions: an Indian and Hindu affinity increasing over the course of time, positive and negative emotional reactions recalled in every early accounting but latterly giving way to consistent affirmation of the traditional way. We see an anger at male control vying with a respect for the relationships which that control engenders; a postmodernist intellectual perspective pushed down, hardly expressed, eclipsed by an absolute belief in the quality of the Hindu religious and cultural tradition; an ultimate respect for patriarchy which is prepared to subjugate the values earlier established. At the same time she evinces an openness to diversity in religion which characterizes the mixed quality of her Trinidad familial landscape.

CONCLUSIONS

All the young women interviewed appear to be moving forward positively, with an essential groundedness in the multicultural environment of present-day Trinidad and Tobago blending comfortably with their ethnic identities as Indians. None of them expresses a strong desire to return to the motherland, their Indianness being worked out in a local Trinidadian context.

They all show strong, though complex, family ties. Their relationships to their mothers are significant, and in two cases conflicted. Both Jameela and Shalini see their mothers as uncertain or ambivalent in their positioning and are seeking a more focused way, but Shalini is having some difficulty finding it. Throughout her interview she expresses more uncertainty as to her positioning than the other two speakers. Both Janine and Jameela seem more rooted in what they perceive as personally determined, deep faith systems which they feel they have rediscovered, their religious backgrounds being mixed. In both cases their male relatives have played pivotal roles in this discovery. Shalini's faith base is expressed more superficially and for her indicates a movement away from traditional beliefs in contrast with the other two.

If we are to define the young women's sources of gender identity, for Jameela it is prescribed by the demands of Islam as she sees them from her own readings of the Qur'an, but also by the ideological positionings on gender she has absorbed from the modern Trinidadian context, which she contrasts with what she perceives as female oppression in the Saudi Arabian context. Her views emanate from close discussions with the men in her life: from her husband and from her father, who is responsible for her broader interest in what is culturally Trinidadian. Elements of two world views have apparently been reconciled comfortably within her, at least for now.

For Shalini, gender identity is conflictual: the demands of tradition contradict the demands of modern education, career and empowerment. A tie to her grandmother makes a link here, as the latter clearly wanted the same for her children as Shalini wants for herself. There is contradiction in Shalini's positioning: dismissal of what her mother represents but a recognition of her mother in herself; a strong desire to cleave to the home environment accompanied by a desire to break free through education and a career path which remains unformulated.

For Janine there has been a passionate and painful shift to acceptance of the doctrines of Hinduism from an early rejection of its values. Patriarchal stricture remains strong in her life yet works itself out with a passionate self-lessness and commitment and a measure of religious tolerance.

These are indeed women in transition, striving to reconcile the complex demands of tradition with their development as twenty-first-century emancipated thinkers. They show little affinity with India per se but more with the cultural values and norms carried over to the diasporic community which gradually established itself in Trinidad from the mid-1900s. For each of them their evolution as twenty-first-century women is very much in process, with conflicts remaining unresolved and ambivalence coming through in manifold ways. Perhaps as educators we focus on these conflicts too infrequently and should seek means of facilitating their resolution more readily to support this complex womanhood in the making.

NOTES

1. Rhoda Reddock and Rosalie Barclay, *2000 Report for the United Nations Inter-Agency Campaign on Gender Violence against Women* (St Augustine, Trinidad: University of the West Indies, 2000).

2. Basmat Shiw Parsad, "Marital Violence within East Indian Households in Guyana: A Cultural Explanation", in *Matikor: The Politics of Identity for Indo-Caribbean Women*, edited by Rosanne Kanhai, 40–61 (St Augustine, Trinidad: University of the West Indies School of Continuing Studies, 1998).

3. Bridget Brereton, "The Historical Background to the Culture of Violence" (paper presented at Seminar on the Culture of Violence, Centre for Gender and Development Studies, University of the West Indies, St Augustine, Trinidad, May 2004), 6.

4. Patricia Mohammed, "Structures of Existence: Gender, Ethnicity and Class in the Lives of Two East Indian Women", in *Trinidad Ethnicity*, edited by Kevin Yelvington (London: Macmillan Caribbean, 1993), 233.

5. Ibid.

6. Niels Sampath, "An Evaluation of the 'Creolisation' of Trinidad East Indian Adolescent Masculinity", in *Trinidad Ethnicity*, edited by Kevin Yelvington, 235–53 (London: Macmillan Caribbean, 1993), 242.

7. Cf. Valerie Youssef, "On Judgement and Justice", in *Writing Rage: Unmasking*

Violence in Caribbean Discourse, edited by Paula Morgan and Valerie Youssef, 41–77 (Kingston: University of the West Indies Press, 2005).

8. Gabrielle Hosein, "Gender, Generation and Negotiation: Adolescence and Young Indo-Trinidadian Women's Identities in the Late Twentieth Century" (MPhil thesis, Centre for Gender and Development Studies, University of the West Indies, St Augustine, Trinidad, 2004).

9. Thomas Hylland Eriksen, "Indians in New Worlds: Mauritius and Trinidad", *Social and Economic Studies* 41, no 1 (1992): 157–87.

10. Barbara Johnstone, *Discourse Analysis* (Oxford: Blackwell, 2002), 98.

11. For example, Valerie Youssef, "Marking Solidarity across the Trinidad Speech Community: The Use of 'an ting' in Medical Counselling to Break Down Power Differentials", *Discourse and Society* 4, no. 3 (1993): 292–306.

5

No Pure Place of Resistance

Reflections on Being Ms Mastana Bahar 2000

– GABRIELLE JAMELA HOSEIN –

WOMANHOOD IS A PERFORMANCE of ethnic, gender, class and other ideals. At other times it is achieved through reinterpretation or refutation of what those ideals, individually and together, insist upon. In this chapter I use my own reflections to flesh out the play of intersectionality common to so many young Indian women, as well as the distinctiveness of each individual's story. Young Indian women transgress as well as reproduce hegemonic meanings simultaneously. My participation in the Mastana Bahar Indian Cultural Pageant illustrates my own playful way of negotiating and navigating expectations of "appropriate" behaviour. Rather than representing a generalized Indian female standpoint, I highlight the embodied ways in which I experience Indian womanhood as well as the politics of its construction and analysis.

Feminist scholarship values seeing and theorizing the personal as political, thus treating women's lives as a source of (self-)knowledge.[1] This scholarship legitimizes using academic life to reflect on the extent to which individual dilemmas, aspirations and choices are collectively experienced ones.[2] Some scholars have argued that a focus on the personal is narcissistic. Others warn that individual stories cannot be generalized or speak to a collective experience and that linear narratives of memory convey a false picture, while still others argue that reflections such as this reify a false notion of the individual.

My aim is to describe one experience that has furthered my thinking about Indian womanhood, and some bases for my understanding of it ten years on. There are commonalities with other young Indian women in my story, and there are differences that reflect a nexus of the personal, academic and political.

Readers of this piece will not end up knowing what it means to be an Indian woman in Trinidad. I write against this, perhaps because of my own continued questioning. Rather, I draw the axes – from cultural inheritances to gender and generation – along which Indianness and womanhood are continually being worked through. Looking back ten years, I focus on the queen segment of the pageant to show an instance when Indian femininity is collectively imagined, and its significance to the cultural politics of Trinidad and the Caribbean region. I draw on scholarly research on Indian girlhood to theorize my participant observation, link fashion and beauty to Indian claims of national belonging, and explore the implications for coming of age at the end of the twentieth century.

Themes of identity, authenticity and the comfort of belonging connect then to now. These first made me ask questions about ethnicity and femininity, then informed my participation in the Mastana Bahar Indian Cultural Pageant, and they still shape my experience of being an Indian woman today. Among other things, both academic life and global and Caribbean feminisms have shaped my perspective and voice along the way. Now my definition of self is more a personal and political one that nonetheless engages with these very desires for community and how they are made real. With these shifts in mind, this chapter explores some of the meanings of young Indian womanhood through my own story.

INHERITANCES

My family's ancestry lies in the migration of Indian indentured labour to Trinidad and other Caribbean islands in the mid-nineteenth century. Some of my father's family came from Hyderabad; some members of my mother's family came from Afghanistan. A few generations later I grew up with a single mother in Barbados and Canada, where we had few extended family members, and with little investment in religion and cultural rituals. My return to

Trinidad in 1995 stimulated many questions about the relationship between gender ideals, ethnic group boundaries and notions of belonging. Having lived outside of Trinidad and Tobago for more than ten years, I sought to re-establish a sense of home and roots. I came back home as an independent-minded twenty-one-year-old, unprepared for the fact that my age, sex, unmarried status, family religion, class and ethnicity would become significant in different and heightened ways.

Almost immediately I encountered rules about how Indian young women should dress, behave and talk in public. In particular, concepts of female shame and reputation seemed to give licence to family, religious leaders and even other community members[3] to discipline young women who disobeyed the informal codes of conduct. I was discovering late a range of rules about how to be the "right" kind of Indian girl. I felt inauthentic as I self-consciously and with uncertainty began to realize what it seemed I should have known all along.

In this context I began thinking about the expectations, meanings and identities that were now shaping me as a young Indian growing into womanhood. I talked about this with other young Indian female friends and family living in the same semi-urban, ethnically diverse area of north Trinidad. Particularly as young, unmarried Indian "girls", we all experienced gendered moral imperatives constraining our choices, mobility, sexuality and relationships with males. Extended family and neighbours helped police and protect girls' virtue and good names for both their own sake and family and community respectability. Across classes and religions, and even taking into account heterogeneity, codes regarding femininity appeared stricter for Indian girls than those of other ethnicities. As one young Indian woman said to me, "More is expected of us because we are Indian."

Talking with others, I found very complex and at times (seemingly) contradictory reasons for asserting particular aspects of self and for negotiating[4] notions such as *appropriate, good, immoral* and *un-Indian*. Using different "tactics",[5] we were individually reproducing, representing and resisting ideals and expectations in a variety of ways. For example, I observed that young Indian women represented a kind of symbolic womanhood at extended family gatherings, in religious settings and at cultural functions; this image could be very different from our everyday and other ways of dressing and carrying ourselves. I wondered if such performances of different feminine identities were a means of navigating the demands of community and belonging and a way of occupying multiple identities. One explanation is that as young women, "girls come to learn how to take up their place in multiple and competing regimes of power" where class and race differences are "important social markers" and hetero-sexuality "confers differing (if troubling) forms of social power associated with girls' different claims upon its prestige".[6] How did we as young Indian women see ourselves in relation to popular (and patriarchal) images of traditional Indian womanhood? Did religious and cultural myths and female icons shape our identities? How did they connect to our present, everyday situations?

In 1995, celebrations of the 150th anniversary of the first indentured Indi-ans' arrival in Trinidad and Tobago, which included the public revitalization of Indian ethnic identities, sparked my curiosity. Personally and academically, I began to explore the ways in which Indian young women were implicated at a symbolic level in the public expression of what was considered pure and enduring about Indian culture. What did our "tactics" suggest about the lim-itations, opportunities and aspects of agency involved in performing gender and ethnic identities?[7] And, further, how were we engaging the boundaries of ethnic belonging? Started in 1997, my Master of Philosophy (MPhil) thesis arose from this period of wondering how young Indian women's daily lifestyles reflected our approaches to the rules establishing appropriate roles, values and behaviour.[8]

Entering the annual national Mastana Bahar Indian Cultural Pageant Queen competition in 2000 was an extension of both my personal explorations and my thesis. I had observed the competition in 1999 and interviewed some of the contestants. This time I was more clearly asking about the traditions and values that underlie Indian gender ideals, the "cultural messageways"[9] that convey authoritative notions of womanhood and the mechanisms for patrolling the boundaries of female Indian identities. These were the ques-tions I had been reflecting on since I arrived back home. My experience as Ms Mastana Bahar[10] also helped me to understand how the late twentieth-century context provided multi-ethnic and intergenerational values about sex-uality and morality. As Cohen, Wilk and Stoeltje point out, "Beauty pageants showcase values, concepts and behaviour that exist at the center of a group's sense of itself and exhibit values of morality, gender, and place."[11] The cultural politics of the Caribbean and Trinidad and Tobago added significance to the meaning of such values.

WINNING PERFORMANCES

The urban-based Mohammed family first began to produce the Indian cultural competition Mastana Bahar in 1970.[12] By the end of the season, the overall winner usually received a car. The family also began to produce an annual live cultural pageant, held on a large stage at Rienzi Complex in central Trinidad,[13] that reflected the same categories. The pageant lasts only one night and is attended by thousands of mostly Indian families. In 2000 the prizes for this competition were a maximum of TT$5,000 in each category. As with the television show, the categories were dance, *chowtal* singing and *tassa* drumming. The queen segment was specific to the staged night.

Historically the Mastana Bahar television and stage competitions have played a key role in supporting and revitalizing local expressions of Indian culture. The queen segment of the pageant provided an alternative to national contests, such as the Miss Trinidad and Tobago pageant, in which Afro-Trinidadian women were increasingly challenging standards of beauty that value whiteness but where Indians continued to be relegated to the periphery by the creole continuum and mainstream.[14] Since beauty "contestants' performances of gender imbue 'naturalness' into political constructs such as nation and citizen",[15] the pageant can be seen as part of ethnic struggles over belonging in post-independence Trinidad and Tobago.[16]

The pageant is one symbol of Indian struggles to be identified as distinct from but involved and embedded in the diverse larger Trinidadian community. This historical tension grew from the early days of Indian indentureship between 1845 and 1917. Waves of indentured immigrants coming from India entered a colonial plantation society where they were both peripheral to and at the bottom of a social order defined by white, creole and African identities. Later on, the movement towards independence was linked mainly to development of and assimilation into Afro-Trinidadian race- and class-consciousness.

By the 1950s, efforts to establish a distinct Indian identity and to compete with African men for political power began to take shape. In the context of Afro-Creole cultural hegemony and post-independence ideologies of miscegenation, Indian women's bodies, dress, deportment, sexuality and respectability were significant and visible markers of both ethnic difference and status. The community was working out its own identity in relation to its internal class, caste and religious differences, Indian notions of patriarchy and (in part the stereotypes of) other ethnic groups.[17]

Becoming part of this movement in the 1970s, Mastana Bahar aimed to give Indian culture and community greater visibility and validity through providing media space for Indian music, dance and aesthetics, including depictions of female beauty. Such symbols of cultural persistence enable ethnicities to mark their presence and their right to define the nation and claim national resources. As Rhoda Reddock has pointed out, ethnic tensions and hierarchies, issues of gender and male control over women, and individual identity choices all inform "contestations" over political power and national culture.[18]

Individual stories such as my own show additional considerations. I wasn't interested only in what it took to be seen as a representative of Indian culture. As someone who rarely wore makeup or high heels, I was also interested in the glamour and pleasures of femininity, with which I felt uncomfortable in daily life. I wondered how such dress influences the ways young women feel about and move in their bodies. Just as I had been reflecting on the ways Indian girls performed gender and ethnic identities in daily life, I wondered about how this occurred in the beauty pageant space, where women express, experience, idealize and affirm femininities even as their bodies are marked in terms of nation, ethnicity and ethnic competition. I entered because I anticipated that the process, from preliminaries to finals, would engage both my personal and academic questions and enable me to experiment explicitly with gender as performance, and be fun as well.

The other contestants were mostly young women from various parts of central Trinidad, a few were from the East–West Corridor in north Trinidad and one or two were from south Trinidad. Most of the contestants were between seventeen and twenty-four years old. I was the oldest at twenty-five years of age. Except for one *dougla* young woman, all the others were (or appeared to be) Indian. About half were involved in Indian culture as dancers or participants in their temples. Two or three, including myself, came from Muslim family backgrounds. About three were attending university but none had a postgraduate degree, nor were any of them enrolled in such programmes. Schooling was prized, however, and audience members would make comments about "how good it is to have education". The class backgrounds of the young women also varied. Most did not appear to be wealthy, seeming to come from lower- or middle-income families. The heterogeneity of the group attested to the pageant's panoramic visibility and continuing significance, despite intra-community differences.

At the preliminaries I wore a simple beige *salwaar kameez*, little dramatic makeup and the only pair of high-heeled shoes I owned. Many other girls were far more glamorously dressed. In particular, the four young women sponsored by a popular dance choreographer – dancers from his troupe – were all in gold, with four-inch heels and glittering saris; their hair had been professionally swept up and curled. One young woman wore Western dress at the preliminaries: a long, close-fitting skirt and long-sleeved top made of stretchy material. This costume elicited comments that it "looked bad" (that is, inappropriate) to be wearing close-fitting and "non-Indian" clothes. Fashion therefore played a role in marking Indian cultural sovereignty and the seemingly contrary pull between East and West. It also highlighted how diasporic trade in Indian fashion provided alternatives to globalized US merchandise and influence.

I made it to the semi-finals. We were chosen to continue on the basis of our dress and introduction and a short speech about an issue, Indian culture or the role of the Mastana Bahar queen. For the next round I wore my mother's green and orange (non-glittering) silk sari and some flowers in my hair. I also wore a few bracelets, a bindi (an essential part of any Indian outfit in this competition) and makeup. Everyone was more ornately attired in saris or *gararas*. Young women also wore dangling, jingly gold earrings and other ornaments, two or three necklaces and large nose rings. It seemed essential to shimmer, glitter and sparkle on stage, merging the ideal presented by Hindu goddesses with a culturally Indian aesthetic and with the material culture expected of beauty contestants.

We repeated our actions from the preliminary round. This involved walking onto the stage and then pausing and placing both hands together as if in prayer; then we bent from the knees in a low dip with eyes lowered in a gesture of modesty. Afterwards the contestants walked to the microphone at front stage centre and greeted the audience by saying "*Namaste* [or *seeterram*], *assalamualaikum*, good evening, ladies and gentlemen." Then, after a short speech, each young woman walked to the right corner of the stage, then to the left, and then circled the stage and exited. Before exiting we would bow again at the centre in a gesture that confirmed beauty, piety, modesty and grace.

It was performance staged to display decorative femininity, Indian iconography and the "appropriate" actions of high-caste Hindu culture, ironically re-centring the Bollywood world of fantasy within India's diaspora. Yet my backstage observations and interactions revealed that most of the young women had not entered the contest because they conformed to the ideals presented on stage. Rather, as in the pageants held on Borough Day or at a national level, the competition appeared primarily to validate the girls' sense of being pretty, allowing them to model and to access the status of being a beauty queen on a stage in front of friends, family and unrelated males.[19]

While "front-stage" overtly counted, the backstage commercial, class-based, personal and political interests of organizers, participants and others also competed to define the meanings of the pageant. As Stoeltje writes, "From the actual process of entering the contest, through the preparation for the performance and the contest itself, women are transformed from girls to women and produced as signs."[20] In the Mastana Bahar Indian Cultural Pageant, the queens become symbolic of their sponsors, the Indian community and the status of ideal womanhood. It is particularly so because this pageant is more than a simple beauty contest. It is valued as a community vehicle for asserting moral values as part of the politics of local culture and tradition. It aims to show Indian ethnicity as beautiful, to give prestige to Indian women and to affirm qualities such as grace, intelligence, humility, upward mobility and self-respect as feminine.

Meeting the young women at these events and talking to their designers and families provided some insights into notions of the ideal Indian female body.[21] In many ways the contest was a "counter-pageant" that explicitly challenged the dominance of both Euro-American and Afro-Trinidadian standards and notions of beauty.[22] While winning could be a stepping stone to competitions at national and international levels, it did not have to filter into this hierarchy and could establish its own competing aesthetic, based on notions of authenticity and purity.[23] Yet amid such an aesthetic, centre stage was a hybrid space where caste and colonial attitudes regarding colour, responses to and expressions of racial othering, and contemporary Western ideas combined in fluctuating ways.

A glance below the surface of the Miss Mastana Bahar competition showed another picture of young Indian (and *dougla*) women attempting to affirm their sense of femininity through one of many possible sources of validation. In deportment, appearance and style, contestants could embody "conventionally idealised versions of femininity" that are symbolic of "the values and goals of a nation, locality, or group". Yet because pageants are ideologically hybrid events, young women who choose to participate "sometimes reject the overt messages, sometimes choose to participate for a range of idiosyncratic reasons, and sometimes get a different message from their participation than was intended".[24]

For example, after the semi-finals, a young gay Indian couple from Couva who owned a sewing shop offered to be my designers. Two years before, their "girl" had "made queen", and they wanted another shot. Also they were competing with the choreographer whose "girl" was currently reigning. My designers decided to act as my sponsors and absorb the costs of "sending up a girl to be queen". Significantly, this couple unobtrusively challenged the assumption of heterosexuality promoted by "authentic" representations of the community. My hairstylist and makeup artist were both non-Indians, and one was also a gay man. Sexual and ethnic diversity were also typical of the other contestants' crews. Over the following weeks I realized that within Mastana Bahar's celebration of purity and heteronormativity, there was a "backstage" openness to sexual and racial hybridity.

The final round was in March, five months after the October preliminaries. Reinzi Complex was lit up and the accompanying live band ready. The queen segment took place in two parts. First the contestants paraded in "modern wear". My outfit was a short fitted top with long sleeves and a flared floor-length skirt covered in appliqué and hand-sewn beads; I also had a large *dupatta*, which was partially transparent. I wore layers of costume jewellery from the top of my head down to my fingers, which had been "finished" with long red fake nails. Unused to this combination of polished "nails", makeup, skirt and heels, I felt a humorously ironic sense of being "in drag" as I performed onstage a femininity that was considered natural but was hardly normal for me.

Midway through my walk across the stage, after stopping at each corner to pose as if frozen in a *kathak*-style dance, I walked to the centre with the *dupatta* in front of me so that my body could be seen through the transparent panels. Then, twisting and raising the *dupatta* as I turned on the spot, I let it fall over my head. Use of the stage and display of outfits and *dupattas* score big points, and my designers had choreographed this routine for me. For the "traditional wear" segment I wore a multicoloured sari and spent about three minutes onstage doing various poses as if in tableau, lifting and displaying the material cascading over my shoulder, exemplifying the impact of Bollywood, as well as the Indian fashion industry, on staged displays of Indian femininities in Trinidad and Tobago.

At question time I was asked whether the rise in drug abuse is linked to family breakdown – a typical question. Generally the questions lead contestants to affirm women's place in the family and the importance of culture and religion. As Cohen, Wilk and Stoeltje point out, beauty contests often affirm a link between women's productive and reproductive roles. In response to my question, I answered that I did not think one caused the other but that they were both products of changing community-level relations, unemployment and other factors. This answer received loud crowd applause, perhaps because it took the question of community survival as complex and serious while layering Western education onto female participation in cultural traditions and appropriate femininity.

Other questions asked were "What does the term 'national unity' mean to you?" and "Who is your favourite local artiste or star?" Some that recognized women's changing roles and current social issues included "Do you think we need a woman as prime minister of Trinidad and Tobago?" and "Do you support the death penalty as a form of punishment in our country?" Contestants often emphasized that problems of "broken homes" and crime could be solved if women took greater responsibility for their families. This was because, they said, the woman is the centre of the family, and "the hand that rocks the cradle rules the world". In instances where family roles were not being questioned, contestants seemed to feel freer to affirm that "women should have a place in all aspects of society". This was seen to be particularly true, it was stressed, as we were in a new millennium.

In addition to individual parading, contestants had to participate in a group presentation with elements of dance and modelling. There was clearly a sense of competition among us as we observed one another's apparel, manner of walking and speech, but there was little overt animosity. However, throughout the contest there was much commotion about bribing judges, contestants getting their questions beforehand and judges being biased, but this seems typical of pageants everywhere.

Many things may have contributed to my winning, including my educational and class privilege, my answer at question time and the stunning outfits my sponsors designed or bought. After the results were announced, many people, including other contestants, came up to congratulate me. One said she did not think I should have won, as my "modern wear" was neither modest nor Indian enough. A letter to the editor of a national newspaper stated that Sham Mohammed (the founder of the contest) would be "turning in his grave" at the outfit I wore, as it did not represent the kind of Indian woman the pageant was supposed to depict. In newspaper coverage following the competition, I was often asked about my aspirations, views on marriage, family and career, feelings about interracial relationships and perspectives on the status of women generally.

I clearly did not fit the narrow stereotypes of Indian women, and more than anything else, the newspapers seized on this point. One headline called me a "militant maharani".[26] Another interviewer asked me if I aspired to get married and have children, and about my views on interracial relationships. I said that I had always wanted to have children but that marriage was not my primary aspiration. I added that I thought race was not always the most important factor when considering a partner.[27] A glaring headline ensued: "Miss Mastana Shocker: Wants Child Out of Wedlock. Could Marry Non-Indian".[28] This emphasis on challenging tradition was highlighted by the Port of Spain Afro-Creole–dominated media and not well received by many Indians.[29] Local feminists also had mixed reactions. Some found the experience an interesting and entertaining story and (usually half-jokingly) told others about it. Others felt betrayed that I, as a young feminist, would enter a beauty contest.[30] I often had to explain that I learned a lot about ideals of Indian womanhood from the experience, and that I had approached the contest as part of my research, with humour and with a sense that there is no pure place of resistance.

FEMINIST THEORY AND POLITICS

In the following sections I reflect my own experience in relation to the literature on Indian womanhood and the conclusions drawn from my MPhil research on Indian girlhood. My observations and experience taught me that there were many parallels between the pageant and daily life for young Indian women. Performance of symbolic womanhood at all levels is rewarded, even if it hides who girls are and how they behave in other settings such as in bars and clubs, with friends, at university, at work and with intimate partners. Young Indian women continue to negotiate expectations that oppose honour, purity and respectability to shame, pollution and reputation, and the pageant is one site where they can make choices about how they can legitimately appear. In reality, "beauty contestants can never fully achieve the idealised role they are performing" and must animate the "form" of the queen without fully "fleshing her out".[31] This is, of course, a gendered experience, not shared by young Indian men.[32] Indianness is not similarly invested in moral impera- tives regarding men's sexuality, hair, bodies, dress or deportment.

Dress is one way that gender status differences are enforced. One could argue that the pageant seeks to elevate Indian women. Certainly audience, organizers, sponsors and especially the young women themselves experience it this way. Yet ideals of femininity which reward women for appearing to be morally upright, dutiful and sexually passive are also the ones that keep girls in check. They send the message that women in everyday life are on display for community judgement and they maintain the sexual double standard between women and men.[33] For women, authenticity is earned rather than ascribed, and is "a matter of social practice and performance rather than mere biological inheritance".[34] In this context, a pageant aiming to affirm and cel- ebrate community especially illuminates that "beauty has everything to do with culture and power".[35]

The literature on Indian womanhood in Trinidad and Tobago places control of female sexuality in the context of "competition among patriarchies"[36] of dif- ferent ethnic, religious and class groups. Historically Indian women's sexuality has represented a source of honour or insult for Indian men or for the com- munity as a whole. The only legitimate option for girls was obedience to family and community, and female retention of Indian symbols was a mark of respectable Indo-Trinidadian male and female identities. Education, class, area of residence, religion, Westernization and acculturation informed both regulatory codes and the extent of girls' obedience.[37] In this regard we still need a more thorough understanding of why, how and with what implications young women renegotiate their options and challenge regulation of their sex- ualities. Clearly age, gender and generation have long been crucial points of intersection with notions and symbols of identity, difference and belonging.

Between the 1950s and 1980s scholars began to theorize the influence of multiple value systems, multi-ethnic strands, intruding urban trends and metropolitan influences on the growing "generational gap" between traditional expectations regarding appropriate roles for girls and their own feelings.[38]

From the 1980s Caribbean feminists began to recognize that study of women's bargaining with the demands of Indian womanhood was crucial to understanding the construction of Indo-Trinidadian femininity *and* community.[39] By the 1990s a focus on Indian women's challenges to and negotiations with patriarchy, yet their desire to retain and claim community, dominated the feminist literature and writings by Indo-Trinidadian women.[40] Attempting to demarcate young women's late-twentieth-century experience highlights the importance of further tracing how evolving ideas about "personal choice" and girls' individuality have established new parameters for construction and negotiation of female gender identities.

Contemporary young Indian womanhood is now marked by a distinct (and expanding) adolescent space and experience between childhood and womanhood, defined by a focus on development of individual identity, aspirations, desires and opinions. This status of adolescence has changed the context within which females are bargaining with (patriarchal) community expectations and traditional gender roles. Put another way, the literature suggests that, increasingly, girls are expected not just to obey but to *choose* to obey parents and authority figures, moral imperatives and gendered sanctions.[41] The legitimacy of exercising personal "choice" and seeking independence and fulfilment provides a new enabling context for young women's exercise of agency. It may also enable young women to feel that they are speaking from a knowledgeable (generational) standpoint. This suggests a fundamental change in the terms of Indo-Trinidadian girlhood and the transition from childhood to womanhood over the past fifty years.[42]

Feminist scholars suggest that the development of feminine subjectivities is a specifically gendered process that rewards young women for presenting themselves in appropriately feminine ways. In this sense, coming to grips with the demands of womanhood and emerging sexuality is also about accepting feelings and representations of subordination.[43] Yet young women use femininity "tactically, when appropriate, and often in contradictory ways".[44] In this sense, the contradictions of young Indian women's lives do not enable a "coherent or 'pure' non-contradictory feminist positioning". Rather, we should recognize that these contradictions produce "competing meanings" and "cultural tensions".[45] This is especially true for young women whose lives are implicated with constructions of ethnic, national, class and religious group boundaries and identities. I reflect on my own negotiations within this historical and theoretical context.

ARRIVAL

This chapter has outlined the questions I was seeking to answer and the kinds of experience and scholarship I have drawn on to do so. Research conducted for the MPhil degree put me in touch with almost 150 young women, 125 of whom filled out questionnaires and participated in short workshops on (Indian) girlhood. By the end of my degree I knew I was not the only one negotiating ethnic and gendered expectations as I grew into womanhood. More important, I knew more about how young women managed their navigations[46] across educational, family, occupational, religious and community-defined spheres, as well as their own feelings about their identities. They did this by reproducing expectations of purity, compromise and respectability in relation to marriage and family while using the public sphere of peer culture, education and employment to legitimize expressions of autonomy, reputation and resistance. In other words, they participated in practices associated with both tradition and modernity by separating them into different spheres and by reworking the dominant meanings within each sphere. Similarly, in the pageant, young women such as myself brought a generational sense of legitimacy to how we both reproduced and refused hegemonic feminine ideals – by using symbolic womanhood to create front-stage and back-stage identities.

My own participation in the Mastana Bahar Indian Cultural Pageant showed how ideals of Indian womanhood can be powerfully influential yet also considered highly symbolic, performative and only one of several compelling ideals. It is likely that any winner of the pageant would have, in her own way, complicated and subverted notions of ethnic identity and markers of belonging. Gender and generation create aspirations for belonging across sites, but on terms for which young Indian women value consent. Participating in the Mastana Bahar Indian Cultural Pageant was part of a process of

developing self-knowledge about "the inter-connection between representation and lived social relations".[47] It helped me to understand more about both
femininity and ethnicity, and to more confidently and tactically choose aspects
with which I identified. Easy assumptions about contemporary girls' relationship to Indian womanhood are impossible, and my story is intended to show
some reasons why.

So many ethnically defined expectations of women are tied to patriarchal
definition and control of their bodies and sexuality, reinforcement of nostalgia
for women as decorative cultural symbols, and differentiation of those considered "good" from those considered "bad". Although I knew the pageant was
culturally significant, at the time I saw it mainly as a beauty contest that
played into these power relations. One thing I have come to appreciate, however, is its role as a "counter-pageant" enabling a range of global, national and
"community"-defined feminine ideals to be reproduced and contested simultaneously. These ideals are lived by organizers, participants, audience members, sponsors and publics of different ethnicities, classes, religions and
geographical locations, in more complex, multiple ways than I understood at
the time.

Ultimately, writing this chapter made me ask myself how I defined my own
sense of being a young Indian woman. The most difficult part of writing this
was articulating transgressive locations and perspectives amid a cultural
unease with hybridity. There are, simply, many ways in which I don't – and
don't wish to – fit. I don't rely on extended family relations, religion, ideals of
respectability, notions of "racial" difference, discomfort with miscegenation,
music, language, dress or popular cultural practices to define my ethnicity. I
continue to bring a critical feminist stance to many patriarchal markers of
ethnic boundaries, and fierce antipathy to being easily fitted into categories.

In *Matikor: A Politics of Identity for Indo-Caribbean Women*, Kanhai writes
that Indian women's demand is that "they take their Indianness and their
femaleness" with them.[48] Yet there are many moments when I neither identify
as Indian, female, feminine, heterosexual or Trinidadian in any stable, constant and exclusive way, nor do I identify as *not* being those things. This was
the difficulty of this chapter for me. Not only have I stopped trying to be an
"appropriate Indian girl" and to manage ethnic or gender expectations, I have
stopped maintaining a claim to a racialized, sexualized, feminized self. At
times I identify with and reproduce these identities, and their hegemonic

meanings, but I do so transgressively, playfully, seriously, rebelliously, performatively and unpredictably, in ways and as forms of power that I am still defining.

Perhaps this is what I have mainly learned from the Mastana Bahar Indian Cultural Pageant, from researching young Indian women's lives and from a long tradition of Indian women's and feminists' search for selfhood, relationship and agency. Even if we win according to accepted categories, "we wish to be looked upon" in personally meaningful ways, as belonging both to communities and to ourselves.[49] Among other experiences, being Ms Mastana Bahar enabled me to see and recognize the different parts and histories of myself that contribute to constituting familiar as well as "new kinds of subjects".[50] As Cohen writes, "If beauty contests are sites for constituting identities at all, these are identities that emerge from the interplay of the differences and similarities of their participants, identities defined not by essence or purity . . . identities that are constantly producing and reproducing themselves anew."[51] Participating in the pageant heightened both my identification with and appreciation for symbols of Indian womanhood. It also strengthened my confidence that I could legitimately choose their meanings and my realities, just as other young Indian women have long begun to do.

NOTES

1. Robyn R. Warhol and Diane Price Herndl, *Feminisms: An Anthology of Literary Theory and Criticism* (New Brunswick, NJ: Rutgers University Press, 1997); Tess Cosslett, Celia Lury and Penny Summerfield, *Feminism and Autobiography: Texts, Theories and Methods* (London: Routledge, 2000); Diane Freedman and Olivia Frey, *Autobiographical Writing across the Disciplines: A Reader* (Durham: Duke University Press, 2003).

2. Sandra Pouchet Paquet, *Caribbean Autobiography: Cultural Identity and Self-representation* (Madison, Wis.: University of Wisconsin Press, 2003).

3. By "community" I do not mean to imply a homogeneous and singular group but rather a sense of an Indo-Trinidadian community that exists in spite of various (inter- and intra-)religious, class, geographical and other differences.

4. I refer here to Patricia Mohammed's useful concept of "negotiation", which she

uses to analyse gender relations among Indians in the post-indentureship period of 1917 to 1947. She discusses negotiation as involving "collusions, compromise and accommodation, resistance and subversion" in the public and private spheres. See Patricia Mohammed, *Gender Negotiations among Indians in Trinidad, 1917–1974* (Basingstoke, UK: Palgrave, 2002), 15.

5. De Certeau argues that strategies have institutional positioning and are able to conceal their connections with power. Tactics have no institutional location and cannot capitalize on the advantages of such positioning. Rather, *tactics* refers to the ways that those with less power to set the rules appropriate, recombine and reinterpret them in new ways. Tactics are not necessarily ideologically consistent but are slippery, subversive, makeshift, unstable and even temporary responses to necessity. They give an appearance of conformity while making rules habitable by actively engaging their legitimacy, meanings and definition of order. Michel De Certeau, *The Practice of Everyday Life* (London: University of California Press, 1988).

6. Valerie Hey, *The Company She Keeps: An Ethnography of Girls' Friendships* (Philadelphia: Open University Press, 1997), 13.

7. I use the concept of performance to describe my original observations and the feeling that I had to "act" in ways seen to be suitable for a young Indian woman when around adults and family, in religious and cultural spaces and in public generally. *Performance* is used here in an almost literal sense, beyond Judith Butler's concept of performativity, to describe a self-consciousness about how my appearance enabled me to be seen as "into my culture", "good", "a role model for Indian girls", "not too Westernized" and "not like others in your generation". See Judith Butler, *Bodies That Matter: On the Discursive Limits of Sex* (London: Routledge, 1993).

8. Gabrielle Hosein, "Gender, Generation and Negotiation: Adolescence and Young Indo-Trinidadian Women's Identities in the Late Twentieth Century" (MPhil thesis, University of the West Indies, St Augustine, Trinidad, 2004).

9. Vera Rubin and Marisa Zavalloni, *We Wished to Be Looked Upon: A Study of the Aspirations of Youth in a Developing Country* (New York: Teachers College Press, 1969), 91.

10. The queen is typically titled "Miss Mastana Bahar", but in all the press interviews that I have given, I have used "Ms" instead, as a small but marked expression of personal agency, feminist reframing and subversive desire.

11. Colleen Cohen, Richard Wilk and Beverly Stoeltje, eds., *Beauty Queens on the Global Stage: Gender, Contests and Power* (London: Routledge: 1996), 2.

12. Shamoon Mohammed, "The Creolisation of Women in Trinidad", in *Mastana*

Bahar and Indian Culture in Trinidad and Tobago: A Study of the East Indians of Trinidad and Tobago (San Juan, Trinidad: Mastana Bahar Thesis Publication Committee, 1982); Aisha Mohammed, "Love and Anxiety: Gender Negotiations in Chutney-Soca Lyrics", *Caribbean Review of Gender Studies* 1 (2007): 1–42.

13.   A site symbolically associated with the struggles of unions in the Indo-Trinidadian–identified sugar industry, and with Indian cultural activities.

14.   Belinda Edmondson, "Public Spectacles: Caribbean Women and the Politics of Public Performance", *Small Axe* 13 (March 2003): 11–12.

15.   Cohen, Wilk and Stoeltje, *Beauty Queens*, 9.

16.   See Natasha Barnes, "Face of the Nation: Nationalisms and Identities in Jamaican Beauty Pageants", in *The Gender and Consumer Culture Reader*, edited by Jennifer Scanlon, 335–71 (New York: New York University Press, 2000) for a discussion of ethnicity and beauty pageants in Jamaica.

17.   Patricia Mohammed, "Gender as a Primary Signifier in the Construction of Community and State among Indians in Trinidad", *Caribbean Quarterly* 40, no. 3–4 (1994), 32–43.

18.   Rhoda Reddock, "Contestations over National Culture in Trinidad and Tobago: Considerations of Ethnicity, Class and Gender", in *Caribbean Portraits: Essays on Gender Ideologies and Identities*, edited by Christine Barrow, 414–35 (Kingston: Ian Randle and Centre for Gender and Development Studies, 1998).

19.   Feminists interpret girls' concerns about "looking good" as both a form of subordination and a source of feelings of power and pleasurable self-esteem for girls who gain "approval". As Hey described, appropriate appearance signifies appropriate class and sexual meanings and enables girls to stake "claims as particular beings on the public stage"; Hey, *Company*, 118.

20.   Beverly Stoeltje, "The Snake Charmer Queen: Ritual, Competition and Signification in American Festival", in *Beauty Queens on the Global Stage: Gender, Contests and Power*, edited by Colleen Cohen, Richard Wilk and Beverly Stoeltje (London: Routledge: 1996), 17.

21.   Height was not important but hair length and skin colour were. Contestants and my designers talked about how the *dougla* young woman would not win because she was too dark and was racially mixed. "Fair" skin was ideal, and sponsors cautioned us to stay out of the sun so we would not look dark. However, brown skin like mine was acceptable. Weight was also important; the skinny look of Western models was not required, but plumpness could attract negative comments. Another contestant was seen as having a big bottom "like dem creole" and was not likely to win for that reason.

22.   See Rebecca King O'Riain, "Making the Perfect Queen: The Cultural Production

of Identities in Beauty Pageants", *Sociology Compass* 2, no. 1 (2008), 79, for literature on other examples of counter-pageants around the world.

23. In 1997 a young Afro-Trinidadian dancer won the title. This was an anomaly and was widely seen as a "national unity" gesture in a post-1995 UNC-dominated era. One letter to the editor protested that she was an unwed mother and therefore transgressed Indian ideals regarding family and marriage. This was the only time a non-Indian won the title. See Brenda Gopeesingh, "What Constitutes Indian Culture?", *Sunday Express*, "Indian Arrival" special, 25 May 1997, 1.

24. Robert Lavenda, "'It's Not a Beauty Pageant!': Hybrid Ideology in Minnesota Community Queen Pageants", in *Beauty Queens on the Global Stage: Gender, Contests and Power*, edited by Colleen Cohen, Richard Wilk and Beverly Stoeltje (London: Routledge: 1996), 45.

25. Cohen, Wilk and Stoeltje, *Beauty Queens*, 9.

26. Tracy Kim Assing, "Gabrielle: A Militant Maharani", *Sunday Guardian*, 23 April 2000, 24.

27. In fact, my boyfriend at the time (now my husband) was an Afro-Trinidadian.

28. Alicia Walters, "Miss Mastana Shocker: Wants Child Out of Wedlock, Could Marry Non-Indian", *Independent*, 19 May 2000, 2.

29. Indians who spoke to me were offended that, in their view, African or white beauty queens in Trinidad and Tobago were never asked such questions about racial mixing; they felt that this was a specific way that Indians and Indian women were targeted in public discourse. Some Indians were simply offended by my answer, especially given the authenticity, purity and tradition associated with my title.

30. Their position is a valid one. I would never have entered a competition involving a swimsuit segment, because in many ways I both understood and agreed with feminist critiques of pageants.

31. Cohen, Wilk and Stoeltje, *Beauty Queens*, 9.

32. Hosein, "Gender, Generation and Negotiation".

33. Penny Van Esterik, "The Politics of Beauty in Thailand", in *Beauty Queens on the Global Stage: Gender, Contests and Power*, edited by Colleen Cohen, Richard Wilk and Beverly Stoeltje (London: Routledge: 1996), 203.

34. Katherine Borland, "The India Bonita of Monimbo: The Politics of Ethnic Identity in the New Nicaragua", in *Beauty Queens on the Global Stage: Gender, Contests and Power*, edited by Colleen Cohen, Richard Wilk and Beverly Stoeltje (London: Routledge: 1996), 86.

35. Cohen, Wilk and Stoeltje, *Beauty Queens*, 6.

36. P. Mohammed, *Gender Negotiations*.

37. Patricia Mohammed, "The Creolisation of Indian Women in Trinidad", in *Trinidad and Tobago: The Independence Experience, 1962–1987,* edited by Selwyn Ryan, 381–97 (St Augustine, Trinidad: University of the West Indies Institute of Social and Economic Research, 1988); "Gender as a Primary Signifier"; "The Idea of Childhood and Age of Sexual Maturity among Indians in Trinidad: A Sociohistorical Scrutiny", in *Caribbean Families: Diversity among Ethnic Groups,* edited by Jaipaul L. Roopnarine and Janet Brown, 115–46 (Greenwich, Conn.: Ablex Press, 1997).

38. Rubin and Zavalloni, *We Wished to Be Looked Upon,* 197.

39. Rhoda Reddock, "Freedom Denied: Indian Women and Indentureship in Trinidad and Tobago, 1845–1917", *Caribbean Quarterly* 32, no. 3–4 (1986): 27–49; Shaheeda Hosein, "Until Death Do Us Part? Marriage, Divorce and the Indian Woman" (paper presented at the 33rd Annual Conference of the Association of Caribbean Historians, University of the West Indies, St Augustine, Trinidad, 2001); P. Mohammed, *Gender Negotiations.*

40. Rawwida Baksh-Soodeen, "Power, Gender and Chutney", in *Matikor: The Politics of Identity for Indo-Caribbean Women,* edited by Rosanne Kanhai, 194–98 (St Augustine, Trinidad: University of the West Indies School of Continuing Studies, 1999); Janis Kanhai-Winter, "My Aaji", in *Matikor,* 130–39; Indrani Rampersad, "Becoming a Pandita", in *Matikor,* 140–43.

41. Gabrielle Hosein, "Ambivalent Aspirations: Assertion and Accommodation in Indo-Trinidadian Girls' Lives", in *Gender in the Twenty-First Century: Caribbean Perspectives, Visions and Possibilities,* edited by Barbara Bailey and Elsa Leo-Rhynie, 528–63 (Kingston: Ian Randle, 2004).

42. G. Hosein, "Gender, Generation and Negotiation".

43. Angela McRobbie, *Feminism and Youth Culture: From "Jackie" to "Just Seventeen"* (Basingstoke, UK: Macmillan Education, 1991).

44. Hey, *Company,* 84.

45. Ibid., 115–16, 125.

46. Negotiation involves agency and engagement with rules and expected roles of various kinds. Young women negotiate, but they are also able (and to some extent compelled) to move among and "choose" from a range of multiple and competing prescriptions and demands. This is a continual process of finding the balance of identities and practices "appropriate" to different spaces and situations. Therefore they navigate different ideals as well as negotiate the expectations of each; G. Hosein, "Ambivalent Aspirations".

47. Tracy Skelton and Gill Valentine, eds., *Cool Places: Geographies of Youth Cultures* (London: Routledge, 1998), 18.

48. Kanhai, "The Masala Stone Sings: Poetry, Performance and Film by Indo-Caribbean Women", in *Matikor: The Politics of Identity for Indo-Caribbean Women*, edited by Rosanne Kanhai (St Augustine, Trinidad: University of the West Indies School of Continuing Studies. 1999), 234.

49. Rubin and Zavalloni, *We Wished to Be Looked Upon*.

50. Stuart Hall, "Cultural Identity and Cinematic Representation", in *Ex-Isles: Essays on Caribbean Cinema*, edited by M. Cham (Trenton, NJ: Africa World Press, 1992), 234–36.

51. Colleen Cohen, "Contestants in a Contested Domain: Staging Identities in the British Virgin Islands", in *Beauty Queens on the Global Stage: Gender, Contests and Power*, edited by Colleen Cohen, Richard Wilk and Beverly Stoeltje (London: Routledge, 1996), 144.

Survival
and
Creativity

6

Women as Invisible Healers

Traditional Midwives of Trinidad and Tobago

– KUMAR MAHABIR –

INTRODUCTION

WHEN THE COST of biomedicine is beyond the reach of low-income families, or when biomedicine is unable to cure certain (culture-specific) illnesses, home and/or traditional health-care givers rise up to fill the void. The services they provide are comprehensive and include aspects of biomedicine as well as traditional medicine itself. In their practice, masseuses in Trinidad[1] represent varying degrees of traditionalism, acculturation and modernism.[2] One reason why the work of masseuses persists to this day is their success in satisfying patients' physical, mental, psychological, emotional, spiritual and social needs. The decrease in both the number of midwives/masseuses and the number of activities they perform, however, reflects the increasing secularization and penetration of Euro-American values transmitted through education, religion, television and other means of mass communication.[3]

TYPES OF CONDITIONS TREATED

Hospitals in Trinidad have usurped most of the traditional functions of midwives, who were until the 1950s very active in attending to parturient women and their newborns. Their services have been truncated to "rubbing" the new mother and her newborn and performing rituals to placate the supernatural spirits. They still, therefore, reaffirm an important link between this world and the other, between natural/traditional medicine and "doctor medicine". In addition, they *jharay najar* (cure the evil eye), deal with neonatal jaundice, treat culture-specific bodily dislocations such as *hassuli* among infants, *boo-chet*, *nara* and *palai*. Most of their therapeutic treatments relate to attempts to relocate bodily organs believed to have been shifted from their normal positions.[4] Traditional masseuses primarily treat non-life-threatening conditions; they often refer their patients to doctors when they feel that curing a complaint is beyond their level of expertise.

FEMALE INFERTILITY

Indo-Trinidadian masseuses boast about how they have successfully treated women who had felt they were infertile for as long as ten years. They claim that doctors are often amazed at the positive results of their cures but have never tried to contact them. It is mainly this specialty that attracts non-Indian women to them. Masseuses believe that female infertility is caused when a woman's womb, or "mattress"[5] is "out of place" or "too low", which has to be corrected by inserting the fingers in the vagina and pushing the uterus upwards. This dislocation is commonly believed to be caused by lifting heavy objects. Infertility may also be the result of improper abortions carried out by doctors or backyard female practitioners. It is also believed to be a result of "cold" accumulated in the womb which, along with other "nastiness", has to be cleaned out. The problem of infertility has to be "fixed" by a masseuse using abdominal massage, cupping (discussed later in this section) and other procedures, rather than through surgery by a gynaecologist. They admit that at times their treatment regimens fail: it is "sometimes God' work that some women can't have a baby".

To treat the problem of female infertility, the masseuse makes a concoction, the ingredients and administration of which vary with her ethnicity. African masseuses use an old Spanish-derived medicine, a brew which consists of honey, aloes and egg albumin. This mixture is drunk and then followed by a purge combined from honey, castor oil, lamp oil, olive oil and boiled ginger. An adhesive plaster is placed on the woman's back; it contains a paste consisting of brandy, egg albumin, flour and vinegar. If the masseuse believes that the infertility problem is caused by inflammation in the tubes, wild coffee roots are collected, washed, pounded and boiled and administered as a purge.

Indian masseuses, on the other hand, make a fertility "plug" consisting of familiar ingredients from their kitchen, household and garden environments. These include *jawine* (a small edible grain), a raw grain of *channa* (chickpeas), dried ground ganja (marijuana) leaf, ground ginger and camphor, which is optional; some masseuses add *harjor* and allium. These are wrapped in a piece of clean cotton *dhoti* (loincloth) and tied into a bunch "like a ball" with sewing thread. The ends of the thread are left long, as on an IUD contraceptive. The plug is dipped into a glass of white puncheon rum, lubricated with petroleum jelly and inserted into the patient's vagina, where it is left until the "mattress" is "set". During the period of treatment the woman is advised not to engage in sexual or vigorous activity. When the "mattress" moves into its natural place, the muscles of the vaginal opening are expected to expel the plug. If it has not discharged after three days, the masseuse extracts it with her fingers.

PREGNANCY AND PRENATAL SEX TESTS

Masseuses claim that they can perform pregnancy tests from as early as three months, by touching the abdomen and feeling "a beat". If the pregnancy is four months gone, the expectant mother can herself feel the heartbeat in her abdomen while she is seated; a "lump" can also be felt. The doctors I interviewed maintain that around the fourth month of pregnancy they can hear the foetal heartbeat without the use of instruments. Masseuses in Trinidad also claim that they can determine the sex of a baby by observing the shape of the woman's swollen abdomen. There is general agreement that if it is a boy, the abdomen will be protruding ("long"), and if a girl, it will be round ("spread out").

ASSISTANCE WITH DELIVERIES

The law in Trinidad now mandates that women should deliver their babies at clinics or hospitals. Before the 1960s, when health facilities were not so readily available, traditional midwives/masseuses attended to deliveries at home ("put ladies to bed").[6] They prepared for deliveries by boiling a pot of water, sterilizing a pair of scissors, cutting pieces of sewing thread and having on hand bottles of antiseptic Dettol and Savlon liquid. They attended to generations of women, sometimes in the same family. One parturient woman reminded a seventy-seven-year-old masseuse of her long service: "*Mai* [mother], you know that you work for me, you work for my mother and now you have to work for my children." The masseuse had birthed most of the woman's eleven children at her father-in-law's house, without the assistance of a registered nurse or local village midwife. It was only after "the baby come out" that she sent her husband to seek help.

Masseuses today continue to attend to home births only when there is an sudden emergency. One masseuse last attended to an emergency home delivery in 1994. The unmarried expectant mother had not made any effort to go to the hospital because "she didn't have soap, towel, nothing, to take to the hospital". She soiled the bed sheets because there was no enema available. The masseuse used sewing thread to tie the umbilical cord and a razor blade to cut it. The afterbirth was not expelled automatically, so the masseuse made her blow into a soft-drink bottle "to add pressure" to her womb. Another masseuse attended to a parturient woman in 1995 who had been sent back home after the nurses at the hospital informed her she was not ready to deliver. She had the baby at home prematurely, after which the masseuse was called to assist. (One of the masseuse's daughters has eight children, seven of whom were born at home with her assistance.)

The masseuse would massage the back and pelvic area of the parturient woman during labour and delivery.[7] Unlike women in the 1950s in Uttar Pradesh, India,[8] Trinidadian Indian women did not squat on a low wooden stool or on the floor for delivery.[9] The majority (85 per cent) of masseuses interviewed said they feel confident that they can assist in a delivery at home or in the hospital (see figure 6.1).

Sixty-two per cent of the traditional masseuses interviewed usually attempt to reposition the breech or transverse foetus of an expectant primigravida mother after the eighth month of pregnancy. Others (38 per cent) refer their patients to an obstetrician, who is likely to resort to a Caesarean section as a last alternative. Less than 10 per cent of women with breech pregnancies seek the aid of a masseuse as their first choice to relocate the foetus into a cephalic

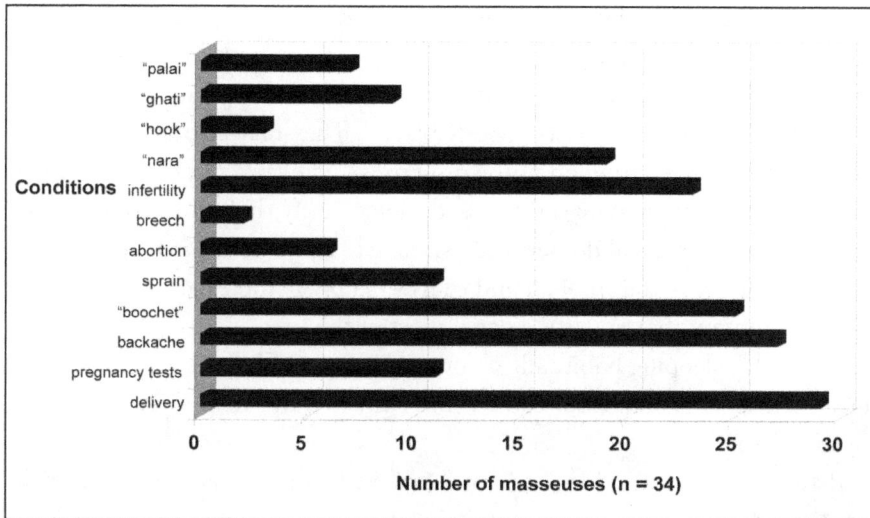

Figure 6.1: Frequency of conditions which masseuses claim they can handle.

Note: Figures exclude basic maternal and infant massage, application of abdominal bands and treatment of the evil eye and *hassuli*, which all of them can treat.

position. These were mainly Indian women whose feelings about their abnormal foetal position were confirmed by their physicians. Women in this condition in Trinidad visit a masseuse as prevention against the risk of foetal death during a breech delivery and the pain of a prolonged labour. Masseuses know from experience that when a baby is born with its feet first, the mother "bear[s] too much pain". Obstetricians say that foetal death can occur from asphyxia or intracranial haemorrhage from a tentorial tear produced by sudden changes in intracranial pressure.[10] A visit to the masseuse could also mean saving about US$2,500, which is the expense of a C-section delivery in a private hospital. The masseuse believes that when the foetus remains in breech ("bridge") presentation at the onset of labour, obstetricians "are quick to put knife on ladies".

Masseuses believe that one symptom of a breech pregnancy is the expectant mother's feeling pain on one side of her abdomen and "emptiness" on the other. The problem may be so acute during the ninth month that the patient is unable to walk, and a masseuse will be asked to make a home visit. ("When the baby resting on one side, the leg does kinda drag with the weight.") Masseuses diagnose whether the foetus is in a breech or transverse position by gently probing the sides of the abdomen with both hands in an attempt to locate its head. If the underneath of the abdomen feels hollow, it is likely that the foetus is not properly placed. They may also place a drop of oil at the top of the abdomen; if the drop runs "sideways" rather than straight down, a breech pregnancy is diagnosed. Some verify their decision by examining the shape of the abdomen and listening to the beat of the foetus's heart. Masseuses believe that breech and transverse pregnancies are caused when the expectant mother is "sitting down most of the time", "sitting too much in a hammock", sleeping habitually on one side of her body or not being consistently active. This behaviour causes "the baby to move to one side and settle there".

If the foetus is found to be "cross" or "sideways" and is more than eight months old, the masseuse attempts to rotate ("fix and straighten") it by external version in utero. Inversion is done by massaging and shaking the woman's abdomen, lightly at first and then vigorously, "to ease up the baby from where it stick up or sink down". The masseuse's palms, lubricated with coconut oil, are always placed on the opposite sides of the abdomen. The procedure is often painful, but since the perceived alternative is a C-section, women prefer to bear these few minutes of agony.[11] Masseuses would like to apply this procedure during labour but are barred from participating in institutionalized deliveries. Obstetricians in Trinidad believe that it is possible to safely turn a foetus by external version, but they choose to deliver babies by Caesarean section, particularly if they are either large or small for their due date. Masseuses recognize that trying to turn a foetus to a cephalic position is a delicate, complicated and dangerous procedure. "You have to know how you turning that baby, otherwise that baby could pass away in the mother belly."

TREATING BACKACHES

Masseuses in Trinidad also treat backaches, by using a variety of traditional cupping methods. One technique is to place a teaspoon of pot salt or rice grains on a piece of cloth the size of a handkerchief. The salt is bunched and the ends of the cloth are tied together with a thread. The masseuse sets the loose ends alight by torching them with a lighted *deeya* (earthen lamp) and the cloth ball is then placed on the affected body part. A *lota* (brass jug) is used to cover the lighted cloth, which "pull[s]", "hold[s] and "draw[s]" the pain. This procedure is done twice daily on the back, and below the navel if the problem is diagnosed to be an abdominal disorder.

A modified traditional variation, used by Hindu masseuses in a hurry and by non-Hindu homecare providers, is "glassing".[12] A one-inch-long piece of candle is mounted on a coin set on the affected area, then a glass is turned upside down over the lighted wick. Another method is to pour a few drops of puncheon rum on a cloth, which is used to wipe the inside of a thick drinking glass. A match is struck, causing flames to engulf the inside of the glass. The lighted glass is quickly placed on the affected area and the flesh puffs up underneath it. The flames consume the oxygen inside the glass after a few minutes and they extinguish. The glass (or *lota*) then falls sideways and the complaint is believed to be cured. Prayers are not recited during this procedure.

TREATING NARA AND BOOCHET

Indo-Trinidadian masseuses also treat Indian-specific physiological complaints such as *nara* and *boochet*. The latter is described as "something like a ball" or "lump" located under the breastbone. The organ drops or shifts when a person lifts or pushes a heavy object or trips and falls suddenly. It is believed that weakness of the body can also precipitate the disorder. The main symptoms are vomiting when anything is ingested and chest pain: "You can't even drink water; it coming back up." The problem is treated by massaging with both hands simultaneously, moving them from the sides of the body to the centre, and then relocating the *boochet* with the index finger. It is also treated by glassing, which "sets" the organ back into place.

Nara is a dislocated vein, characterized by abdominal pain, nausea ("bad feeling") and vomiting with or without diarrhoea ("belly going off"), lethargy, poor appetite and general malaise. Physicians whom I interviewed approximated this condition with "torsion of the omentum", which is an abnormality caused when the omentum – "an apron of fat that hangs from the stomach and covers the intestine" – twists on itself, cutting off the blood supply and sometimes causing abdominal pain. Masseuses diagnose *nara* by placing their thumb firmly on the abdomen just above the navel, where they feel a rhythmic "beat", "grumble" or "bubble". Medical practitioners suggest that this sensation is the pulsation of an aortic aneurysm, which is a balloon-like swelling of an artery caused by weakness in the vessel wall. Folk medical practitioners claim that while appendicitis feels soft, *nara* is hard like a lump, so there is no danger of rupturing an inflamed appendix while massaging, as doctors fear.

Like *boochet*, both men and women suffer from *nara*, and it is possible for a person to suffer from both complaints concurrently. But while *nara* in men is usually treated by "cracking" by male bone-setters, in women it is treated by "rubbing" by masseuses.[13] Treating this condition is done by a series of firm strokes directed towards the navel. Physicians maintain that vigorous massaging can be dangerous because it can cause an aortic aneurysm to rupture and can lead to "instant death". Based on my knowledge as a person who has spent almost all his life in Trinidad and that of my folk medical and postnatal informants, there is not a single known case of a person dying "instantly" under the hands of a masseuse. Trinidad physicians do admit, however, that these manipulations can "somehow help to untwist the omentum in the abdomen when the folk practitioner puts her hand on the patient's belly".

In treating *nara*, the bone-setter ("massage man") usually instructs his patient to lie flat on his belly on the floor and relax ("to get the bones loose"). He "crack[s]" him by asking him to turn on his side while he sets his foot on the patient's waist and jerks one arm. The procedure is repeated on the other side. The patient is then asked to stand and lace the fingers of both hands behind his neck with his elbows pointing towards his toes. The bone-setter stands behind him, wraps his hands around the patient's arms, lifts him off the ground and jerks him until he hears a "cricking" sound emanating from the spinal column. The patient is also asked to lie on his back on the floor and flex his knees. The bone-setter places his hands on each knee and pushes the knees suddenly towards the abdomen. Again a "cricking" sound is expected to emit from the hips and lower spine. It is believed by folk healers that, if left untreated, *nara* can form a hard lump ("knot") around the navel which would have to be dealt with by a specialist physician.

TREATING SPRAINS

While Trinidad bone-setters treat sprains by manual traction ("cracking"), masseuses treat the same problem, mainly among women, by "rubbing" and the application of herbal poultices. The latter method, however, has become almost obsolete with the promotion and availability of pharmaceutical products such as "soft candle". Only 12 per cent of the masseuses in my sample said that they still use brown paper soaked in vinegar as a compress. About the same proportion of them treat sprains by cutting an eggplant (*baigan*) in half, spreading salted butter on the insides and tying them on the affected body part.

The masseuses recall that the generation before them treated sprains by applying wild saffron, *harjor*, wild onion, white lime, talla grease and rope imported from Germany. Some of the ingredients would be chopped and then placed in a mortar, where they would be pounded. Then they would be heated in a pot and the moist mass would be spread on a castor oil leaf, which would be placed in a headscarf (*orhni*). The poultice would be wrapped around the inflamed part of the limb and remain in place for about four days. It was applied "as hot as the person could bear". When the cataplasm was removed, the masseuse would rub the affected area and apply a new poultice. She would "massage the nerves, the veins . . . and shake the foot . . . and the bone would go *crick!* and it set". Masseuses nowadays believe that commercial adhesive plasters are not satisfactory: "It falling off in two, three days." Until the 1940s they used the sap of a chataigne, matapal or breadfruit tree as an adhesive. The "wax" used by cobblers was also a good substitute for treating any dislocated ("unranged") musculoskeletal problem.

TREATING *PALAI*

Palai, or "pressing" – recognized by physicians as asthma or bronchitis – was last treated by masseuses in Trinidad in the 1950s. Masseuses diagnosed this respiratory problem by observing that the area around the person's umbilicus was "jumping" and the chest was "beating hard hard". They would *jharay* (treat) the complaint by joining the thumb and smallest finger of one hand together and making a circular motion. The motion was performed five or seven times around the affected navel while a mantra was recited. Instead of the fingers, a knife could also be used.

PERFORMING ABORTIONS

Abortions are illegal in Trinidad except for the highly restricted "therapeutic abortions", which must be carried out within the first trimester of pregnancy by licensed medical practitioners. However, some family doctors routinely perform abortions in their private clinics for any woman who has the money to pay. The cost of an abortion depends on how advanced the pregnancy is – currently US$170 per month.[14] Other doctors are unknowingly misled by their clients, who tell them that they need medication to resume menstruation.

Backyard abortionists, who are usually females, are the locally known specialists in this secretive operation. Because of how they think human's/women's bodies work, they seldom use sharp instruments such as wire hangers or poisonous cassava sticks to puncture the foetal bag of water. As Sobo found in Jamaica, purgatives are more often used, because it does not make any sense to "pull out" what can be "washed out". This procedure also minimizes the risk of permanent disability or death from sepsis, haemorrhage, uterine perforation, lower genital tract injury, renal failure or embolism.[15] In any case, women who visit backyard abortionists sometimes end up in public hospitals seeking post-abortion treatment[16] when pain and bleeding increase or when the foetus and its sac are not expelled.[17] The post-abortion ward at Port of Spain General Hospital is popularly referred to as the "slip and slide" ward because of the high number of women (50 patients weekly) who are admitted for botched or incomplete induced abortion.[18] When questioned by the hospital staff about their condition, most women claim that they miscarried because they had accidentally slipped and fallen.

Most women try self-inducing methods at home before visiting a doctor, backyard abortionist or masseuse. The use of home remedies varies with the availability of the ingredients and the stage of the pregnancy.[19] Home remedies often include the ingestion of substances considered to have "strong", "bitter" or purgative qualities. Parturient women stress their bodies with hard manual work or they jump to "bring down" the foetus. Another home remedy increasingly used in Trinidad to induce abortion is the over-the-counter drug Cytotec (misoprostol), which is sold without a prescription.[20]

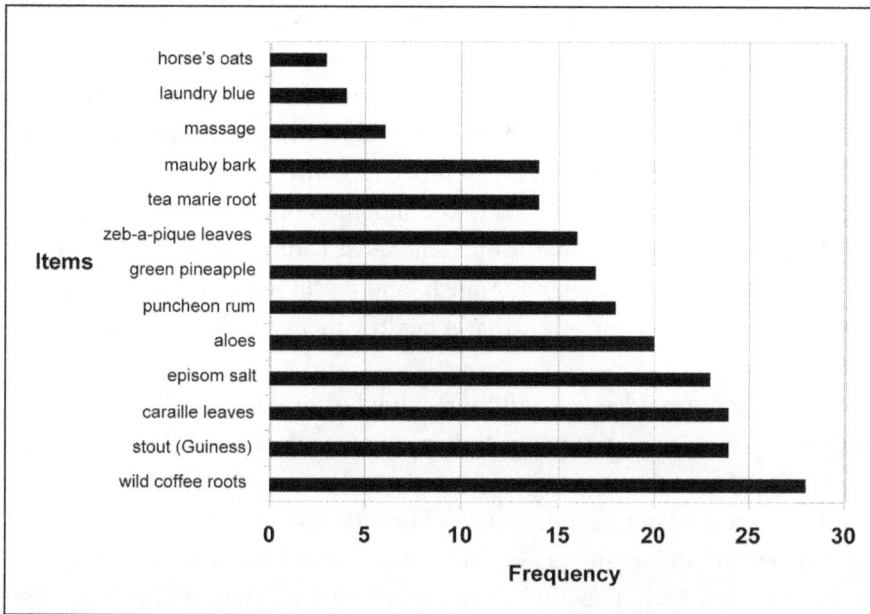

Figure 6.2: Frequency of abortion items used by masseuses (N = 34).

It is not unexpected that masseuses, who are the recognized folk gynae-cologists and obstetricians in the community, sometimes provide this kind of lucrative service. However, only 6 per cent of the masseuses I interviewed confessed that they performed clandestine abortions. They did not want to be publicly identified for fear of the law and social condemnation. Those who do not perform the service do so for religious and moral reasons: "You can't save life and then you want to destroy it." One elderly masseuse whispered mischievously to me about another village colleague, "It had a time when she used to dig out child and throw away. But now she go down deep in [religious] devotion and she stop now."

The procedures the masseuses prescribe are often the same as those used by pregnant women at home. Traditional masseuses' methods of abortion may also include the use of horse's oats boiled in stout and laced with a few drops of puncheon rum. The potion, taken by mouth, is expected to "make two-month and three-month baby fall". Another potpourri is made by boiling young guava, black sage, carailla and cashew leaves; a cup is drunk for three morn-ings consecutively. The roots of a wild coffee plant are also boiled and drunk to "pass out" the foetus. Other abortive brews include green pineapple soaked in white rum, boiled mauby bark, the boiled roots of the ti-marie plant, the boiled leaves of the zèb-a-pik tree, aloes, stout and Epsom salt. Figure 6.2 illustrates the frequency of items mentioned by the thirty-four masseuses I interviewed. As in Asia,[21] a follow-up procedure involves the masseuse pressing deeply with her hands on the lower abdomen of the pregnant woman in an effort to "squeeze" the foetus out. Masseuses admit, however, that sometimes "you could drink all kind of bush, and it still wouldn't go". This belief is consistent with doctors' view that a healthy foetus is almost impossible to dislodge.

Like their knowledge and skill in making fertility "plugs", the specialty of performing abortions attracts non-Indian clients to these mainly Indian/Hindu masseuses. An examination of 210 randomly selected medical records of postnatal women at Mount Hope Women's Hospital reveals that more non-Indian (56 per cent) than Indian (44 per cent) women had had either a spontaneous or induced abortion. This finding is consistent with that of Harewood and Abdulah,[22] which reveals that the proportion of women who had an induced abortion was higher for women of African descent than for those of other racial groups.

SUMMARY

Since masseuses in Trinidad are the key custodians and practitioners of traditional medicine who specialize in treatment of mainly low-income women, they represent a symbol of resistance to the dominance of capitalistic male medicine.[23] The socio-economic divergence between healer and patient is small compared to that between the physician and his client. Being skilled as a folk medical practitioner does not automatically place the masseuse in a separate privileged class or set her apart from the exigencies of life in the low-income community in which she lives and serves.[24] The low-income patient is not constrained in expressing her most private problems to the masseuse in the Trinidad English dialect that both of them habitually speak. In Trinidad society, where the activities of the majority of women were up to the 1960s confined to the domestic sphere, massaging provided the only avenue for low-income women to participate in community service in the public domain.[25]

Massaging, therefore, can be seen as a thinly disguised protest movement directed towards wage-earning male physicians.[26]

NOTES

1. I define a traditional masseuse as one who has had no formal training in massage therapy and is recognized by the community as having specialized knowledge and skill in treating patients. See also Carolyn F. Sargeant, *The Cultural Context of Therapeutic Choice: Obstetrical Care Decisions among the Bariba of Benin* (Dordrecht: Reidel, 1982), 63.
2. Sheila Cominsky, "Childbirth and Change: A Guatemalan Study", in *Ethnography of Fertility and Birth*, edited by Carol P. MacCormack, 205–29 (New York: Academic Press, 1982).
3. Daniel Miller, *Modernity: An Ethnographic Approach* (Oxford: Berg, 1994).
4. George Foster, "Relationships between Spanish and Spanish-American Folk Medicine", *Journal of American Folklore* 66 (1953), 201–17.
5. There is no anatomical term in Western medical science synonymous with "mattress". Masseuses indicate that it supports the uterus and grows as big as a marble during pregnancy.
6. There is still a vestigial belief in *rakshas* – deformed foetuses with hair, two long teeth overlapping the lower lip and a rat-like face. Their ears are described as "flatty flatty" and their eyes as bulgy; their limbs are long, thin and crooked – "like a *crapaud* [frog]". They were almost always stillborn but it was believed that, if born alive, they had the capacity to jump and crouch on the mother's chest or fly through the window to the top of the roof, to await a convenient time to pounce and kill both parents. This fear led midwives to suffocate them instantly upon delivery. *Chuggalias* or *bhillinays* (village news-carriers) of course exaggerated the physical features and capacities of these foetuses. Only two of the thirty-four masseuses I interviewed claimed that they had actually got a glimpse of a *raksha*, which did not have wing-like limbs. The other descriptions were based on second-hand sources. My belief is that *rakshas* were the result of a malnourished mother and/or an incomplete abortion. Masseuses think that these are the living results of the parents' or grandparents' *karma* (retribution): "You can't plant mango and expect to reap tamarind. My old parents say, 'Your deeds have to run for seven generations.'"
7. Margaret Kay, *Anthropology of Human Birth* (Philadelphia: F.A. Davis, 1982).

8. Mildred S. Luschinsky, "The Life of Women in a Village of North India: A Study of Role and Status" (PhD diss., Cornell University, 1962).

9. Feminist childbirth educators (e.g., Miriam Stoppard, *Woman's Body* [New York: Dorling Kindersley, 1984]) argue that when a birthing woman is squatting and supported by others, her pelvis will be completely open and she will be able to take full advantage of gravity.

10. See G.D. Pinker and D.W. Roberts, *A Short Textbook of Gynaecology and Obstetrics* (London: English Universities Press, 1967), 153.

11. Bridgette Jordan, *Birth in Four Cultures: A Crosscultural Investigation of Childbirth in Yucatan, Holland, Sweden and the United States* (Montreal: Eden Press, 1978).

12. Ruth Behar, *Translated Woman: Crossing the Border with Esperanza's Story* (Boston: Beacon Press, 1993), 108.

13. Another method by which to *jharay* (treat) *nara*, practised up to the 1950s in Trinidad, was with bamboo strips and prayers. The healer stood in front of the patient holding two strips of bamboo, about one foot long, outstretched in his hands. While the healer was reciting mantras (sacred formulae), the two strips would draw towards each other as an indication that the complaint was being cured.

14. In 1995 the death of a woman from an attempted abortion performed by a medical doctor was reported in the local newspaper. The woman was about four months pregnant and had been injected with a controlled poisonous drug to induce an abortion.

15. See United Nations, *The World's Women* (New York: United Nations, 1995), 79.

16. Sandra Chouthi, "Doctor Earns $6,000 a Day Doing Abortions", *Trinidad Express*, 12 July 1988, 17.

17. D.N. Marshall et al., eds., *A Guide to Family Health* (Grantham, UK: Stanborough Press, 1983).

18. Kamla Rampersad, "Deaths from Abuse of Cytotec on the Rise", *Trinidad Guardian*, 2 March 1996, 11.

19. George Simpson, "Folk Medicine in Trinidad", *Journal of American Folklore* 75 (1962): 326–40.

20. Rampersad, "Deaths".

21. J.S. Sambhi, "Abortion by Massage", *IPPF Medical Bulletin* 11, no. 3 (1977): 2–3.

22. Jack Harewood and Norma Abdulah, "What Our Women Know, Think and Do about Birth Control" (St Augustine, Trinidad: ISER, University of the West Indies, 1972), 32.

23. Merrill Singer, "Postmodernism and Medical Anthropology: Words of Caution", *Medical Anthropology* 12 (1990): 289–304.

24. See also Barbara Kerewsky-Halpern, "Trust, Talk and Touch in Balkan Folk Healing", *Social Science and Medicine* 21, no. 3 (1985): 319–25.

25. See also Sargeant, *Cultural Context.*

26. See I.M. Lewis, *Ecstatic Religion: An Anthropological Study of Spirit Possession and Shamanism* (London: Penguin, 1971).

7 ❧

Identity, Activism and Spirituality in the Art of Bernadette Persaud

– BRENDA GOPEESINGH –

AN INDO-CARIBBEAN WOMAN artist is not a common feature in the anglophone Caribbean. That such an artist thrives on confronting issues of cultural and political sovereignty is simply extraordinary. This chapter examines the work of Bernadette Indira Persaud as she explores her ancestral heritage, which leads her towards a path of spirituality and activism. It also discusses her views on the distribution of political power in the global context and her outright challenge of the suppression of Caribbean artists through the imposition of Western standards. This chapter is the outcome of conversations I had with the artist at her home in Chateau Margot, Guyana, in March 2007, supplemented by several newspaper clippings, pamphlets and journals which she kindly passed on to me, as well as other relevant research material.

INTRODUCTION

Bernadette Indira Persaud, a citizen of Guyana, stands tall as one of the most prominent contemporary artists in the English-speaking Caribbean. Some of her earliest works explore the political, religious and cultural aspects of life in her homeland. She is relentless in her search for truth and rummages into the depths of religious texts in order to study them and test the accuracy of her own perspectives. What concerns us here is the degree to which her role as activist and educator thrusts her into a select group of thinkers motivated by radical patriots such as Martin Carter, Cheddi Jagan, political activist Walter Rodney and others.

Persaud had just established her presence in the Guyanese art community in the 1980s when she became the first woman to win the National Visual Arts Exhibition and Competition in 1985, with her painting titled *The End of a Season* (oil on canvas, 48 inches by 25 inches). This painting was done shortly after the death of her father in 1984. Its title is taken from the poem "Reluctance", by the American poet Robert Frost. The painting depicts birds (gaulins) coming home to rest in the trees of the Botanical Gardens in the evening. The colours are the colours of autumn and decay. But Persaud was to move far away from this theme and style.

Since then she has exhibited extensively in Canada, the Caribbean, India, the United Kingdom and the United States. She retired from the position of senior lecturer at the University of Guyana in 2007, having taught at the Burrowes School of the Arts between 1991 and 1998. Her paintings continue to grace the walls of private homes and corporate halls. They can also be viewed in Castellani House, which accommodates the national collection of Guyana.

In as much as there was no documented tradition in Caribbean art[1] from which she could draw upon to develop her work, nor was any locally written art history available to her, Persaud relied upon her own culturally and politically specific circumstances to provide her with subject matter. In the absence of permanently installed works of art in the 1980s – when she started painting seriously – she relied upon textbooks (like other artists), photographic models and the images around her, even when they were devoid of history and context.

Persaud ranks among a small group of Indo-Guyanese artists who emerged in the 1980s – Philbert Gajadhar, Betty Karim and the Amerindian-Indian artist Desmond Ali – whose art finds its inspiration in the rich depository of their ancestral legacy. Persaud's work treats current societal issues such as oppression, identity and politics, which continue to crowd the psyche of the world's migrant peoples. It is here that Persaud has reached the peak of her ability to arouse, to agitate and to motivate. Persaud has become the voice for those artists who, because of the peculiar brand of cultural politics practised by the art establishment in Guyana, have been excluded from the mainstream, the beacon of light for those whose work would have faded into the shadows of marginality.

In May 2002, on the occasion of the International Conference of the Indian Diaspora which marked the 164th anniversary of the East Indian presence in Guyana, the Arts Forum in collaboration with the Berbice campus of the University of Guyana presented an exhibition of the visual arts by contemporary Guyanese (East) Indian artists who were living and working in Guyana at the time. Although the exhibition highlighted the contributions of East Indian artists, Persaud took issue with statements in the Guyana Carifesta 1976 catalogue by the late Dr Denis Williams, a highly respected authority on Guyanese arts. It was in Jamaica, at the premier regional exposition of the arts, that Williams sought to explain in his curatorial statement the absence of Indo-Guyanese art: "Despite their numerical superiority over any other ethnic group and their potent commitment to Guyanese nationhood, East Indians in Guyana have remained generally aloof from the mainstream of creative expression in the arts."[2] Williams expanded on these remarks by saying that "East Indians, like the Chinese, Portuguese and Amerindians, had made no distinguishing contributions to the creative arts".

In responding to these remarks, Persaud noted that East Indian artists had been members of the earliest organizations of artists: the Arts and Craft Society, founded by British expatriate amateurs in 1929, and the first nationalist Guianese Art Group, founded in the 1940s. Persaud made the connection between "Indian invisibility/marginalization and the ethno-cultural-political hegemony – called the 'socialist revolution'". She spoke out against "the narrowness of vision, cultural limitations and biases of those who control the spaces in which the artist exhibits". She charged Williams with charting the course of mainstream art during the 1970s and 1980s, determining what constituted the national patrimony and who represented Guyana in the national collection. More specifically, Williams was among those "who determine[d] what is officially accepted as art". Her discourse continued with a strident plea for recognition of the pluralism contained in the contemporary international art scene. She condemned "the thick skinned insensitivity to the art which derives from the non-western cultural sources", lamenting the fact that "this art is quickly dismissed, belittled, marginalized or subjected to inappropriate models of analysis". In tracing the history of ethnic/cultural marginal-ization in Guyana, Persaud's daring should be understood within the context of the ethnic/cultural conflict in that country.

HISTORICAL AND POLITICAL BACKGROUND

Guyana, formerly known as British Guiana, is geographically part of the South American continent. With most of its population made up of two large groups – people of African and Indian descent, the former descended from slavery and the latter from indentureship – it resembles Trinidad and Suriname. The emancipation of African slaves in 1834 brought about the introduction of indentured labourers in 1838. After the long, perilous journey across the Atlantic, they had no alternative but to work for wages, which undermined the bargaining power of the former slaves.[3] The resulting hostility and con-frontation can be held as partly accountable for the recurring ethnic strife which plagues the country to this day. These ethnic conflicts came to a head during the independence movement of the 1950s and early 1960s.

As with many such struggles around the world, the demand for national independence from the country's colonial rulers coincided with the introduc-tion of socialism/communism as an alternative economic system. C.L.R. James, a world-renowned West Indian intellectual, saw this as "the most pro-found historical movement of the twentieth century". He cited "a whole body of intellectuals who believed that the world revolution was to be led by the communist parties with their ideological and organizational headquarters in Moscow".[4] The black American artist and actor Paul Robeson was also given to this type of thinking, declaring "that only the world revolution could save humanity from the crises and catastrophes of capitalism".[5]

Without doubt Dr Cheddi Jagan, the political leader who championed the cause of an independent Guyana, was influenced by this movement as he sought a solution for saving Guyana from the oppression brought on by cap-italism. Jagan was first elected to the Legislative Council in 1947. By 1950 he had formed the People's Progressive Party (PPP), which became the governing body of Guyana.[6] Jagan's alliance with Georgetown-based poet Martin Carter, who was well respected, as well as his collaboration with well-known black leaders such as Rory Westmas, Ashton Chase, Forbes Burnham and other left-wingers, reduced some of the social and ethnic hostilities which plagued the country for a brief halcyon period.

Conflicting attitudes emerged between the British and Americans over what exactly Jagan's ideological position was.[7] The British regarded him as a "democratic socialist", similar to members of the British Labour Party, while the Americans viewed Jagan as an outright communist, determined to perpetrate the same brand of communism as espoused by Fidel Castro in Cuba. When the PPP won the elections of 1953 by a two-thirds majority, the anxiety of the British was that Jagan's voice was strengthening anti-imperialism in various parts of "their" empire. They suspended the British Guiana constitution to arrest and jail several party activists.[8] In the early 1960s, as the struggle for independence intensified, the Kennedy administration, fearful of Jagan's communist leanings, intervened with the British to dismantle Jagan's PPP. By then, ethnic tensions were increasing and Forbes Burnham, leader of the Afro-Guyanese community and Jagan's former comrade, got the support of the United States. Not one murmur was heard from the Caribbean leaders about disrespecting the sovereignty of a nation, nor about the overt racial violence against Indo-Guyanese.

At that time Bernadette Persaud was attending high school in Georgetown. She recalls that when a combination of Afro-Guyanese, "red" (racially mixed Euro-Afro) and Portuguese opposition elements erupted into violence against the Indo-Guyanese, her two uncles hurried from different directions to escort her home to safety. Her father, a school principal, along with her mother and other prominent Indo-Guyanese citizens of Linden/Mackenzie, had to be air-lifted out of the area by the Demerara Bauxite Company. Other Indians crowded into the police station, from which they were taken to safety by boats. Several Indian men were pushed off their bicycles into the Wismar River and many Indian women were raped. Following the Wismar massacre the *Sun Chapman*, which was transporting both African and Indian passengers from Wismar and Mackenzie, was blown up.

Violence continued to escalate throughout the country as PPP elements retaliated. The opposition, the trade unions, the Catholic Church and the American CIA joined forces to bring down the PPP government. The British were pressured by the Americans into using their constitutional authority over Guyana. They introduced an electoral system of proportional representation, which removed the PPP from power in 1964.[9]

After the first eruption of ethnic violence in the 1960s, Persaud's parents returned to live in Bushlot, an Indian village in Berbice (fifty-six miles outside Georgetown) where they had been born. Up to that time Persaud admits to having no profound consciousness of race. Most of her school friends in Mackenzie (renamed Linden in 1970) were black. That being Indian made her different was an overnight discovery, and "it was very, very shocking". Relations with people in the neighbouring black villages had always been cordial, but now she would have to be on her guard.

During the 1970s Persaud spent her time reading for a Bachelor of Arts degree (English major, history minor) at the Turkeyen campus, University of Guyana, as well as a diploma from the Burrowes School of Art in Georgetown. Teaching was an obvious career choice, but after teaching English and art at the O and A levels from 1977 to 1980 at St Rose's High School in Georgetown, Persaud became a target of political victimization, like many others under the Forbes Burnham regime. The principal of the high school was transferred to another school in Georgetown as a form of punishment. After taking part in protest activities against the tightening of the dictatorship, government interference in the schools and the assassination of Walter Rodney, Persaud was assigned to a school in Kaituma. This she likened to being sent to Siberia. When she declined the transfer, she was unceremoniously dismissed on the pretext of failing to take up her position.

Persaud then directed her energies into painting, as she considered it "a point of departure for exploring themes of political oppression, identity and mortality". This, she says, "was tied up with the quest for creativity, originality and an authentic god/self". Her expressed goal is "to challenge, subvert and redefine existing notions and perceptions about one art and the nature of our reality here in Guyana". She pursues an indiscriminate yearning to chronicle the value of her surroundings, to engage with subjects which justify her attention and to interpret them with an exactness which stimulates the thought processes of her compatriots. Her scrutinizing gaze has fixed itself upon the everyday realities which impede Guyana.

ESTABLISHING HER PRESENCE IN THE ART WORLD

Unemployed and deprived of the right to work, Persaud found more time for painting, a pastime she had always enjoyed. More importantly, it allowed her

the freedom of uninterrupted contemplation of the natural beauty of her surroundings, the political manoeuvrings that had prompted her dismissal, and
her cultural heritage, upon which there had been little focus because of her
Christian upbringing. For a while, painting the lotus flower was enough to
repress the anger she felt at being victimized, but soon she became infused
with larger issues. Persaud's fascination with nature may have provided a temporary escape from the political atrocities of life in Guyana in the 1980s, but
later those very atrocities would consume her. For Persaud, to accept everything, to question nothing, was to deny her potential for critical thinking and
diminish her capacity for engagement with the external world. Without an
oppressive regime to expose, without the need to extricate herself from a cultural void, without the urgency to speak out on behalf of Guyana's marginalized artists, could Persaud have targeted more intimidating issues?

Persaud was determined to insulate herself from the deepening state of
oppression which enveloped her country. To this end her challenge became
the pursuit of unlimited development which derived from her penetrating
observations and intense sense of awareness. She identified the need to substantiate her own prerogatives and refused to retreat from the findings she
would encounter. Her capacity for research and analysis, along with her
unflinching determination to treat with critical interpretations of each circumstance, placed her at risk of being excluded from the ranks of Guyana's
artistic milieu. She confronted this possibility with a strength which could
only have come from within. Her search for authenticity has never been
dependent upon the least consideration for personal benefit, real or potential.

The brutality and injustice that characterized the paramilitary state in
which she lived called for arousal of her compatriots to the debilitating effects
such a society would have on their own humanity. As I sat in her studio, Persaud explained that "painting fragments of the [Georgetown botanical] Gardens in 1983 started out as an escape from Guyana's oppressive political and
economic conditions". "But," she added, "I soon discovered that even in the
peace and serenity there, the Man with the Gun intruded.[10] Later, ironically,
I discovered that the Man with the Gun is himself overtaken by another, a
more powerful gentleman – Death." The painting, *A Gentleman in the Gardens: Counterpoint*, can be interpreted at three levels: the transient beauty of
the lotus lily which dominates its presence; the inclusion of the Man with
the Gun, who represents the military state; and the grim personification of

death. The Man with the Gun is purposefully separated from the image of the lotus by a narrow elongated space which signifies the separation of the theme of nature and the theme of political oppression. The split also symbolizes the suppression of what is ugly from the nation's consciousness.[11]

It was indeed a dark time; her family was in crisis – her brother had recently died in a plane crash – and now her country was quickly falling into a state of degradation. The media were censored. Her reflections nestled within the beauty that surrounded her; however, her deeper contemplation was drawn towards the darker side of Guyana's reality, which manifested itself in the cold embrace of the military. The nation was experiencing such disquiet and fear that people could not bring themselves to speak about the presence of the army; there was some kind of unified denial that this was happening.

But it was ever present: soldiers in the Gardens, soldiers marching in parades, soldiers in their Jeeps cruising through the city. The residence of the president overlooked the Botanical Gardens, and amid the variety of birds and different species of flora a soldier stood guard, looming at the entrance. From this painting Persaud developed a series which grew from *A Gentleman in the Gardens: Counterpoint* to *The Gentlemen in the Gardens*. For this series Persaud utilized the poetry of Martin Carter to show that one oppressor (under colonialism) was being displaced by another in the post-colonial dispensation. The title of the 1987 painting *The Slender Grass* (oil on canvas, 21 inches by 33.5 inches), for example, was inspired by this poet – Guyana's most illustrious – who captures the tragedy of Guyana's circumstance in his poem "This Is the Dark Time My Love":

> Who comes walking in the dark night time?
> Whose boot of steel tramps down the slender grass?
> It is the man of death, my love, the strange invader
> Watching you sleep and aiming at your dream.[12]

It was in 1984 that the Barbadian calypsonian the Mighty Gabby released his composition "Boots". One line says, "left, right, left, right, boots, boots, government boots". This was a time when soldiers had also begun to have an impact on the tranquillity of the Barbadian citizenry.

Persaud discerns the blatant injustices in the daily struggle for life and of some imposing their will upon others. She seeks to nurture the relationship between her art and society by dispelling "the conditioned blindness and igno-

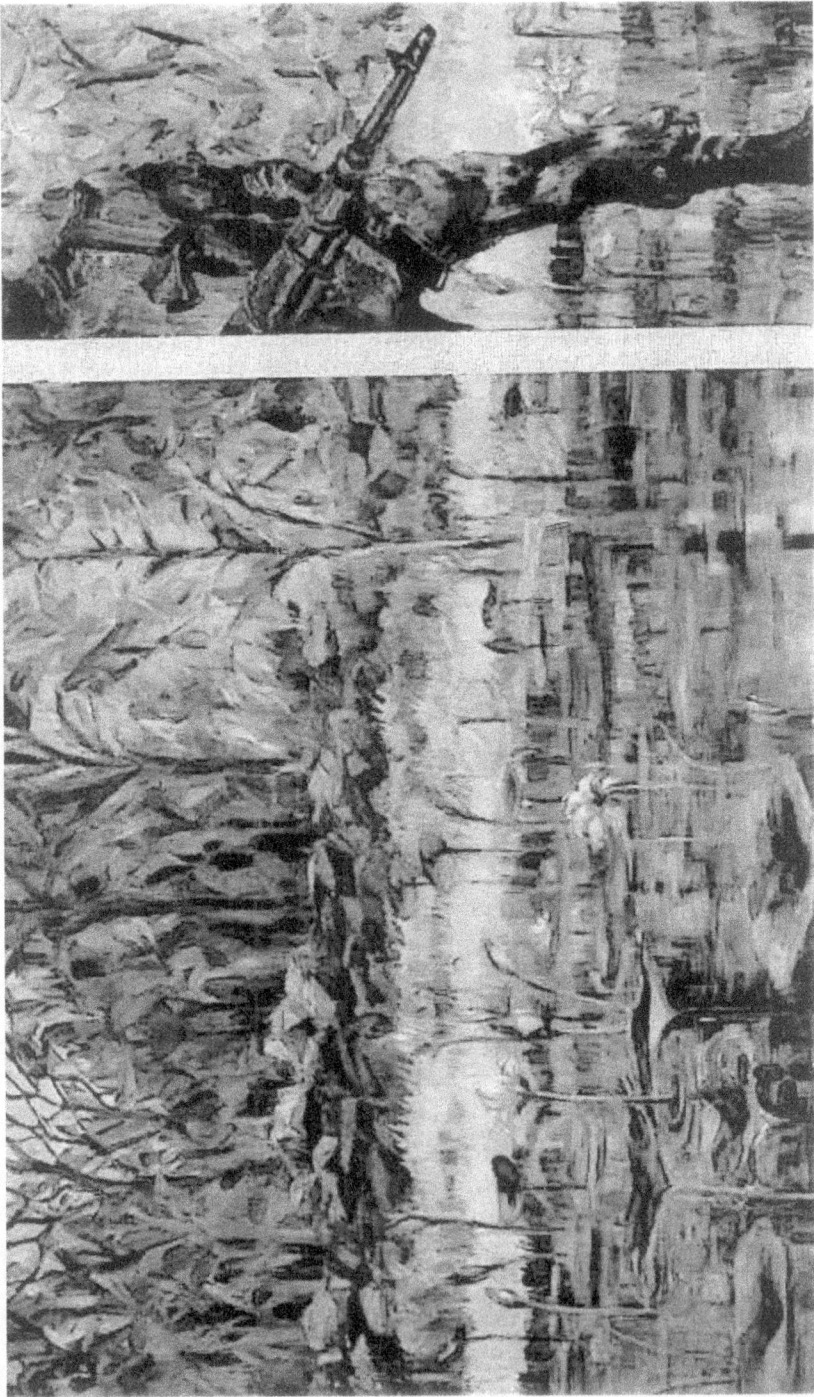

Figure 7.1: Bernadette Persaud, *A Gentleman in the Gardens: Counterpoint*, 1983. Oil on canvas, 16½ × 27½ in. Collection of the artist.

rance" which have been evoked through their "own cultural limitations". While she uses her canvas to conduct a dialogue with her audiences, provoking their consciousness into connecting with their cultural aesthetic, she is not satisfied that their interpretation of her message is enough. She compels them to empathize with the deep-seated discontent which engulfs her, and persuades them that her reality is theirs. "For me," she says, "the Gardens with their primitive beauty and the Man with the Gun are dominant symbols of life: the serpent in Eden, a dream of innocence gone awry. At another level, these images represent the essential paradox of Guyana – the core of our political dilemma, not unique in most of the militarized and totalitarian societies of the Third World." Her later paintings would dramatically capture the universality of these conditions.

With the *Gentlemen in the Gardens* series Persaud brought a consciousness to bear upon those Guyanese who failed to acknowledge the painful reality that enveloped them. For her, unmasking the realities of an oppressive regime was paramount to her existence at that time. Had not her imagination intervened, the significance of what was embroiling her country could have remained buried in the subconscious of many. When the series was first viewed by the public, she was asked whether she was depicting Grenada. Sadly, her response had to be, "No, I am depicting Guyana." Ironically, her political paintings evoked such wide interest that there were times when she questioned the artistic value of her work.

ANCESTRAL CONNECTEDNESS

Persaud cultivates an affinity to the lotus lily, which sprouts in colourful clusters intermittently throughout Guyana's countryside. Its seeds were brought to Guyana by the indentured labourers, and its blossoms infused beauty into their degrading life conditions and brought centrality into their religious rituals. In her own words, the lotus "became more than a simple flower for me – it became a powerful symbol. It opened to me ancestral cultural ideas." Persaud's creativity knows no bounds as she incorporates this spiritually significant ancestral symbol into the indigenous landscape of Guyana with the political reality that she lives. This early series of paintings draws heavily upon the Impressionist style with their subtle shades of lemon, yellow, sap green and ultramarine.

The first phase of the lotus paintings (from the 1980s) is a collection which the artist calls the "Lotus of Time" series. Persaud explains that these early pieces – *The Lotus of Time, The Lotus of Pain, The Lotus of a Hundred Petals* and *The Lotus of a Thousand Desires* – deal with transience, ambivalence, mortality, death and decay as they seek to "interrogate the relevance of certain ancestral, philosophical ideas and explore the distance I have travelled from the ancestral 'home'". Her 1987 statement sums up this complexity:

> For Hindus and Buddhists, the lotus is a symbol of the Eternal, the Timeless: its petals fall but it constantly renews itself as it scatters its seeds and blossoms afresh. I question all of this. For me, the lotus does not represent what is timeless and eternal, rather what is beautiful, frail and temporal. And so I paint a withering lotus, the lotus of pain (not joy), the falling petals, the lotus of Desire (not detachment).

Her painting *The Lotus of a Thousand Desires* won the judges' award for outstanding painting in the annual national exhibition of 1989. This presentation speaks to the sense of cultural ambivalence and loss which the Indian migrant experienced. Here the luxuriant pink lotus is represented in such profusion that it compels the Guyanese art community – which is mainly Euro- and Afrocentric – to look at the significance of this flower to the Hindu sector in which it is so highly prized. This is not a field of daffodils or sunflowers; it is not the homage of Wordsworth's poetry for the English countryside nor is it the adulation of Van Gogh for the French landscape. The lotus is part of the value system of Indo-Caribbean people. A part of its message may have been lost in the perils of indentureship, but today the artist draws on its image in a vigorous effort to strengthen the self-image of the Indo-Caribbean person, who can now reclaim it, as she has done, as a significant part of his or her heritage. Persaud describes this painting as representing "the transience of life, it captures the ever expanding fecundity of nature and the human condition". Succumbing to desires is against the Hindu philosophy of detachment, but in this piece the artist defiantly celebrates the blossoming of desire.

For thousands of years the lotus lily with its soothing aura has symbolized spiritual enlightenment and healing on every level of existence. The goddess Lakshmi is depicted as emerging from a lotus which blooms in murky waters.

One aspect of its symbolism lies in the idea that if such beauty can emanate from a contaminated environment, so too can we as human beings follow the dictates of dharma, or righteousness, despite the negative elements which pervade our surroundings.

By the 1990s, the timeless and eternal qualities of the lotus had begun to spark a new consciousness within the artist, which manifested itself in the piece *The Birth of the Lotus*. This painting, along with *The Lotus of a Thousand Petals/Tantric Lotus, Coolie Colours* and *The Lotus of Pain*, form part of a group which the artist calls the "Timeless Lotus" series. The "Lotus of My Great Grandmother" series reflects the second phase of this new consciousness, which "investigates the philosophical retentions and colour aesthetics of my great grandmother, India". Here Persaud pays tribute to her great-grandmother Mahadai Lachmansingh, who refused to be converted to Presbyterian Christianity when her husband, John Lachmansingh (Baba), was converted by Reverend Cropper in the 1930s.

On the one hand Persaud is sometimes dissatisfied with the response to her philosophical and political paintings at an official level, while on the other hand she revels in the fact that the flash of colour in her exhibitions appeals to many of her students and their parents. Nothing pleases her more than knowing she has reached out to the specific sensibilities of the simple rural folk, who often feel intimidated by formal works of art. She relates with pride how after looking at the paintings called *Readings from the Koran*, an elderly Muslim woman suggested, "We should get some paintings for the *masjid*." She wants her work "to be accessible to all, for even if they do not understand Arabic, they do not need to, because they identify with Arabic writings – they are familiar with them". Her paintings reflect her reconnection with ancestral values and usher in some measure of dignity, respectability and beauty for those whose religions were once dismissed as unworthy. Even as Persaud's compositions stimulate the social consciousness of her viewers, her overriding concern with ethno-cultural identity is consistent with artists such as Trinidadians M.P. Alladin, Isaiah Boodhoo, Leroy Clarke and Guyanese Philip Moore.

THE MIGRANT'S DILEMMA

Through his insightful treatment of themes such as uprootedness, isolation and alienation in his prolific writings, V.S. Naipaul has generated extensive scholarly discussion about the psychological realities of migration. One of his early novels, *The Enigma of Arrival*, aptly describes the migrant's position as "one's lack of representation in the world; one's lack of status".[13] In a similar vein, the German writer Gunter Grass describes the predicament of the migrant as being deprived of "roots, language and social norms", three of the most important qualities which define him as a human being. "The migrant, deprived of all three, is obliged to find new ways of describing himself, new ways of being human."[14] Caught between the agony of losing his homeland and the anxiety of adjusting to his new surroundings, the migrant must choose what he would discard of his culture and what he would incorporate from his new experience. Only after a prolonged period would his ongoing negotiation with "ambiguities, ambivalences and contradictions" enable him to move from the position of Other to become part of the mainstream.

Persaud reflects on the experiences of Indian immigrants, among whom were her own ancestors, as they sought to eke out a living on the fringe of a host society that was both hostile and diminishing to their psyche. She is familiar with the historical reports that, as indentured labourers, they existed in a system of servitude that was little short of slavery. She knows just how much their religions were despised, how they were regarded as "barbaric" and how they were referred to as "heathens". She recognizes that, despite the advancement of Indians in education and commerce for more than one and a half centuries, there had been only slight changes in the attitude of conde-scension from the Euro- and Afrocentric society of Guyana. Even as a fourth-generation Guyanese woman artist, and despite her status as a Christian from a highly respected family, Persaud was not shielded from the discriminatory stance against Indo-Guyanese. How much worse was it for the less educated Hindus and Muslims?

PROTESTING EUROCENTRISM

In the 1960s, 1970s and 1980s, Guyanese artists gravitated towards Western Modernism, which was regarded as the ultimate expression of the twentieth century. It claimed a particular brand of universality which evoked the disso-lution of all national, cultural and social boundaries. It also spelled the erosion of the diverse strands of indigenous art which had painstakingly survived the dominance of mainstream artists. Even after a little more than four and a half centuries of colonial rule, mainstream art in Guyana and the Caribbean region was located in European civilization, to such an extent that all visual expressions of alternative cultures had been confined to the periphery.

In making a presentation to the Race Relations Forum at the John F. Kennedy Library in Georgetown in May 1993, Persaud made reference to the debates and analyses as made by noted French intellectuals, such as Jean Bernabé, Patrick Chamoiseau, Raphaël Confiant and others, who represented "a dominant strand in West Indian literary thought".[15] In her view, what came out of that debate was a general consensus that the discovery of the ancestral self was a necessary dialectical stage in the quest for an authentic identity. She continued, "At the root of this quest lies that profound historical self-doubt or self-diminution characteristic of all colonized peoples and the psychological unease and perpetual self-questioning/self-defining which a society with our peculiarities generate." She saw this as being of tremendous importance to artists of all ethnic groups, as there is evidence that "the ethnic ancestral past is indelibly woven in the present and the future". She recognized the risk for the artist who pursued this path, as it diminished the importance of the market, the state, the patron and the critic. She opined that such an artist "runs the risk of being incomprehensible to his fellow human beings who remain culturally limited". She was apprehensive that in "a society filled with racial antagonisms and competition, the ethnic character of his work may cause unease and even anger". Through the quest for self, Persaud became familiar with those repressed religious practices with which so many in our plural societies identify. For her, "painting leads to a discovery of the self and paradoxically a transcendence of self, it is a dialogue with self and a dialogue with God".

Persaud has become one of the forerunners in negotiating the interplay of tensions between Western and Caribbean art. Her work reveals an obvious departure from that of pioneering Guyanese artists – such as E.R. Burrowes, Aubrey Williams, Hubert Moshett, Marjorie Broodhaagen (all deceased) and, later, Stanley Greaves – who adopted European standards without challenging the perpetuation of colonial values. These artists were very conscious of their cultural dilemma and sought to fuse European styles with local subject matter. Despite their efforts, they could not escape European standards and values. Contemporary artists who follow the mainstream Eurocentric tradition established by their predecessors – such as Terence Roberts, Carl Anderson and most of the contemporary women artists – continue in the Eurocentric tradition established by their predecessors.

Convinced that Western criteria should no longer be the yardstick for measuring the value given to the artistic expressions of Caribbean peoples, Persaud is adamant in her pursuit of "a vision of inclusion which speaks for the most obscure artist whose ancestry is mirrored in his art, a vision which encompasses the transference of Caribbean art from the periphery". Persaud recognizes that the Eurocentric education to which Caribbean peoples have been exposed has moulded our aesthetic sense, but embedded deep within us are dimensions which, although they have been suppressed for so long, cry out for expression. Pursuing a continuum with the Western contemporary style of painting would invariably amount to mimicry. Consequently, she avows that "our artists should formulate an alternative aesthetic which would strengthen our fragmented selves as we seek to become whole". Her response to our cultural deprivation is purposeful as she declares, "the artist whose psyche has been shaped, not only by heredity, race and culture but also by our peculiar geophysical and colonial circumstances, follows a quest for an authentic vision, for wholeness which is perhaps compulsive. This is one of the conscious imperatives of my impulse to paint."

Unlike some of her Caribbean contemporaries who live in a metropolitan society, Persaud is not "talking back to the Empire" but directs her work to an audience right here in the Caribbean. She underscores the distinction between herself as a visual artist and as a writer who has to pitch her work against the language of the Other, the idea being that the language of art is universal whereas the Caribbean writer is caught in the interchange between Standard English – the language of authority – and Creole – the language of the people. She explains that her work transforms "the specificities of the here and now" and emphasizes that her canvas responds not to historical theories relevant to the more "advanced" societies but to the tangible issues which surround her. There are times when the severity of these issues gives way to a total disregard for style as her imagination is fired by new interrogations which compete for expression.

RESEARCHING ISLAM

Muslim Guyanese are both self and Other to Hindu Guyanese: self along the lines of ethnicity and Other along the lines of religion. Curiosity about this group lured Persaud to her first reading of the Holy Qur'an. By the early 1990s her political consciousness was being reactivated by the subjective reporting of CNN journalists covering the Gulf War. Islamic civilization is also Other to Western civilization; consequently the Gulf War created a pressing impulse for Persaud to think through her own perspectives on Muslims. She embarked upon a second reading of the traditional text of the Qur'an. What we find is that her treatment of the Other is all-embracing. Her view is that "when we reject the Other's 'music' or the Other's 'song' there is no chance of it impacting upon us, no chance of experiencing its existing beauty and as a result such beauty is lost".

The effects of the Gulf War – its lifeless bodies, its missiles, its demonic destruction – so overwhelmed Persaud that she integrated them with the poetic beauty of the Qur'an and the delicate calligraphy of the Islamic galaxy along with the symmetrical lines of Muslim architecture in the painting *A Gentleman under the Sky* (1991).[16] For her the elegance of the mosques interspersed around the countryside, defining the minority presence of Muslims in Guyana, acquired new significance. She pays homage to the local craftsmen who were able to replicate the intricate geometric designs of mediaeval buildings, complete with domes and minarets, embellishing them with expressive arabesque calligraphy. It is within the mosque that the Qur'anic cosmos comes to life in the spirited treatment of space as an infinite, expanding design of sun, moon and stars.

Convinced that there were many unresolved issues in her understanding of Islam, Persaud engaged in a succession of readings which clarified her vague, hazy areas in relation to the Islamic concept of God and the cosmos. The series "Readings from the Koran" validates Persaud's efforts to combine "the poetry of God and man, the fusion of heaven and earth, man and God" – a commitment she had undertaken in her Hindu-based work. Paintings such as *A Gentleman under the Sky*; *Koranic Study*; *The Architecture of Time/Man/God*; *In the Name of Allah, the Beneficent, the Merciful*; and *The First Reading* are but part of this series.

EXHIBITING IN INDIA

In 1996 the Guyana Carib Artists – Philbert Gajadhar, Bernadette Persaud
and Doris Rogers – were selected to represent Guyana at the Carib Art Travelling Exhibition (1993–96), sponsored by UNESCO. When Guyana was
invited to participate in the celebration of India's fiftieth anniversary of independence in 1997, it was most fitting that these same artists were called upon
to exhibit their works at what was considered a most prestigious event. The
Ninth International Triennale of Art – an exhibition of contemporary art –
took place in New Delhi, where the trio presented their pieces. As the
spokesperson for the group, Persaud applauded the fact that despite "the hor-
rors of the Middle Passage and the Kala Pani, despite the persistence of more
insidious forms of post-colonialism, the gods dwelling within us and without,
have survived! No one is truly dispossessed. This is the message that our
paintings proclaim."

    Among her offerings was *Colours of God/Self* (1996).[17] This *jandhi* (flag)
installation portrays the pantheon of indigenous ancestral gods of India, which
includes Christ on one flag and an Islamic emblem on another. In so doing it
recognizes the universality of all religions when the divide between religion
and spirituality is transcended. Persaud says, "It underlines the quest of an
aesthetic of colour that is truly expressive of the self/Self. It also seeks to challenge the aesthetic canons of Eurocentric elitist taste in Guyana and the
Caribbean, for it brings into the realm of art an aspect of our grassroots religious culture." She ascribes new meaning to this painting, which she says
within the context of the Triennale signifies "a symbolic representation of the
return of the gods to their ancient homeland". Through this exhibition she
communicated the philosophy of Hinduism as one of accommodation. The
colours of the *jandhi* are "not just the colours of God, but the colours of Self.
For when you are invoking God, you are invoking the power of God within
yourself." The idea of divinity dwelling within the human personality is as
ancient as Hinduism itself.

    For the Hindu, the act of hoisting a *jandhi* is filled with emotion. As part
of worship, the entire family wends its way to the site, which has already been
established as holy ground, for this is where all family *pujas* have culminated
in years gone by. The hole has already been dug; the family lodges the bamboo
pole deep into the ground in one unified action, to the accompaniment of

sacred mantras recited by the family pundit in Sanskrit. It is an act which has been performed by our grandparents and their parents before them; it establishes our reconnection with antiquity. The words of V.S. Naipaul reverberate: "we go back and back forever: we go back, all of us to the very beginning; in our blood and bone and brain, we carry the memory of thousands of beings".[18] It is a moment when one tends to reflect upon this as a conscious act of commitment to a higher power by one's ancestors. For just as the notches in the bamboo pole represent the obstacles one faces in life, so too the hoisting of the *jandhi* towards the high heavens signifies one's aspiration towards a higher level of existence – towards spirituality.

ALTERNATIVE INTERPRETATIONS

Persaud was invited to exhibit her flag installations – both *Colours of God/Self* and *Colours of America* – at the Philip Sherlock Centre for Creative Arts on the Mona campus of the University of the West Indies during International Women's Month in 1999. Retired Caribbean actress Jean Small was so inspired by the presentations that she created a spectacular display by hoisting fifteen-foot-high bamboo poles, *jandhis* attached, outside the centre to signal the arrival of the "gods" on the campus. Surely being recognized by the Caribbean's highest seat of learning can be considered no mean feat for a woman artist of East Indian descent, especially in light of the fact that some of her work venerates the cultural aesthetics of a seemingly polytheistic religion. The boundless enthusiasm with which Persaud was received in Jamaica is reflected in an article written by Small titled "How the Gods Came in a Suitcase".[19]

Years later, in an interview with Ruel Johnson, Persaud explained that her role of artist as messenger is reflected primarily on two issues.[20] "One, the political thing, was the gentleman with the gun, who became the international soldier – who became, more specifically, the US soldier. The other, what I call the cultural thing, concerned my own predicament as a Christianized Indian." She describes her work as seeking "to reveal beauty in all things". Despite this, one can detect an ever-present dichotomy in her paintings: peace versus violence, beauty versus ugliness, power versus powerlessness, visibility versus invisibility. Even as she relates an incident which demonstrated her greater understanding of why Hindus frown on conversion, she noted that "in all of my work, whether I'm dealing with the ancestral cultural aspect of it, or whether I'm dealing with the man with the gun, I'm trying to show everyone that here is beauty – which though it may be close to you, you don't see, you don't notice, because of your own conditioned blindness and ignorance, your own cultural limitation".

The Hindu deity Kali is always represented as ugly, dishevelled, with a ferocious demeanour and a bloody tongue hanging out. Persaud actualized her determination to show beauty by depicting Kali with her mouth closed. In the interview with Johnson, Persaud says, "There was the case where I showed a painting to a neighbour of mine, an ordinary working man, a Hindu, and he understood it; and he pointed out what he saw as its one flaw to me. I was trying to make Kali beautiful and I painted her with her tongue in her mouth. In pointing this out to me, he said that her tongue should be hanging out." This "flaw" as pointed out by the "ordinary working man, a Hindu" raises some interesting observations. For while the average Hindu may be elated by Persaud's presentation of Hindu imagery to a wider audience, it is more than likely that the orthodox Hindu would totally reject her tampering with the intrinsic characteristics of Hindu iconography. Although the act of painting Kali with her mouth closed may conform to her objective "to reveal beauty in all things", it does not substantiate the premise that "the cultural aspect of her work emerges out of her concern for the preservation of certain things".

I am tempted to question whether Persaud's own cultural estrangement does not permit her to discern the dedication the devout Hindu has for ritual and tradition. In Hinduism the reliance on symbolism is manifested by the use of detail in conferring powers and attributes to a deity. In *The Elements of Hinduism*, author Stephen Cross declares:

> every aspect of the image of a deity is made meaningful. It is not simply a beautiful object, but a complex statement, a product of the intellect: The image of a deity is not merely a group of symbols, and no element of its forms should be the fruit of the inventiveness of the image maker. Every peculiarity of the attitude, the expression, or of the ornaments is of significance and is intended as a fit object for meditation.[21]

Altering the inherent characteristics of Kali is clearly not permissible.

For Rosanne Kanhai, Persaud is documenting the silencing of women in

Hindu-based communities, particularly in the Caribbean.[22] Kanhai pondered on the early period of indentureship, when Indian women were encouraged or coerced into silence and were assigned roles of passivity and obedience. They were expected to suppress their pain when faced with violence in the household lest it splinter the family unit and expose the weaknesses of the group to the wider, hostile society.[23] Said Kanhai, "Perhaps Persaud's Kali is a protest of this silence!"

PROTESTING ATROCITIES

Men murder men as men must murder men
To build their shining government of the damned.
– Martin Carter[24]

Persaud's unprecedented visibility in the art world was further enhanced in 2005 when she was invited to exhibit at the Eleventh International Triennale of contemporary art at Lalit Kala Akademi in Delhi, where she continues to nurture an ongoing relationship between the personal and the geopolitical which ultimately treats with the merging of local and global concerns. Her chosen title, "The Struggle of Man against Power Is the Struggle of Memory against Forgetting", adopts the theme of a novel written by Milan Kundera in which he graphically exposes the ruthlessness of the politician who thrives on propaganda for influencing public opinion.[25] The novel is used as a medium to establish how the official version of events invariably differs from reality. As an artist, Persaud is keen on establishing the alternative reality of art which records historical facts devoid of politicization. Two of her most vivid exhibits emphatically recount the horrific incidents which occurred amid the land-scape of Guyana towards the turn of the century.

The first painting, *A Flag on Earth*, is a symbolic representation of a series of beatings, rapes and kidnappings of Indo-Guyanese and the destruction of the predominantly Indian business sector of Georgetown. A little boy accompanying his father to catch shrimp at 3 a.m. one day was killed along with his father. A man who was riding his bike witnessed the horror, and he too received a bullet. In the painting the Kali flag is perched atop the planet/ Guyana and a map of Guyana is depicted on the side. Kali is depicted as wearing three skulls: two large skulls and a little one. The three killings heralded

Figure 7.2: Bernadette Persaud, *A Flag on Earth: Guyana,* 2001. Mixed media and acrylic on canvas; Earth 20 in. diameter, flag 20 × 14 in., flagpole 33 in.
Artist's note: In this construct, Kali plants her victorious flag on the planet/Guyana. Guyana is consumed by fire, within and without, in the aftermath of the elections of March 2001.

the start of a fresh round of ethno-political killings on the east coast of Demerara which lasted for more than two years.

The second painting takes its title from verses of the Holy Qur'an. According to the artist, "it represents the burning inferno, in which we live and die, here in Guyana". More specifically, it memorializes the daily ethnic atrocities which took place on the east coast of Demerara from 2001 to 2003. On the burning ground Kali dances wildly, adding more skulls to her never-ending garland, while soldiers look on passively at the orgy of rape, killing, beating and burning. Such was the chaotic condition of Guyana under the PPP government.

Also on show was *Colours of America* (1999), in which Persaud expressed her outrage at the attempts of one superpower to control the universe.[26] The circular design on the canvas features the stars and stripes of the American flag, with the central motif highlighting Shiva Nataraja, the Lord of Dance. Here Persaud rejects the rectangular flag of the Western mode and adopts the triangular flag of Hinduism, which is symbolic of earth/hell and space, while the third point reaches towards God and the heavens. The narrative installation she constructs transforms the local soldiers into the American soldiers carrying long rifles, effectively dramatizing the imminence of militarization on a global scale. The notion that the soldiers are our new gods is left to interpretation.

In the composition *Gentlemen on the Moon* (2000) the iconoclastic gentleman is poised arrogantly on this sacred golden object – God – symbolizing American military and technological supremacy. But the god/the moon/the self wears a sardonic grin. The moon goddess in the painting has been described as combining both Greek and Hindu iconographical features. From these four paintings, etched in the firmament of time, one can perceive the artist's intensity of feeling, her energetic spirit and her dismay for humanity. These characteristics infuse her paintings with an undistorted reality, such that their political pronouncements assume the distinction of being irrefutable.

THE ARTIST'S PERSONALITY

Persaud's emboldened narratives of the Burnham totalitarian regime attest to her innate fortitude. It is the profound sense of justice embedded within her

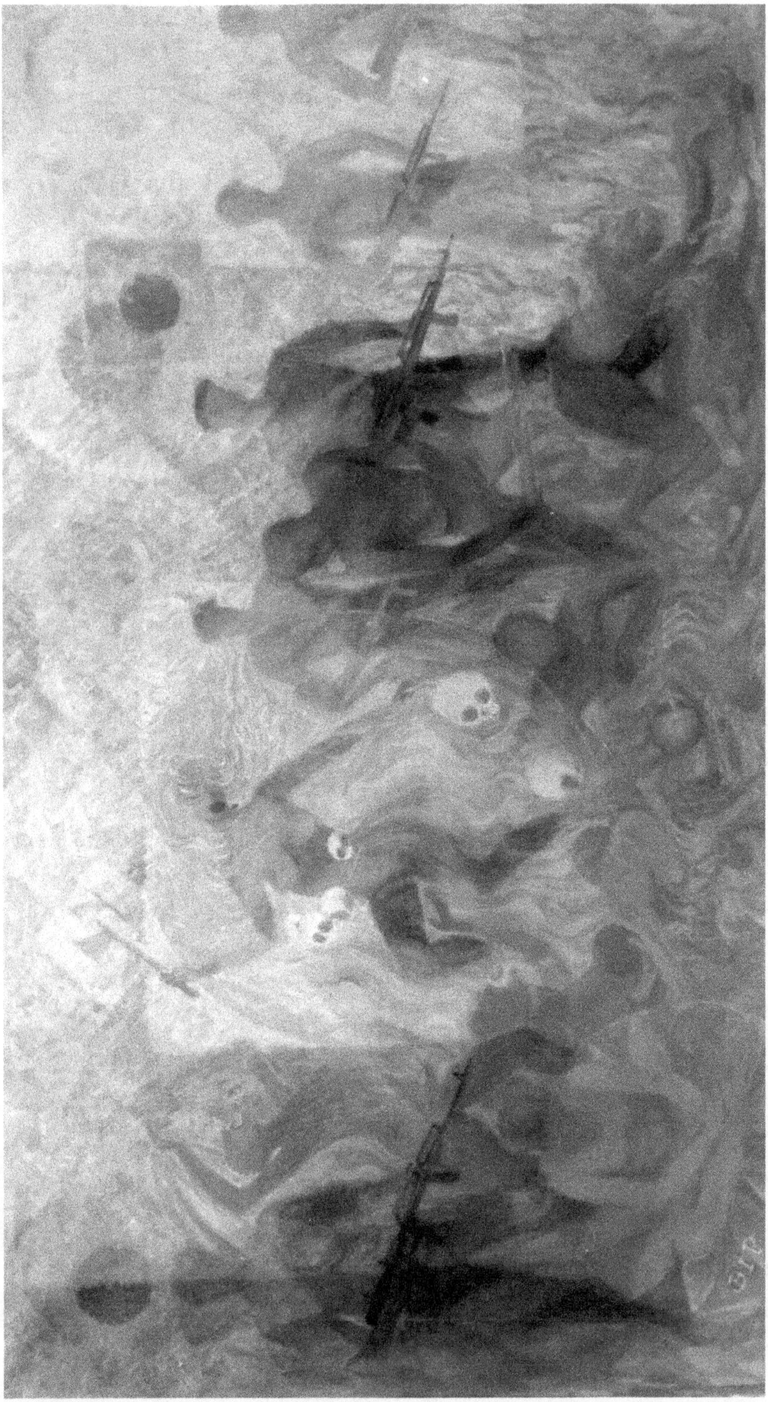

Figure 7.3: *The Burning Square: Lo We Live and We Die*, 2003. Acrylic on canvas, 44 × 79 in.

personality that triggers her dissatisfaction with the exclusion of artists whose genre of expression differs from what is considered acceptable. This trait in her character does not reflect the uncertainty which resides in an insecure mind; rather, it generates a creativity which is so vigorous and so confident that it demands to be taken seriously. Persaud has positioned herself to explore the role of art in nation building, its intellectual power, its ability to transform the individual and collective consciousness and ultimately its political functions. Art has become such a significant part of her life that she cannot possibly think of directing her focus elsewhere. The energy and grit with which she pursues a continuous path of art and activism attest to an image of this Indo-Caribbean woman as resilient, resolute and civic-minded. It is within the context of recognizing painting as a serious investigation that she senses the human suffering of a people whose culture was continuously diminished by colonial rule, forcing them into a spectrum of duality.

For Persaud, painting is a form of self-expression, a passion. She is not interested in painting anything that is politically correct, neither is she motivated by the idea of selling her art, for being an artist is not her primary source of income. She may sell her paintings to offset the cost of materials, or sometimes, when there is not enough space for her new work, she reluctantly parts with some of her pieces. Being an art teacher meant that she could take up her paintbrush with ease, "like I never left off". In reminiscing about her adolescent years, Persaud recalls that among the many prohibitions laid down for her as an Indian female in Guyana, she could not go anywhere unescorted, nor could she wear trousers. Another severe restriction was that she was not allowed to wear red or yellow. She was so agitated by this constraint that in her early years of marriage she quickly acquired a wardrobe filled with red dresses. It was during this period that she deliberated upon the oppression of women in her culture and the political dictatorship which was surfacing in her country.

A major source of grief was that one of Persaud's sons was born with brain damage. She was riddled with self-doubt for a while, but even this misfortune did not deter her from her chosen path. As she spoke during our conversation of her compatriots who had fled the country in droves, her words revealed her compassionate nature as a wife and mother. She related accounts of heart-rending scenes which took place at the Timehri Airport as she witnessed families saying goodbye to each other in the unending exodus from Guyana. She told of letters written by waves of emigrants to their parents while they were trying to get legalized. "Mammy, don't dead", they said to their mothers. "The country was like a prison," she said, and with a handicapped child, she felt trapped.

Persaud also recalled that her family was very proud of being one of the first Hindu families to convert to Christianity in the area where she lived; many years would pass before it was divulged to her that her mother's uncle was a pundit. She admits to having had "a very iconoclastic view of everything – of life, of religion and God" when she began her artistic career in her adult life. She reflected upon her mother's infirmity as a victim of Alzheimer's disease, expressing her own sense of loss at her mother's being unable to recognize her:

> When you experience your mother losing her memory, you are dying. For you are alive in the eyes of others . . . . their perspective of what you are. When your mother fails to recognize the nuances of your relationship with her, that is terribly diminishing. You are ceasing to exist. When your mother is losing her memory, she is at the mercy of others, she is at the risk of being manipulated.[27]

CONCLUSION

In January 2004 an exhibition of Persaud's paintings titled "Recent Paintings" was mounted at the National Museum of Trinidad and Tobago as part of the Cultural Studies Conference. It was there that Kenwyn Crichlow, a lecturer at the Centre of Creative and Festival Arts, University of the West Indies (St Augustine), described her as "painting with an expressive palette on some innovative shapes in pursuit of a vision of Caribbean spirituality from the provincial margins of a gendered, Hindu, Indo-Guyanese persona".[28] In an age when popular acclaim garners more prestige than ever before, Persaud has secured for herself an undisputed position in the historiography of Caribbean art.

NOTES

1. Since then, Veerle Poupeye's *Caribbean Art* has been published. Poupeye is a Belgian art historian based in Jamaica. Prior to this there was no published history of Caribbean art. See Veerle Poupeye, *Caribbean Art* (London: Thames and Hudson, 1998), 97, 130, 145.

2. Denis Williams, "Aloof from the Mainstream", *Daily Chronicle*, 23 May 2002, 13.

3. Judaman Seecoomar, "Ethnic Conflict in Guyana", in *Guyana and the Caribbean: Reviews, Essays and Interviews*, edited by Frank Birbalsingh (Chichester, UK: Dido Press, 2004), 56.

4. C.L.R. James, "Paul Robeson: Black Star", in *Spheres of Existence: Selected Writings* (London: Allison and Busby, 1980), 261.

5. Ibid.

6. Frank Birbalsingh, "Dr Cheddi Jagan: Interview", in *Guyana and the Caribbean: Reviews, Essays and Interviews*, edited by Frank Birbalsingh (Chichester, UK: Dido Press, 2004), 77.

7. Ibid., 84.

8. Frank Birbalsingh, "Martin Carter: Interview", in *Guyana and the Caribbean: Reviews, Essays and Interviews*, edited by Frank Birbalsingh (Chichester, UK: Dido Press, 2004), 95.

9. Birbalsingh, "Cheddi Jagan", 84.

10. The artist explains: "We all refused to see the man with the gun standing at the gate of the Botanic Gardens, concentrating only on the beauty of the trees, the birds and the flowers. I was reluctant to 'spoil' my painting by including him in it, but he kept intruding in my thoughts. So I painted him 'cut off' from the main scene."

11. This 1991 painting can be seen in Guyana's National Collection at Castellani House. In 1993 it captured the Purchase Prize in the Caribbean art competition sponsored by UNESCO in collaboration with the Dutch Antilles.

12. Martin Carter, *Poems of Resistance* (London: Lawrence and Wishart, 1954).

13. V.S. Naipaul, *The Enigma of Arrival* (New York: Random House, 1987), 157.

14. Salman Rushdie, *Imaginary Homelands: Essays and Criticism 1981–1991* (New York: Penguin, 1992), 277–78.

15. Bernadette Persaud, "Ethnicity and Art", *Guyana Sunday Chronicle*, 20 June 1993, 14.

16. *A Gentleman under the Sky* depicts the war in Iraq, that is, the Gulf War. It shows the American soldier as master of the universe, standing arrogantly on the

planet. In the background is the Islamic cosmos with missiles flying, creating an effect like the Fourth of July. The Arabic refers to the cities destroyed: Babylon (destroyed in history) and Baghdad and Basra (bombed during the Gulf War). The colours represent the Islamic cosmos: blue fused with green − the union of heaven and earth. It was after this painting that the series "Readings from the Koran" began, where Persaud's focus shifted from the local soldier to the American soldier.

17. First presented at the Philip Sherlock Centre of Creative Arts, University of the West Indies, Mona, Jamaica, *Colours of God/Self* depicts Shiva Nataraja, the Lord of Dance. When Shiva is viewed as the supreme god, he possesses all three functions of the Trimurti within himself − those of creator, preserver and destroyer. As customary, deities are depicted with more than two arms in order to establish that theirs is a greater power than that of mortals. Shiva is placed in a circle which signifies the cyclical concept of time and life. Here his four arms denote universality; in his upper right hand he holds a small drum, which corresponds to creation. In the Hindu view it is through sound that everything that exists came into being.

18. V.S. Naipaul, *A Way in the World* (New York: Random House, 1984), 11. Stephen Cross summarizes the concept of self/Self as follows: "This idea of two orders of reality existing within man had existed in embryonic form within Vedic thought from a very early time." Stephen Cross, *The Elements of Hinduism* (Australia: Element Books, 1994), 27–32.

19. Jean Small, in the endnotes of her pamphlet "How the Gods Came in a Suitcase" (Kingston: University of the West Indies Library, June 1999), explains: "The word Kali means 'time' and time is an all destroying, all consuming power. Here the symbolic colour is deep blue bordering on black. She is fearful and awe-inspiring and is usually depicted wearing a garland of skulls around her neck. Her nakedness symbolizes what cannot be manifested. She dances triumphantly on the body of her husband, Shiva, wearing an axe in one hand and holding a severed human head in the other. She personifies destruction and an energy that is responsible for the dissolution of the universe."

20. Bernadette Persaud explains, "I am trying to show that here is beauty." Interview by Ruel Johnson, *Caribbean Beat* 68 (July/August 2004).

21. Cross, *Elements of Hinduism*.

22. Rosanne Kanhai, interview by author, February 2008.

23. Rosanne Kanhai, "The Massala Stone Sings: Poetry, Performance and Film by Indo-Caribbean Women", in *Matikor: The Politics of Identity for Indo-Caribbean Women*, edited by Rosanne Kanhai (St Augustine, Trinidad: University of the West Indies School of Continuing Studies, 1999), 216.

24. Martin Carter, "After One Year", in *Selected Poems* (Georgetown, Guyana: Red Thread Press, 1997), 119.

25. Milan Kundera, *The Book of Laughter and Forgetting*, translated by Aaron Asher (New York: HarperCollins, 1996).

26. Reference is made to the rectangular design commonly used for national flags in contrast to the triangular flags which accompany Hindu rituals such as the *jandhi*. There is some suggestion that the arrangement of the flags on the canvas was prompted by the circular arrangement of flags at the Rockefeller Center in New York. This explanation is given in the endnotes of Jean Small, "How the Gods Came".

27. Shortly after my visit Persaud's mother came to live with her; she died within a year.

28. National Museum of Trinidad and Tobago, *Recent Paintings* (exhibition catalogue), 2004.

8

Breaking with Tradition

Hybridity, Identity and Resistance in
Indo-Caribbean Women's Writing

– ANITA BAKSH –

SINCE THE LATE 1980s, when Indo-Caribbean women began publishing significant works of literature, they have contested the stereotypical images of
themselves portrayed by male Indo-Caribbean writers and writers of other
races who do not speak to the realities of their multi-dimensional experiences.[1]
As writers they have also transgressed societal borders of public and private
domains, challenging specified gender roles established in Indo-Caribbean
communities. Given that their writing addresses and overcomes marginalization from outside the Indo-Caribbean community as a whole and from within
it because of gender, they disclose the oppression and abuse as well as the
struggle and resistance that exist within Indo-Caribbean communities –
details usually kept insulated within the home or within the racial community.
The political and social implications of their fiction position Indo-Caribbean
women writers as brave border-crossers; they follow the tradition of courage
displayed by indentured Indian women who embarked on the original oceanic
crossing, facing abuse, rape, starvation and alienation among the dangers
ahead.

Using post-colonial and feminist theory as a framework to examine Lakshmi Persaud's *Butterfly in the Wind* (1990), Jan Lo Shinebourne's[2] *The Last*

English Plantation (1988) and Shani Mootoo's *Cereus Blooms at Night* (1996), this chapter examines the ways in which Indo-Caribbean women writers challenge hegemonic colonial and patriarchal domination and thus uncover marginal spaces in their fiction, in both form and content. First by drawing on theories associated with African oral traditions to analyse the techniques used to incorporate Hindu mythology into Persaud's and Shinebourne's novels, I argue that the structure of these novels reflects what Shalini Puri terms a *"dougla* poetics", a hybrid form that incorporates Indian, African and European cultural traditions.[3] Based on the figure of the *dougla* – offspring of the interracial union of a person of Indian descent and one of African descent – *dougla* poetics offers a way to discuss the specificities of hybridity in the Caribbean context. While Puri develops the theory particularly in reference to Trinidadian cultural productions, the term also applies to those associated with Guyana, where there is a similar ethnic history and dynamic.

While my analysis in the first section uncovers the possibilities of a *dougla* poetics as a theory to describe hybrid cultural productions, the second section, which focuses on themes of identity formation, exposes the limitations of a *dougla* poetics as it applies to hybrid identities. I analyse the extent to which characters in each of the novels employ creative modes of resistance to negotiate a sense of self in colonial societies. These acts of defiance reflect what Ketu H. Katrak refers to as "covert resistance", which is "couched in folktales, mythology, religious scripture, popular culture, uses of magic, and obeah".[4] To Katrak's list I add the use of subversive language, creation of alternative realities, and forging of coalitions with other oppressed individuals. Katrak identifies covert resistance as a significant means of survival for women, for whom overt acts of resistance may have serious repercussions. The images of resistance portrayed in these texts oppose stereotypes of Indo-Caribbean women as docile, passive and culturally essentialist beings in colonial and post-colonial environments. More broadly, my analysis explains that these Indo-Caribbean women writers challenge Western definitions of feminist agency by illustrating that for women of colour in the Global South, resistance is enacted in forms that evolve within their own culture.

Lakshmi Persaud and Jan Lo Shinebourne transform the genre of the European realist novel through their use of oral techniques to record Hindu epics
within their novels. Their chronicling of Hindu mythology also fills an important gap in Caribbean literature. Edward Kamau Brathwaite and other
Caribbean writers have demonstrated the centrality of African oral traditions
to Afro-Caribbean literature and culture; however, less attention has been
given to the ways in which oral traditions have shaped the literature and culture of non-African peoples in the region. Relevant to the Indo-Caribbean
community of Hindu descent, it is important to understand that the Hindu
epics, including the *Ramayana* and the *Mahabharata,* were recorded in Sanskrit before 300 BC but have been rerecorded, translated, reinterpreted and
retold ever since.

Brought to the Caribbean by Indian indentured labourers during their
crossing of the *kala pani* (dark waters), these epics are recounted by Indo-
Caribbean pundits during Hindu prayer meetings as well as performed at
community events such as the Ramleela festival. In *Literary Occasions*, V.S.
Naipaul's admission that as a teenager in Trinidad he was more interested in
performances of the Ramleela – a dramatization of the story of Lord Rama –
than in the films *The Prince and the Pauper* and *Sixty Glorious Years* attests to
the major role Hindu epics play in Indo-Caribbean communities. His satirical
depictions of Hanuman House in *A House for Mr Biswas* and the comical
figure of pundit Ganesh in *The Mystic Masseur* also speak to the ways in
which these epics have influenced both Naipaul and the Indo-Caribbean
community.[6]

The themes, and sometimes actual narratives, of the *Ramayana* and the
Mahabharata are incorporated into Jan Lo Shinebourne's *The Last English
Plantation* and Lakshmi Persaud's *Butterfly in the Wind* as a counter-
hegemonic discursive strategy to negotiate the complexities of colonial realities. However, the *Ramayana* and the *Mahabharata* as refashioned by male
Hindu sages, such as Valmiki and Tulsidas, depict culturally prescribed roles
for Hindu women.[7] Since these stories were told mainly by male pundits,
points out Patricia Mohammed, "it was no coincidence that the symbols and
images of women which were focused on are those which ensured a patriarchal hold on the definition of Indian femininity".[8] As Mohammed suggests,
the Hindu epics were retold and modified by male storytellers to mould the
behaviour of a Hindu diaspora, particularly that of Hindu females. However,

as Mehta argues, "[t]hrough story telling, women have tried to affirm their subjectivity, using these stories as sounding boards to question issues of gender inequality, sexual oppression, female marginalization and invisibility, thereby creating a revisionist version of the primarily male-centered epic tales".[9]

While I agree with Mehta's assertion and plan to further discuss the ways in which orality can be used as a tool of empowerment, I also argue that these novels are not in themselves examples of orality, but rather of how techniques of orality, drawing on influences from India and from the Caribbean with its mix of Indian and African oral traditions, have impacted the development of writing by Indo-Caribbean women. In their novels, Shinebourne and Persaud challenge the patriarchal tradition of transferring the Hindu epics both orally and literally in two significant ways: by recording these tales as female authors and by depicting women as the tellers of the tales. In order to collapse this division, they employ techniques used in oral cultures to depict these epic tales in their novels. In fact what we are encountering is not orality per se but the "literary" – the way in which oral traditions inform literary traditions.

Before proceeding with the analysis of Persaud's and Shinebourne's novels, it is necessary to briefly discuss theories of African oral traditions as they apply to Hindu mythology. In his book *Encounter with Oral Literature*, Okumba Miruka argues that none of the major theories that underlie the study of oral narrative, including evolutionism, diffusionism, functionalism, formalism and structuralism, are completely correct, but all are considered "to be complementary in understanding the nature of the narrative".[10] Following Miruka's assertion, the following analysis considers concepts of various theories as they apply to Indo-Caribbean women writers' use of oral texts.

The Hindu mythology that is incorporated into these novels can be classified using certain aspects of the evolutionist theory. The philosopher David Hume argues that "primitive societies" created their gods "by deifying societal heroes", and " 'all tales, especially of the heroic kind, primarily have to do with antecedent historical personalities and their experiences' ".[11] Hume's declaration holds true for the *Ramayana* and the *Mahabharata*, which are believed to represent the origins of contemporary Hindu society. Together these important Indian epics attempt to prescribe gender roles, to define relationships between individuals and to explain an individual's relationship to society. Although they are linked to Hinduism, the values perpetuated in them are derived from Sanskrit literature, which predates contemporary Hinduism and was symbolic of Indian culture in general. Hindus and also Indo-Caribbeans who were Muslim or Christian were also influenced to some extent by these cultural values.[12]

Narrated in the first person, *Butterfly in the Wind* is a coming-of-age text that depicts an Indian girl's struggle to forge a sense of cultural and sexual identity in colonial Trinidad. The mother of the protagonist conveys a story from the *Mahabharata* to her daughter in an attempt to socialize the young girl into Indian womanhood and, more generally, to preserve Hindu culture. Kamla, the protagonist, relates the Indian epic as her mother tells it to her:

> In the dark age . . . there lived a young lady of great beauty called Draupadi who was about to have her nakedness revealed in the pavilion of the king's court by the courtier Dur-yodhana . . . [She] cried out to the heavens and appealed to Lord Krishna to come to her rescue. The bemused courtier . . . began to unwrap her loveliness. Her soft silk sari glided through his arrogant fingers as he pulled – and pulled and the more his desire grew the more he pulled – and as he pulled, yards and yards of silk passed through his now moist fingers. . . How long he persisted at this devilish act I can not say, except to point out that when he fell with exhaustion to the ground there was a high mountain of the softest strongest silk behind and fully-clothed, beautifully-chaste Draupadi before him.[13]

This passage is significant for several reasons. First, it illustrates the role of the mother as cultural repository and transmitter. Read in a colonial context, Kamla's mother transmits Hindu mythology as an act of covert resistance to undermine the attempt of British colonialism to devalue Indian cultural beliefs and behaviours. Second, it draws attention to the novel's use of modes of orality. Kamla's retelling of the story begins with "in the dark ages", a phrase that Miruka calls the "historical setting"[14] that gives the narrator several advantages: it establishes that the storyteller is not speaking of current times and therefore is not required to give all the facts, and by extension is licensed to make revisions. In other words, the retelling of the story may not be a factual account of what happened or what was written in the Sanskrit version of the text. However, the use of a "historical setting" frees both the fictional character and the real author from being accused of distorting the epic by community members who view epic storytelling as a male endeavour and/or believe that the epics hold incontestable truth claims.

Persaud also makes use of alliteration and repetition as modes of orality.

While these elements are also considered to be literary devices, in oral traditions they are used particularly to emphasize the theme of the narrative. The
narrator uses alliteration to describe Draupadi's clothing, which symbolizes
her sexuality: she wore a "soft silk sari". The softness of the sari represents
the vulnerability of her sexuality, and the silk material represents its precious-
ness. Later in the story alliteration is again used to describe the sari, but as
Lord Krishna intervenes in Draupadi's defilement the adjective that described
her sari as "soft silk" becomes "the strongest silk"; this change reflects the
transformation of the cloth from a garment to a shield that protects her body
from the rapist.

The narrator also employs the oral technique of repetition to describe the
way Dur-yodhana tries to remove Draupadi's attire: "he pulled – and pulled
and the more his desire grew the more he pulled – and as he pulled, yards
and yards of silk passed through his . . . fingers". Using repetition allows the
narrator to establish the force that Dur-yodhana uses against Draupadi and
to create a sense of time. As the narrator points out, "How long he persisted
at this devilish act I cannot say." While the exact length of the incident is
unknown, the fact that Dur-yodhana "pulled and pulled . . . yards and yards
of silk" from Draupadi's sari signals to Kamla and the reader that the torturous
episode persisted for a long time. The novel's use of African oral techniques
– including a historical setting, alliteration and repetition – to record traditional Indian tales exemplifies a *dougla* poetics. This hybrid form of narrative
structure is ironic, considering that *Butterfly in the Wind* focuses on a Hindu
middle-class enclave in colonial Trinidad that eschews hybridity as a subject.

In the novel the storyteller's use of modes of orality allows her to highlight
to her daughter how important it is for young women to guard their sexuality
from men. Kamla's internal struggle with her sexual desire suggests that the
oral techniques used by her mother are indeed effective. Consequently, *Butterfly in the Wind*'s engagement with the theme of female sexuality fails to
transform the gender biases imbedded in the epics.[15] Perhaps this failure is
due to the narrative structure and the immaturity of the young narrator. On
the one hand, the narrator attempts to stay true to her mother's account of
the tale by inserting her mother's voice into the text. On the other hand, the
passage undercuts Kamla's efforts by calling attention to her youth and her
inability to recognize the gender bias of the tale and her mother's attempt to
socialize her into a proper Hindu woman. Even if we attribute Kamla's lack

of analysis to her youth, later in the novel, when as a young woman she experiences sexual desire towards a colleague, she suppresses these desires rather than subvert the patriarchal ideals of Hindu womanhood by acting on them. Her final exit in the novel – to study abroad in a Western nation – problematically suggests that for Indo-Caribbean women, sexual (and cultural) identity formation can occur only in the West.

Shinebourne's *The Last English Plantation*, like *Butterfly in the Wind*, makes use of oral techniques to record Hindu legends but more overtly positions these epics as a method to counter colonial domination. Rather than relate all the details of the myth as Persaud does, Shinebourne emphasizes the context in which the story is told and the act of storytelling. The third-person narrator tells us that when the Hindu matriarch Nani Dharamdai relates a story from the *Ramayana* to the children of the fictitious colonial Guyanese village New Dam, "it seemed to lift her to another plane and she rolled the legend off her tongue like a visionary, conjuring the mythical scene".[16] To conjure is to make magic and enact transformation. In her conjuring of the traditional Hindu tale, Nani employs her own style and interpretation, making it what Ruth Finnegan terms an "aesthetic product" that is shaped by the interaction between the storyteller and her audience.[17] In other words, the creative process becomes a process of transformation of the teller, the audience and the community as a whole. In the case of Shinebourne's novel, Nani is the storyteller, the children are the audience and the context is an Indo-Caribbean community in colonial British Guiana. As a result, the aesthetic product emphasizes the present moment in which the Indian myth is relayed in the novel, rather than the context and content of the myth itself.

In addition, this section reflects the structuralist theory of oral narratives, which declares that myths are attempts by humans to understand the "contradictory concepts" that exist in reality.[18] Rather than give details of the story, Shinebourne chooses to juxtapose the contradictory concepts of the myth of Lord Rama's exile: it is a "myth of the Indian kings, queens, princesses, princes, and the Indian empires of Koshala and Sri Lanka; the movement of royal deities between the celestial and the earthly, between exile and return, their confrontations with humanity and nature . . . the monumental battle between Hanuman the monkey god and Ravana the demon king of Sri Lanka".[19] This list of contradictory concepts can be viewed as an attempt to deal with the seemingly opposing forces of the Indo-Guyanese experience that the novel explores, including negotiating differences between and among rural and urban communities; British, Asian and African cultures; the English, Hindi and Creole[20] languages; Christianity and Hinduism; and India, Britain and British Guiana as home spaces.

The telling of the epic tale transcends time and place, allowing the realities of the Indo-Caribbean experience to be explored. The myth allows Nani to interrogate her colonial subjectivity and indentured past as well as to preserve and transfer elements of Hindu culture to the village children. While she embodies the prescribed role of woman as guardian and teacher of indigenous culture and values, she appropriates the epic as an act of covert resistance to subvert systems of colonial domination – such as the colonial education system – that attempt to eradicate the languages, religions, cultural norms and history of Indians in the Caribbean.

The Last English Plantation exemplifies Puri's *dougla* poetics in a number of ways. As in the case of *Butterfly in the Wind*, Shinebourne's hybrid form that results from the use of African oral techniques to chronicle Indian mythology within the novel illustrates this concept. Given that Hindi appears in the text as a language facing extinction in the Caribbean landscape – because of the widespread use of Creole in everyday activities and Standard English in formal colonial schools, a point I will discuss further later in this chapter – we can safely assume that Nani uses a Hindi-Creole mix in her telling of Rama's tale. While Creole cannot "keep up with her feelings" as Hindi can, Nani has to use a creolized language so that the village children can comprehend the tale.[21] The novel emphasizes the Indian contribution to cultural mixing in the Caribbean, which is often overlooked in favour of the European and African mixtures referred to as creolization. Puri's theory circumvents the tendency of proponents of creolization to exclude Indians by making "visible *as Indian* the Indian elements of a dougla poetics".[22] Shinebourne participates in this project by recording Hindu mythology in a hybrid form, thereby simultaneously demonstrating the ways in which Indian culture has been transformed by cultural exchanges in the Caribbean and acknowledging and celebrating the contributions of Indians to the Caribbean's cultural milieu.

In *The Last English Plantation* Shinebourne uses the coming-of-age motif to call attention to the difficulties of negotiating identity in a multiracial and multicultural society. Born to an Indian mother, Lucille, and a half-Indian/half-Chinese father, Cyrus, June has her mixed-race identity written on her body. Her inability to pass as Indian becomes problematic at an Indian-dominated school, where her Chinese features are ridiculed; the other students brand her as a "Chinky chinee", leading June to recognize that "she was not Indian like them, not the country girls, or the town girls, not what they called 'pure' Indian".[23] Ironically, while June's phenotypical differences exclude her from acceptance into "pure" Indian circles, culturally her Indian ancestry overshadows its Chinese counterpart; in other words, her physical appearance does not match her cultural consciousness.

June's struggle for self-affirmation arises as a struggle with the different linguistic modes circulating in her Caribbean home. African theorist and writer Ngũgĩ wa Thiong'o explains: "Language carries culture, and culture carries . . . the entire body of values by which we come to perceive ourselves and our place in the world."[24] While Ngũgĩ is speaking about the African experience in particular, his statement can also be applied to the Caribbean experience, where the act of speaking English is layered with contradictions. On the one hand, English symbolizes the tongue of the colonizers and the devaluing of other available languages. On the other hand, without it one cannot gain economic mobility in British colonial society. Shinebourne's text demonstrates the important role language plays in the development of cultural identity, through June's relationship with the prominent female characters in the text.

June's mother, Lucille Lehall, insists that her daughter "[s]peak proper English", which includes "the imitation of an English accent".[25] Lucille recognizes the link between language and culture; she believes that if English becomes June's primary language, then English culture will dominate all the other cultural influences, which will help their family gain access to middle-class society. While June once spoke Hindi, "Lucille and St. Peter's school erased it from her tongue".[26] In her rejection of Indian – or what she terms "coolie"[27] – culture, Lucille mimics the colonial education system. Shinebourne interrogates the important trope of mothers as cultural transmitters, seen in many texts written by Caribbean women, by depicting a mother who attempts to transfer the culture of the colonizer rather than that of her ancestors. A stark contrast to Lucille's view of culture is that of Nani Dharamdai. Although Nani communicates in Creole, Hindi remains her primary linguistic mode of communication; her incessant use of Hindi can be viewed as an act of covert resistance against the evolving Afro-Creole culture, as well as against the dominant British culture.

June becomes caught between the Indian, British, Chinese and African influences that exist in her community. The climax of this battle comes when she returns from school disillusioned by the realization that "[a]ll the things she saw and heard were turning her against herself, making her own people look like nothing".[28] This alienation leads June to Nani's house, where "her tears dried and her tension eased".[29] Surrounded as she is by Hindi prayers and the traditions of her ancestors, June's trip to Nani's house becomes crucial to the development of her identity; here Nani shares the story of Le-Hau, June's Chinese-Guianese grandfather, whose name was recorded accidentally as Lehall. This act of renaming symbolically negates the possibility of transferring Le-Hau's Chinese heritage to his descendants. Although June and her father, Cyrus, are part Chinese, they have largely assimilated into the dominant Indian village, which is evident in Cyrus's ability to speak Hindi and his inability to speak Chinese. Nani's telling of Le-Hau's story ensures that it is not forgotten and enables June to symbolically reclaim her Chinese ancestry. Nani's ability to both recite Hindi mantras and tell the story of Le-Hau heals the schisms in June's psyche.

The recuperation of June's psyche becomes visible at the end of the novel, when she journeys to school: "[as] she cycled to and from the villages she was part of the movement between country and town. It was a continual movement of people which did not allow her to feel alone . . . If in the end she did not have to remember the lessons which she learnt in the classroom, she would be sure to remember [these people]."[30] Recognizing the multiplicity that is inherent in problems of constructing identity enables June to move freely through the various cultural influences of her society. Her cultural identity is not completely linked to India; it is also tied to China and, to some extent, to Africa and Britain. Discursively it belongs to all of these places. The fluidity with which June moves between various groups at the end of the novel signals her ability to navigate through the multicultural milieu of her environment, and her recognition that she does not have to deny her Asian ancestry in order to exist as a Guyanese individual.

June's Indo-Chinese ancestry problematizes the notion of *dougla* poetics. Importantly, it reveals the way in which *dougla* poetics describes a certain form of hybridity that does not take into account non-Indian and non-African groups, including Amerindians, Chinese, Lebanese and Syrians – a point that Puri herself acknowledges. Additionally, while the term proves to be useful in discussing cultural productions and political coalitions,[31] in terms of describing hybrid identities its inherent heterosexual bias can lead to other exclusions. Despite its idiosyncrasies, the notion of a *dougla* poetics is a significant contribution to discourses of hybridity and provides a vocabulary with which to discuss certain forms of cultural mixture in the Caribbean context.

Situated in the period of political turmoil when Guyana divided along African and Indian racial lines, *The Last English Plantation* promotes a model of Indo-Guyanese identity that acknowledges racial and cultural exchange without the erasure of Indianness, thereby challenging essentialist notions of cultural identity and authenticity. Importantly, it unravels the myth that one's outer (racial) appearance mirrors one's cultural alliances. By depicting a character whose cultural identity does not fit rigidly into predetermined categories, Shinebourne's fiction uncovers the impossibility of dividing the different groups existing in Guyana along distinct racial and cultural lines. Ultimately she shows that being Indo-Caribbean does not require denial of African, Chinese and English influences, but it does require acceptance of the inevitable cultural exchanges that occur.

In her novel *Cereus Blooms at Night,* Shani Mootoo complicates the notion of identity in her depiction of a subject that is to some extent taboo in the Indo-Caribbean and the larger Caribbean community: non-heteronormative sexual identity. A number of critics have noted Mootoo's nuanced treatment of sexual difference in a Caribbean space. While I also consider the theme of sexuality, I would like to point to an issue that has been neglected in discussions about this novel: its construction of "madness". Mootoo's protagonist, Mala Ramchandin, becomes mentally ill after being abandoned by her mother and sister and being incessantly raped by her father. Caribbean texts[32] usually identify mental illness as "madness"; however, I propose to examine Mala's condition as a mode of resistance employed to combat an oppressive reality. The novel portrays both madness and alternative sexuality as social constructions in the fictitious community of the text, Lantacamara; however, it suggests that this marginalization can be overcome through coalition.

In the text, Mala's life story is narrated by her (male) nurse, Tyler, who inhabits a non-heteronormative sexual identity. Through his reconstruction of Mala's story, Tyler reconstructs his own story as a marginalized subject within the colonial history of Lantacamara. By granting agency and voice to Tyler, the novel demonstrates that people with ambiguous sexuality not only exist in Caribbean society – and therefore within its literature – but are active participants in the creation of Caribbean history. The almshouse, the site of Tyler's employment and Mala's rehabilitation, becomes a microcosm of the attitudes and behaviours of the larger community that it serves. Tyler's position as the sole nurse trained abroad (in the Northern Wetlands, a fictional country that resembles Britain) is overlooked; he is given the menial chores of cleaning the home and scrubbing its floors. His feminine mannerisms and way of dressing provoke "condescending" comments and gain "the kind of notice that one might shower on a child".[33] Because Tyler does not fit the normative identity of a heterosexual, the community ostracizes him, clearly sending a message that he will not be accepted as a full citizen despite his professional training and service.

Tyler's ambiguous sexual identity and his relationship to the transgendered[34] character Otoh challenge fixed notions of sexuality. Otoh and Tyler's relationship seems to be one between a transgendered female who has relations with both males and females (Otoh) and a homosexual male who cross-dresses (Tyler), but the novel resists such clear-cut sexual identifications, calling attention to these ambiguous characters' ability to inhabit both genders simultaneously. Gloria Anzaldua says:

> There is something compelling about being both male and female, about having entry into both worlds. Contrary to some psychiatrics tenets, half and halfs are not suffering from a confusion of sexual identity, or even from a confusion of gender. What we are suffering from is an absolute despot duality that says we are able to be only one or the other.[35]

Anzaldua views a sexually ambiguous body as natural and empowering, and she argues that the confusion about this situation lies not within the individual but in the outside society's "absolute despot duality", which attempts to force individuals to define their gender and sexuality under the dominant rubric. Otoh and Tyler's relationship demonstrates the possibility of the existence of non-normative sexual identities that do not neatly conform to the categories of homosexual, bisexual or heterosexual.

As with Tyler, the almshouse is the site where Mala's marginalization first becomes visible in the chronology of the novel. Upon her arrival at the home she is placed on the floor as if she were an unwanted animal and is branded by the head nurse as a "psychiatric" who usurps resources from the poor. No nurses except Tyler want to touch her body. Some members of the community even rationalize her sexual abuse by her father, Chandin: "While many shunned [Chandin] there were those who took pity, for he was once the much respected teacher of the Gospel . . . Whether they disliked him or tolerated his existence, to everyone Chandin was Sir."[36] Ironically, Chandin, the rapist, is respected while Mala, the victim, is socially rejected. The fictional community's passive attitude mirrors the silence of Mootoo's own family when she disclosed that she had been sexually abused by her uncle. She admits, "it was something that I learned very young not to talk about".[37] Mootoo's real story and Mala's fictional one uncover the community's indirect complicity in the sexual abuse of young women. Rather than confront male abuse of power, the community often shames the victim, thus silencing her.

Mala's strategy of survival becomes her psychic crossing of the border between reality and fantasy. In this split psyche, Mala creates an alternative world where her childhood self, Pohpoh, embarks on nightly missions into the yards of the neighbourhood: "she was able to find her way, to survive in the dark, to name plants and insects with only their scent . . . Like a moth, she breezed through the hole and out the other side without a scratch."[38] Pohpoh becomes one with nature, giving Mala the control, security and sense of self that she was not able to have as a child and that she cannot attain in her present reality. In other words, Mala crosses the borders of self and recreates a stronger, more powerful version of herself through Pohpoh. As the novel juxtaposes Pohpoh's adventure with Mala's isolated reality, both Mala and the reader are unaware of "how much of it actually took place".[39] Furthermore, while Mala's crossing takes her to another place, she is still fully cognizant of the occurrences of the real moment. Her memory and the narrative of the text blur reality and fantasy, drawing attention to the fact that Pohpoh's adventure is a natural alternative for survival in an impossible reality. Rather than buy into the community's warped perception of her abuse, conform to its expectations or actively fight against its tyranny – options that can have severe consequences – Mala excludes herself physically and mentally from its every-day reality. Mala's madness is thus a psychic crossing to resist and challenge the dominant order.

Both Tyler and Mala begin to overcome their marginalization from the out-side community in the relationship that develops from their "shared queer-ness". *Cereus Blooms at Night* suggests that while the dominant culture constructs restrictive models of identity and uses those constructions to police individuals who do not conform, the possibilities of transcending these arti-ficial borders can be strengthened through coalition. Through their union, Mala and Tyler are on the road to overcoming their oppression and they encourage the community to change their attitudes towards marginalized indi-viduals. By the end of the text, the workers at the almshouse treat both of them with more care and respect; their change in attitude suggests the pos-sibility for social change in the larger community.

This chapter has discussed two generations of Indo-Caribbean women writ-ers. Those of the first generation, Lakshmi Persaud and Jan Lo Shinebourne, have laid a solid foundation for Shani Mootoo and other Indo-Caribbean women writers to interrogate more complex issues of Indo-Caribbean expe-rience, going beyond race, culture and gender to include sexual abuse and sexual orientation. *Butterfly in the Wind* and *The Last English Plantation* illus-trate that, consciously or unconsciously, their Indo-Caribbean female authors have been influenced by the Afro-Indo cultural syncretism of their environ-ment; their use of techniques associated with traditions of African oral nar-ratives to represent the Hindu tales they record broadly exemplifies a *"dougla poetics"*. While *dougla* poetics proves valuable in discussing hybrid forms of cultural productions, it can be a problematic marker of cultural and other forms of hybrid identity, as seen in Shinebourne's *The Last English Plantation*.

Read side by side, *Butterfly in the Wind*, *The Last English Plantation* and *Cereus Blooms at Night* demonstrate strategies of resistance that combat hegemonic domination, strategies which can often be overlooked if measured by Western notions of feminist resistance. Indo-Caribbean women writers' engagement with the themes of hybridity and resistance makes their novels invaluable contributions to Caribbean writing and the writing of the Indian diaspora, particularly the indentured diaspora and places to which Indian indentured workers migrated, including Fiji, Mauritius and South Africa. Their fiction reminds us that, while diaspora dismantles previous borders, it also retains some of those borders and sets up new ones that continue to be challenged in a never-ending fluidity and ambiguity.

ACKNOWLEDGEMENTS

I wish to thank Rosanne Kanhai and Merle Collins for their patience, guidance and insight in the development of this chapter.

NOTES

1. Researchers, including Rosanne Kanhai and Brinda Mehta, have documented the struggle of Indo-Caribbean women writers' coming into voice.
2. Jan Lo Shinebourne, who is part Indo-Caribbean and part Chinese-Caribbean, is arguably the first Indo-Caribbean woman to publish a novel.
3. Shalini Puri, *The Caribbean Postcolonial: Social Equality, Post-nationalism and Cultural Hybridity* (New York: Palgrave, 2004).
4. Ketu Katrak, *Politics of the Female Body: Postcolonial Women Writers of the Third World* (New Brunswick, NJ: Rutgers University Press, 2006), 58.
5. V.S. Naipaul, *Literary Occasions* (New York: Alfred A. Knopf, 2003).
6. In *A House for Mr Biswas* the protagonist, Mohun Biswas, labels the multi-generational home of his in-laws Hanuman House, after the Hindu monkey god and Lord Rama's soldier Hanuman, because of the family's attempts to cling to the Hindu culture and lifestyle they brought over from India. See *The Mystic Masseur* (London: André Deutsch, 1957) and *A House for Mr Biswas* (New York: Alfred Knopf, 1961).
7. Brinda Mehta, *Diasporic (Dis)locations: Indo-Caribbean Women Writers Negotiate the Kala Pani* (Kingston: University of the West Indies Press, 2004), 31.
8. Patricia Mohammed, "From Myth to Symbolism", in *Matikor: The Politics of*

Identity for Indo-Caribbean Women, edited by Rosanne Kanhai (St Augustine, Trinidad: University of the West Indies School of Continuing Studies, 1999), 71.

9.   Mehta, *Diasporic (Dis)locations,* 137.

10. Okumba Miruka, *Encounter with Oral Literature* (Nairobi: East African Educational Publishers, 1994), 138.

11. Quoted ibid., 134.

12. Ramabai Espinet's *The Swinging Bridge* (Toronto: HarperCollins, 2003) portrays the ways in which Indo-Trinidadian Christians were also affected by Indian mythology, particularly in regards to Indian femininity.

13. Lakshmi Persaud, *Butterfly in the Wind* (Leeds, UK: Peepal Tree, 1990), 102–3.

14. Miruka, *Encounter,* 168.

15. Espinet's *The Swinging Bridge* also addresses the theme of female sexuality; however, unlike *Butterfly in the Wind,* it demonstrates the ways in which women appropriate Hindu mythology to undercut prescribed notions of female sexuality. For example, the character Baboonie, a widow who is sexually abused by village men, appropriates and revises the songs of the *Ramayana* to voice her marginalization.

16. Jan Lo Shinebourne, *The Last English Plantation* (Leeds, UK: Peepal Tree, 1998), 175.

17. Quoted in Miruka, *Encounter,* 135.

18. Ibid., 138.

19. Shinebourne, *Last English Plantation,* 176.

20. The term *Creole* refers to both a grassroots language and a culture based on synthesis of European and African influences. While Creole is largely upheld as a mode of resistance against European domination, historically it has marginalized Indo-Caribbean culture and people.

21. Shinebourne, *Last English Plantation,* 129.

22. Puri, *Caribbean Postcolonial,* 221.

23. Shinebourne, *Last English Plantation,* 72.

24. Ngũgĩ wa Thiong'o, "The Language of African Literature", in *Colonial Discourse and Post-colonial Theory: A Reader,* edited by Patrick Williams and Laura Chrisman (New York: Columbia University Press, 1994), 441.

25. Shinebourne, *Last English Plantation,* 8.

26. Ibid., 32.

27. The term *coolie* originated in India and refers to cheap unskilled labourers, who occupied the lowest class and caste. It was appropriated during colonialism to describe indentured servants from India and China who were transported to the

Caribbean, South Africa and the islands of the Pacific and Indian Oceans; see Mehta, *Diasporic (Dis)locations*, 54. After colonialism it has remained a derogatory term which the Indo-Caribbean community has resisted and actively fought against. This "fight" takes place in *The Last English Plantation* through the figure of the protagonist.

28. Shinebourne, *Last English Plantation*, 116.

29. Ibid., 126.

30. Ibid. 175.

31. In her lecture titled "From Matikor to a Caribbean Dougla Feminism", given at the Centre for Gender and Development Studies, University of the West Indies, St Augustine, Trinidad, on 10 February 1999, Rosanne Kanhai puts forth the notion of a *dougla* feminist space which would be more inclusive of groups who have been marginally represented in Caribbean feminist discourse. As Mehta points out, in this move Kanhai makes a significant political statement in proposing a hybrid feminist space instead of a separatist affirmation of Indo-Caribbean feminism; see Mehta, *Diasporic (Dis)locations*, 14 and 231n21.

32. See Evelyn O'Callaghan, "Interior Schisms Dramatized: The Treatment of the 'Mad' Woman in the Work of Some Female Caribbean Novelists", in *Out of the Kumbla: Caribbean Women and Literature,* edited by Carole Boyce Davies and Elaine Savory Fido (Trenton, NJ: African World Press, 1990), 89–109, and Liz Gunner, "Mothers, Daughters and Madness in Works by Four Women Writers: Bessie Head, Jean Rhys, Tsitsi Dangarembga and Ama Ata Aidoo", *Alif: Journal of Comparative Poetics* 14 (1994): 136–51.

33. Shani Mootoo, *Cereus Blooms at Night* (Vancouver, BC: Press Gang, 1996), 15.

34. The use of the term *transgendered* is mine, as Mootoo avoids using labels such as *transgendered*, *lesbian*, *gay* and *queer* in her novel.

35. Gloria Anzaldua, *Borderlands/La Frontera: The New Mestiza* (1987; reprint, San Francisco: Lute Books, 2007), 41.

36. Mootoo, *Cereus*, 195.

37. Shani Mootoo, "Interview with Shani Mootoo", *BC Institute against Family Violence Newsletter* (Fall 1993), http://www.bcifv.org/resources/newsletter/1993/fall/mootoo.shtml (accessed 13 December 2006).

38. Mootoo, *Cereus*, 156.

39. Ibid., 159.

9

Beyond Fragile Homes

Indo-Trinidadian Women
Constructing Habitable Narratives

– PAULA E. MORGAN –

THIS CHAPTER EXPLORES THE most recent efforts to address a perennial task undertaken by Caribbean writers of all ethnicities and genders – and, indeed, practically all architects of the post-colonial house of fiction. Indo-Trinidadian female writers are adding their versions of "writing home" from diasporic locations to explore the potential and pain of coming of age and assuming viable adult identities within culturally polyglot island societies, and subsequently building on this foundation habitable identities in lands of their migrations.[1] This chapter reads Ramabai Espinet's *The Swinging Bridge* (2003), Niala Maharaj's *Like Heaven* (2006) and Joy Mahabir's *Jouvert* (2006) as narratives of development with a specific focus on cross-gender and cross-ethnic representation, and as evocations of the making of the artist as a young woman. In the process it explores the unremitting quest for home, nation and belonging, given the complex and problematic social locations which the characters inhabit, in relation to gender and ethnicity as well as ancestral, natal and adopted lands.

Since Jan Lo Shinebourne penned the first female-authored Indo-Caribbean novel (*Timepiece,* 1986), several Indo-Caribbean women writers have emerged to offer their perspectives on what has now become a perennial issue for people of the region who are still grappling with the aftermath of the historic encounter between worlds. Protagonists are faced with competing claims in relation to subject construction rooted in gender, nation and ancestral and migratory cultures. Ironically, for some individuals and people-groups born at increasingly distant reaches from inherited cultures, ancestry as competitor for the overriding determinant of identity construction has, in contemporary times, strengthened instead of lessened. For these Indo-Caribbean women characters and the writers who tell their stories, the issue is made more complex, since adherence to ancestral culture tends to be at odds with the expanded terrain which women have gained in this time; in other words, the tug towards what Arjun Appadurai terms "reconstructed primordialism" stands to erode personal freedoms.[2] In practice within the Caribbean scenario, some of the gains for women are secure and holding steady. These include access to educational opportunity, professional occupations and personal mobility. Others, such as control of wages and property, are still very much the subject of individual negotiations. Yet others, including a woman's choice of marital and intimate relationships outside her ethnic group, which thereby abrogates her culturally assigned location as ethnic boundary marker, remain hotly contested issues.

In *Swinging Bridge*, Espinet writes back from metropolitan Canada to explore the conditions under which her foremothers arrived in Trinidad as indentees, planted a stake in the land, thrived as an extended family and eventually, because of financial pressure, sold their land and opted for secondary migration to Canada. The central motif of the swinging bridge speaks about the potentialities as well as the ruptures and perils inherent in crossings between lands and cultures, times and seasons. Mona's emotional underdevelopment, coupled with her brother's deathbed request that she return to repurchase the family lands on Manahambre Road, Princes Town, precipitates the quest for origins with the imperatives to unearth family secrets, valorize her matrilineage and test the ongoing potential for belonging to multicultural Trinidad. Belonging in this novel is vested in lineage, indigenous foods, nation language and the intimacies of childhood, but also, most significantly, in claiming a stake in the land – not as a transient who has become more tourist than national, but as a propertied citizen and landholder.

Joy Mahabir's *Jouvert* picks up a remarkable number of the resonances of *Swinging Bridge*. Writing out of a shared vantage point of metropolitan residency, Mahabir positions her protagonist as a recent immigrant whose heart, sensibility and sense of being at home remain firmly rooted in the Caribbean rural environment. Indeed, a major focus of the narrative is the breakdown of values and duty of care among the extended family members who have migrated to Canada. Family and community have been compromised. Reclaiming family land and unearthing bizarre secrets are again at the core of the narrative. *Jouvert*, which makes the pre-dawn Monday Carnival revelry its central motif, deals with the interplay between artist, community and representation. In this case the issues are several: Who is representing whom, on behalf of whom? What is the nature of the representation fed to an avid metropolitan market hungry for "authentic" Caribbean images? And what accounts for the intrusive and mercenary manner in which the "native informer" artists serve up their representations?

Like Heaven, by Niala Maharaj, differs radically, in terms of the cross-gender representation of a male protagonist, but fundamentally is not that divergent from the other two narratives. Trinidad-born Dutch resident Maharaj sketches the businessman and financial wizard Ved, who pens his first-person self-exonerating confessional to explain to his daughter his only failure – a most spectacular transgression indeed – his separation from and the eventual murder of his once beloved wife, Anji, by his family; her frank journalism was interpreted as disloyal to ethno-political interests and her divorce settlement was perceived as making an unfair claim on the family's million-dollar empire. The novel, which delivers a severe indictment on its tainted social and family relations, deals with the multiplicity of issues which make up Trinidadian society – what its epigraph, quoting Walcott, terms "mongrelized, polyglot, a ferment without a history, like heaven".[3] The novel examines the ambivalent position given to this near-stereotypical protagonist in the complex social and cultural melee of multi-ethnic Trinidad society; the intimate relationships of such men within the extended family network and particularly their relationships with mothers and wives; and their quest for privacy and self-affirmation, which is often at odds with familial demands.

Like Heaven, despite its tight focus on a single character and even more so the deployment of a first-person narrative voice, brings a large, seething community alive. Indeed, all three novels under study bring a world to life in a manner reminiscent of V.S. Naipaul's classic *A House for Mr Biswas*. Together these fictions demonstrate why a novel about this social group at this period in its history can never be about an individual; it must necessarily be about family and community. The female-authored *Like Heaven* represents the Indian male as sharing the quest object of myriad female protagonists: a search for self-affirmation which will transcend the worse legacies of community while not destroying its best elements, which lend strength and cohesiveness. Espinet's statement defines a central issue common to all three narratives:

> If you happen to be born into an Indian family, an Indian family from the Caribbean, migratory, never certain of the terrain, that how life falls down around you. It's close and thick and sheltering, its ugly violence and secrets locked inside the family walls. The outside encroaches, but the ramparts are strong, once you leave it you have no shelter and no ready skills for finding a different one.[4]

Significantly too, the three authors are domiciled outside of the Caribbean in what I have termed (privileging my own Trinidadian birthplace and homeland) lands of "secondary migration". Paradoxically, conferring an aura of disadvantage upon these migrants – who are otherwise generally perceived, by virtue of their migration, as socially advantaged and poised to enjoy First World privilege and prospects – Brij V. Lal in "People In-Between" deploys the term "the diaspora of the *twice banished*" (my emphasis). Lal's perspective captures effectively the increasingly complex web of migrations and returns and the increasing occurrence of double diasporas in today's globalized world. A substantial cross-section of these migrants, who are by now twice removed from India, have never visited the ancestral land, have lost the language, adopted Western values and adapted to living in multicultural societies. They are

> descendents of Indian settlers in the plantation colonies in the West Indies, Fiji, Mauritius, Africa and parts of South East Asia. Although ancestrally Indian, they are products of many influences, including the West and others peculiar to the region of residence. They acknowledge their Indian roots and can identify with the broad contours of Indian culture, but they are also acutely aware of their separate non-Indianness as well. Questions of "culture", "homeland", "territoriality" and "nation" so intimately tied to the diaspora identity, always problematic even at the best of times, acquire a particular niche in their psyche.[5]

What, then, do the literary evocations indicate about these vexing issues, as inscribed by female writers who are writing narratives of subject formation based in their island birthplace, but from their locations in double diasporas?

NATION AND BELONGING

In the quest for a prototype of belonging which was powerful enough to bring coherence to multi-ethnic, multicultural populations in contestation, Caribbean nations have come to rely heavily on the creolization paradigm, which valorizes indigenous fusions, cultural practices and expressions generated on the islands, such that the sum of the unified nation culture is reckoned to be greater than its potentially divisive parts. Within this paradigm, Indo-Caribbean culture, and particularly its festivals and foods, were welcomed as imparting a colourful flair to the diverse Trinidad and Tobago rainbow republic. This is supported by a plethora of popular contemporary myths, expressions and icons of "Trini" harmony, including instructions on how to "spot a Trini". Creolization as a paradigm has more recently faced contestation, including that argued by Aisha Khan, who evokes an anthropologist's focus on lived experiences as opposed to commitment to ideological strongholds. Khan argues that the creolization rhetoric which has been so inherent to Caribbeanness has served to mask the predominant Afrocentricity of the creolizing impulse.[6]

While the novels under study express divergent perspectives on this issue, they are all clear about the anguish caused by neglect and marginalization of persons of Indian origin on Caribbean soil. This was bred initially by the oppressive labour and immigration laws which governed the indentureship scheme, and the adversarial terms of the indentees' introduction into the chaotic social milieu. The hostility with which the workers were greeted by the Afro-Caribbean population – as scab labour – in no small way fed their desperate attempts to maintain cultural distinctiveness and integrity. These factors fused with early physical isolation (predominantly in rural village communities), vestiges of caste sensibility and fear of miscegenation to create the complex and ambivalent social locations which are evident in the texts. There are predictable outcomes, a major one being, although the nation's responsibility to craft habitable narratives for all of its people-groups is held sacrosanct in theory; in practice, there is keen ongoing contestation over its ethno-political configuration and its mytho-cultural symbols of belonging.[7]

A fundamental challenge is yoking the modes of being and value systems of the range of people-groups into a viable social order. Where are the shared values and relational harmonies which would mobilize the nation to function as a coherent whole? For Espinet, the central motif of the swinging bridge represents transitions between moments of history, potentially empowering and potentially dangerous points of rupture of continuities of language and culture. Migration is figured as producing an aching absence which calls adults back to submerged, never forgotten markers of belonging, such as long-disused names of places and foods – phrases which erupt, displacing the present and tugging one back into a past which is also a beckoning future. Home here becomes the place in which we speak the same mother tongue, crave the same food and understand each other's body language and expressions. It is the place in which we need no translation and interpretation, but essentially it will remain exclusively a site of powerful, sustaining nostalgia unless a re-rooting/routing proves viable.

These fictional texts read the quest for home as rooted in the land; the state's capacity to keep its citizens safe; marginalization versus inclusion of persons of Indian origin, including representation in the political and socio-symbolic systems of belonging; and the ideologies of artistic representation of the ethnicity and of the nation.[8] In *Like Heaven* the issue of being at home hinges on effectively grappling with tough everyday, ever-present economic, social and familial issues. Ved functions centrally in the narrative – and arguably in the nation – as a test case of an ideal citizen of the young republic of Trinidad and Tobago. Maharaj fleshes out a young Indian male who deploys what appears to be supernatural wizardry to amass wealth and to rise to the upper echelons of the corporate business world. He is centrally located as a supreme cross-cultural communicator at the core of a complex web of relations which includes representatives of all groups in the multicultural social fabric.[9] The task of cross-cultural appreciation and accommodation which poses itself in all multicultural societies is heightened in the tiny twin-island republic, which is homeland to the descendants of Europeans, Africans and Asians, all of whom confront the challenges of constructing a viable social order on the bedrock of genocide of the indigenous tribes.

The French Creole former estate owners – who once conceived of themselves as the islands' true aristocrats – in the present time of the novel are ancient relics clinging to decaying homes and overgrown lands desperately in need of rescue, driven to the brink of insanity by the enormity of their loss of privilege.[10] Ved befriends Mr Guillame, and "living good" combined with a dash of opportunism redounds to handsome material gain, when after years of renting space he takes over the impoverished landholder's mortgage. He becomes the rescuer/supplanter of this representative of the island's old aristocracy and eventually comes to occupy the abandoned great house.[11] For the displaced European craftsmen, he creates a market. In relation to his own family, he rescues the business from failure, his family from impoverishment. He becomes a paterfamilial figure to a wide cross-section of his Afro-Trinidadian employees, and particularly to young males who, because of an absence of fathering, are otherwise vulnerable to being seduced into the criminal underworld.

The protagonist is an undisputed hero to all of these people-groups, yet the focus of the narrative is on his inner struggles and insecurities, which he carries like a festering sore. Ved possesses all that he can materially own – money, luxury cars, homes, contracts aplenty. Yet an essential insecurity gnaws at his soul, rooted in the fact that he has never attended university despite his native brilliance, which is heralded on page after page of the narrative. He internalizes what is inherently a class-based tension between an emergent business class and the emergent intelligentsia, the locus of which is the University of the West Indies (UWI). This contestation is implicit in the relative social benefit of monetary – as opposed to intellectual – currency to construction of the emerging nation-state. The repositories of the latter hold the former in contempt as capitalists who are withered by soul-destroying materialism, which requires that they close their eyes to the exploitation, the corruption and the range of dishonourable strategies which are engrained in operations of the business sector.

These class tensions merge with the emotional strain generated within the traditional co-residential extended family that concerns another deep root of insecurity: how can even successful Indian males face the challenges posed by their highly educated, upwardly mobile, independent thinking and articulate wives? Both sources of contention come home to roost in the gap between *Like Heaven*'s husband and wife, a promising young UWI doctoral candidate and assistant lecturer. This is where the text resonates with numerous historical and contemporary discourses on domestic violence and wife-murder. The spectre of domestic abuse, which remains legendary even in contemporary times, figures prominently in all three narratives being examined. Representing a salient departure from widely held assumptions about the vulnerability of passive, uneducated rural women, today's fictional and other discourses also number among the abused those who are too articulate, too aggressive and disinclined to comply with the traditional expectations for Indian women.

The Hindu daughter-in-law occupies a significant symbolic location in the Trinidadian imaginary. Michael V. Angrosino, in his 1973 anthropological study "Sexual Politics in the East Indian Family in Trinidad", identifies the Indianness of the family as vested in "male dominance and the dominance of the mother-in-law over the daughter-in-law who is symbolized as property owned, an object of spiritual degradation to the family".[12] Ethnic identity and adherence to tradition are somehow signalled in the harsh treatment meted out to the daughter-in-law. In *Like Heaven,* Anji's frank public criticism of the Indian party to which her husband's brother hitches his political fortunes, along with her claim to a substantial portion of the million-dollar empire, constitutes her death warrant. The fictional debacle parallels a real-life case, the June 1994 murder of Dr Chandra Narayansingh and the attendant trial. Allegations of the Chief Justice's interference to save the husband accused of murder were in themselves sufficient to threaten the stability of the judicial system of Trinidad and Tobago and to warrant intervention by the London-based Privy Council.[13]

Like Heaven, though light, humorous and eminently readable, remains a virulent critique of Indo-Caribbean family life. This female-authored novel has cast aside the shroud of secrecy and put on display greed, acquisitiveness and compromise for wealth and social advancement. In the process it demonstrates the pitfalls of claims of belonging, solidarity and secrecy based on ethnicity. It critiques – perhaps even chastises – the assumption that the individual's deepest loyalties and basis of belonging are inherited, and moreover that an individual's dominant characteristics are formed in response to communal expectations and aspirations. When the amiable and tolerant Ved has to deal with whether to expose his brother and cousin as the instigators of his wife's murder, he covers up the murder but walks away from the group ethos and group loyalty into the arms of his faithful Muslim employee. His action foregrounds the salient subcultural cleavages which exist even within the ethnic group. The reality – both fictional and social – is that common ethnicity in and of itself does not create social cohesion, and in the absence of a common core of focalizing and empowering values, community has to be maintained by force rather than by consent. Ethnic regimes – both familial and nationalistic – are by definition more authoritarian than democratic. These female writers, though committed to belonging and to family, will not broker evasion and romanticization of its myriad issues in the interest of maintaining a facade of ethnic solidarity.

TERRITORIALITY AND CULTURAL BELONGING

A primary maker of belonging in all of these novels is attachment to the land. The ignominies and anguish of cultural dislocation during indentureship were alleviated in some small measure by the promise of a land grant at the end of the period. For the indentees and their immediate descendants, the decision to accept a parcel of land meant choosing to remain to build a life and a future. Land meant roots, livelihood, community, ritual, seasons, religious observances; the planting of the *jandhi* on the family plot symbolized inter-connectivity between the earth and the heavens, the natural and the super-natural intertwined. The historian Brinsley Samaroo argues: "to a region in which the relentless pursuit of profit has destroyed so much of the flora and fauna, the Indians came with a profound reverence for the land which they called Mother Earth (*Dharti Maa* or *Prithvi Mata*). In this view, the earth is regarded as divine and plants and animals are seen as elements in an eternal cyclic cosmic order."[14] The point is that a stake in the land was very much connected to ontological and communal wholeness. An ethic of accumulation, both generally and particularly in relation to land, would seem a predictable ongoing cultural pursuit for a people-group whose ancestors had migrated to the islands in quest of a better life, lured by the reward of land. As indicated in the novels under examination, this attachment to the land has jumped the generations to survive in its best and worst forms.[15]

In *The Swinging Bridge,* migration to Canada sets up in the younger generation a nostalgic longing to be home, not just as itinerant "local tourists" but as persons with a stake in the land. This generation stands poised between cosmopolitan citizenship of a global, market-driven world, in which place of work is paramount in determining residence, and a nostalgic hankering for a portion of the land of birth. This tension between conflictual realms and codes of belonging remains unresolved to the end of the narrative. The strong implication is that Kello, who greatly longs to regain possession of the family land, would have been excluded from the Caribbean familial and social landscape had his sexual preference been articulated. Conversely, *Jouvert* foregrounds attachment to the land in its worst possible form. When the prosperous Toronto relatives return to claim the portion of land Larry gave to the impoverished Black Maharajin, they offend this complex of values for the sake of greed and ownership as an end in itself.

If land ownership figures prominently as symbolic of rootedness and belonging, Carnival – that swirling amalgam of calypso, street theatre and steel pan – figures prominently in all of the novels as an icon and agent of cultural hybridity.[16] In *Like Heaven,* Carnival ironically contributes significantly to Ved's business acumen. His capacity to negotiate the cultural complex of Trinidad society is rooted in his youthful sojourn in mas camps, where he learned not to fear but instead to understand and appreciate the lower-strata Afro-Caribbean population, their flamboyance, love of celebration, and overt, aggressive sexuality. In his business dealings he addresses a major national issue: how can the creativity, flair, discipline and hard work expended in annual Carnival celebrations be put to productive use year-round? And while the culture of carnival administration has not traditionally lent itself to profit, Ved puts the carnival arts and its grandmaster to work, deploying his astute business sense to channel the originality and love of showmanship into lucrative commercial enterprises.

While Carnival does much to make the businessman in *Like Heaven, Swinging Bridge* foregrounds its unbridled, terrifying and compelling sexuality. In this novel, as well as in *Jouvert,* the girls bond with their father over their right of measured access to that space where social prescriptions lose their hold and primal forces are released beneath the safety of the mask, to prowl the streets for a season. In *Jouvert,* Carnival provides the fragile space of creativity which gives father Larry and daughter Annaise release from the stultifying strictures of their Presbyterian background. Despite his consistent attempts to make an impact through the more socially acceptable middle-class "pretty mas", the father fails yearly to bring out the planned Carnival band and manages instead a subversive hybrid Jouvert creation of pretty mas gone awry.

If *Jouvert* is the most repetitive term in Mahabir's narrative, then *fragile* runs a close second. Used together as they invariably are, they convey a potentially easily ruptured and insecure space in which oppressed people are allowed to generate art. The carnival designers and mas makers create through their artistry an order which defies hegemonic prescriptions and distributes power laterally to all who come to "lend hand" to the feverish creative process. The power shifts in turn to the man in the street, who can wear and dance his art in displays of resistance, solidarity and cathartic abandon. All are invited to contribute to the costume-making and to fill the performance space of the street parade – all ethnicities, all islanders, all returning residents, all tourists – all. According to Rawle Gibbons,

> At the aesthetic level, its impulse is to "fill the space"; instinctively inclusive, it achieves this in several ways, from the enlarging of the self in costume to the prancing and swaying, jumping up and rolling on the ground that claim the horizontal and vertical dimensions of space. Through performance, mass and mass (the movement of crowds) claim the streets, asserting the freedom so intrinsic to Carnival.[17]

The process and the space are both intensely communal and highly politicized. If carnival artistry subverts the hegemonic social order, it also potentially holds the power to undermine ethnic divisiveness by crashing creative and representational divides. Jouvert emerged as an Afro-Trinidadian intrusion into the Christian ritual calendar and the "respectable" mas of the ruling French plantocracy as they took to the streets for *"carne vale"* – to bid farewell to the flesh before Lent.[18]

In Mahabir's text, Jouvert is simultaneously the ground of her artistic impulse and a stage on which Indian-African politics of inclusion and inclusion play themselves out. The father is one of a handful of Indian males who have been regularly producing mas bands at great personal expense. Touted as the greatest show on earth, Carnival is quintessentially Trinidadian, and linked to nationalism as a sweeping stage on which to showcase the harmony of its multi-ethnic society. Mahabir's fictional scenario reveals that, given the Afrocentric nature of the nationalist project in the mid-1900s, Indians were welcomed as consumers and players of mas but unacknowledged and even erased as mas band producers. This link to nationalist politics and its attendant anxieties are played out in a Ministry of Culture exhibition to which

Larry has been invited to send his carnival artistry – only to find his work
omitted and his person made embarrassingly visible by virtue of difference.
The exhibition is predictably staged in a marker of the centrality of European
culture: one of the "Magnificent Seven" heritage buildings which are themselves emblematic of Old World art and architecture. Here its representatives
– the diplomatic corps and the island's Euro-Creole elite – gather to witness
a Carnival exhibition mounted by a state agency, nervously displaying its
indigenous products for validation. In this scenario, class and ethnic divides
use and exclude the festival's producers, both the pan men from the urban
ghetto of Laventille and the Indian mas man from rural Mount Stewart. Indians are welcomed into this space only as gardeners. The other problematic
on the locus of inclusion and exclusion, which has long contributed to a siege
mentality within segments of the Indo-Trinidadian population, rears its head
and, at least in the father's mind, eclipses the grave insult of his exclusion.
For Larry, brooding over his daughter's mild flirtation with the French ambas-
sador at the exhibition, the overriding concern appears to be the potential of
their presence within the broader social sphere to lead to loss of control over
his daughter, with the possibility of interethnic sexual interests.

The task and desirability of bridging the gap between Jouvert "slackness"
and the order, discipline and management required to produce pretty mas
become the point of departure for grappling with related issues, such as the
role of the artist in the multicultural society. What ideologies, if any, should
art legitimately express? Who is the artist representing in her work and to
whom is this representation directed? What calibration of artistic expression
would best accomplish this purpose? And for the migrant artist, how to transition from the rich, fertile creativity of the Caribbean landscape into the
world of cool, sassy metropolitan art galleries?

Mahabir affirms artistry which is rooted in family and invariably in matrilineage. While the father opens the door to the Jouvert space of diversity, creativity and potentiality, he remains a marginalized artist and, by the end of
the narrative, an impoverished and broken man. Much of Annaise's creative
strength and nourishment springs out of her connection with her mother and
her other mother, Black Maharajin. The instruction received from the latter
transcends the severe schooling in technique proffered by the mother, a gifted
art teacher whose own creative process has been stifled by domesticity. This
is the life instruction on location imparted through the wisdom and words of

Black Maharajin, including tales of long dead foremothers who visit festooned with garlands of heady ylang-ylang.

The root of artistry draws from the past, the submerged history of Mount Solitude (later Mount Stewart), an old Maroon hideaway which forms a unique refuge, set apart from the ethnic divisiveness which was a major strategy for imperial divide-and-rule. Not surprisingly, Africans and Indians meet and intermarry freely. Here the past needs to be unearthed cautiously, because "In the way of maroonage, things were hidden, invisible. Histories preserved from the times of slavery and indentureship unfolded slowly, obliquely, in whispers."[19] Recovery of this past requires inclining one's ear to the whispers, reconstructing a family tree in which each person becomes a point of access into deep and complex personal histories, which themselves encode suppressed histories of collective traumatic encounters. Indeed, the entire narrative which chronicles the emergence of the artist is structured around a series of paintings, each of which represents the recovery of personal, communal, national or diasporic history. And each step through the process is significant for the emergence of the artist.

For as many as manage to carve out a tenuous belonging to the Caribbean environment, there are those who carry a permanent sense of being alienated in a strange land. The dislocation trauma cannot be resolved; the wound of rupture cannot be healed. Hence the portrait of Black Maharajin standing with her *churias* (bracelets) before the ylang-ylang tree (itself a well-established blossoming import into the Trinidadian landscape) is the point of access for her hard-won rootedness and the entrenched displacement of Daniel, her first husband, whose yearning to return to India is flouted as his meagre earnings are leached away by living expenses. The racial slur *coolie* spurs him to murder, emanating out of rage at his displacement and at the careless hostility of the predominantly Afro-Trinidadian society.

Mahabir inscribes her chapter in the torturous history of domestic abuse against Indian women through the portrait of Pani, who represents the location of Indian women as what I have termed "bearers of the psychic laceration of indentureship".[20] The violence which erupts out of public flouting of traditional patriarchal dictates and severe displacement trauma is imbricated through murderous abuses rained on the female body within the domestic enclave. Venting her own murderous rage against her drunken and incestuous father, Pani's anguish only intensifies on the day that she chops him to death.

This scenario resonates with the central incident of Shani Mootoo's *Cereus Blooms at Night*. The first-person artist narrator discovers that, despite her fantasies to the contrary, Pani is not named after the fragrant and delicate frangipani flower – a correlation of the night-blooming cereus which is the central motif and emblem of redemptive possibility in Mootoo's novel.

Indeed, Pani – *pani* is Hindi for "water" and an anagram of *pain* – is so named by the taxi driver who finds her in Iere village after her family expels her – wet, wandering, possibly an amnesiac – "like the rain bring she from nowhere".[21] The rain parallels the gushing water from the downspout under which she crouches to wash the blood-guilt of patricide from her hands. She returns to the cascading water on a grim day when a sudden storm and trauma's repetitious intrusions tug her to relive the anguish and to howl in grief for her womenfolk. The catalyst of the trauma is so horrific that it cannot be grasped at once in its entirety; it must belatedly and repeatedly revisit the conscious mind in its attempt to compel recognition and acceptance of its totality. The name *Pani* locates the domestic crisis as an eruption of the group trauma attendant upon crossing the *kala pani*. Centuries may have passed, but *kala pani* anguish remains.

And what is the role of the artist in bringing these traumas to articulation? If the sufferers cannot give them voice then what is the protocol for the creative artist who engages the unrepresentable on behalf of the voiceless? What boundaries do artists need to observe? What is the motive behind the process and expressions? The creative artist becomes within this context a seer/healer who looks into the veiled, the guarded, the violent, the unlovely, the unwanted to map the pain and anguish at its root. The quest for the emergence of the artist is complicated by the quest for authority and legitimacy to reveal what Toni Morrison terms "unspeakable acts"[22] and Erna Brodber identifies as "the half that has never yet been told".[23]

This is the journey which Annaise traverses with sensitivity: "When it came to my own painting I didn't know how to tell Pani's story without transgressing those fragile barriers that Pani had never given anyone permission to cross."[24] These are the barriers which her cousin Vash, who is also a Caribbean artist based in the metropolis, tramples upon. Vash wrests her inspiration from the suffering, hurt, inarticulateness of the broken and wounded pasts. She would have painted Pani "facing the viewer, covered with rainwater and blood", whereas Annaise allows the victim to control the unveiling thus: "I see that the dull green and red shades, distorted by rain occupy most of the painting, and the figure's back is turned to me and she crouched under the spouting. She is in outline, barely distinguishable, abstract, and this is all of her that I am allowed."[25]

Vash, who invites her younger cousin to show her work and then crowds her out of the exhibition, parallels the Trinidadian state authorities who earlier excluded her father's work from the Carnival exhibition, as the betrayer of yet another season of migration. Vash's point of access into sophisticated metropolitan galleries is the portrayal of caricatures and stereotypes of Caribbeanness and Caribbean social relations as commodities to delight metropolitan audiences. She adopts the role of the quintessential native informer. Her signature piece, *Peasant Missives*, prostitutes Annaise's family by creating a collage out of fragments of the letters sent from home by Annaise's father, Larry, begging assistance from the prosperous Toronto relatives so that his daughter can have an opportunity to study abroad to develop her artistry. This flagrant betrayal of trust, which plays into structural First World–Third World inequities, freezes the Caribbean peasant into a mendicant posture and thereby affirms the superiority of the metropolitan viewers.

At an even deeper level, Vash's act is also subtle punishment for injustices perpetrated a generation earlier, when Vash's mother, while still a child, was raped and subsequently punished and temporarily excluded from the family in disgrace. Resentment at this exclusion is focused on Larry, who was dispatched by his mother to carry food weekly to the banished daughter – veiled animosities never resolved, offences never articulated, a beg-pardon ritual never executed – and so the bitterness festers, to work its insidious poison through the generations. Submerged historical and domestic traumas do not simply vanish with time. Indeed, in this and countless other Caribbean texts they flaunt their intergenerational staying power. One resource for their alleviation is an appropriate mode of representation, which requires depth of understanding and sensitivity, because it must speak on behalf of the voiceless and simultaneously return to the wounded control over the revealing. The text transmits a warning that migration can lead to a betrayal of rootedness, community and culture.

The quest then is for place, a meeting ground, a *gayelle*, a site for a ceremony of souls in which the hidden, submerged, shameful and silenced can be brought to light so that healing processes can begin. This is the space that

Mahabir's Annaise occupies. This is the space rejected by Kello in *The Swinging Bridge*, who, in response to strong familial pressure towards conformity and the extreme stigmatization attached to same-sex liaisons, carries the secret of his homosexual orientation and HIV/AIDS status to his early grave. An alternative pathway is signalled early in the narrative and in his life, when a popular Carnival character, a black devil – *djab-molasi* – tempts him to display his same-sex attraction, smearing its body indecently against him and swiping its tail between his legs. As a result of this onslaught, the young boy determines to reject the Jouvert space of inversion that would have allowed even momentary exploration and parading of alternative sexual identities. Instead he dies in hiding.

Mahabir's narrative starts from the ground of shared though contested cultural belonging as reflected in the appropriation of Jouvert as a trope. Her central metaphor travels into metropolitan scenarios in much the same manner as the actual carnivals have taken root, morphing into vibrant festivals of significance to millions of metropolitan dwellers who take to the street annually to dance their unique expressions of celebration, resistance and catharsis. Mahabir's deployment of Jouvert recalls Keith Nurse's assertion "that the Trinidad carnival and its overseas or diasporic offspring are both products of and responses to the processes of globalization" as well as the "intercultural and transnational formations that relate to a concept of a Black Atlantic".[26] The text draws on Jouvert's power as a counter-hegemonic expression uniquely shaped to interrogate hierarchies of class, nation and race and makes it accessible to all who stand in need of such a space. In the process, Mahabir works towards a transnational sensibility which remains rooted in and nurtured by its past. The process is not without disquiet. At points her overt narrative insistence on the Jouvert trope becomes too formulaic. Similarly, the intrusion of the word *Caribbean* into every possible nook and cranny of the narrative (including three times in a single paragraph on pages 12 to 13) itself speaks of distancing and anxiety about the rooted vantage point which she claims.[27]

Evidently the quest for home is heightened, not alleviated, by successive migrations. In *From Pillar to Post*, Frank Birbalsingh speaks of the ongoing pursuit of home for Indo-Caribbean migrants to Canada:

> The irony for Indo-Caribbean Canadians is that while they have escaped from

psychological insecurity caused by political instability, marginalization, lack of opportunity and inter ethnic tension at home, coming to Canada has brought its own insecurities caused by urban-industrial alienation, race and colour prejudice, impersonal, secular mores and the hectic pace and pressure of modern city living.[28]

Moreover, he identifies the multiple challenges inherent in these migrants' being designated as "South Asian" in this new land of their migration, especially for a people who may be phenotypically South Asian but are unique because of their tastes in food, speech habits and other cultural markers of their island birthplaces. This recalls Shani Mootoo's playful allegations in "Out on Main Street", which is set in an Indian sweet shop in Toronto: "We is not grade A Indians", and the tongue-in-cheek, more "positive" assertion, "We is kitchen Indians." Birbalsingh argues that displacement and alienation will be transcended only if Indo-Caribbean identity is properly appreciated for both its similarity and differences from Afro-Caribbean and South Asian cultures.

All of the texts delineate the challenges inherent in the traditional Indo-Caribbean extended family network's being and becoming the primary locus of belonging for the contemporary man and woman alike. For Maharaj in *Like Heaven,* the failure is rooted in the same qualities Espinet identifies: "close and thick and sheltering. Its ugly and violent secrets locked inside the family walls."[29] Maharaj's protagonist – that emblematic national citizen – opts for a swiftly encroaching though not altogether welcome future, including an uneasy truce with its women, embodied latterly in the aggressive, articulate and adversarial daughter whom he loves more than life. In terms of the nationalist project, he exemplifies also his incapacity to contribute to the civic nationalism which is vital to propel the region into its future. Once regimes persist in which ethnic and familial loyalties buttress violent and murderous practices to lend cohesion – at the expense of equity, complementarity, justice and the rule of law – the nation stands at risk. Ved and his generation have been proven incapable of delivering on this imperative; his wife's life was snuffed out because of her valiant efforts to effect the same.

In Espinet's *Swinging Bridge,* the protagonist's quest for an alternative shelter – having stepped outside of family's intimacies and defilements – proves more hopeful. The pathway resides in a cultural hybridity, which becomes the beat to which she now moves in the land of her migration. The Caroni Dub, made by fusion of the hosay drum with the steel band, chac-chac, dholak, dhantal, cuatro and iron, becomes the beat to which she dances her new terrain. Significantly, the rhythms of cultural fusion remain unsupported by any evocation of a real-life community within which to dance and to live.

Mahabir moves beyond these offerings to what, in my view, is a more viable alternative. The closing symbol of the narrative is Indira, the maternal ancestress and freedom fighter who was martyred by the colonial authorities for leading an estate strike. Clothed in bloodied cane-cutter garb – an old blue skirt and an oversized long-sleeved white shirt – Indira recalls the double jeopardy of women in the plantation – that most brutal and brutalizing of regulatory regimes, the site of cultural disruption and enforced acculturation, where women were pillaged as labouring bodies and ravished as sexual bodies. Moreover, the slain woman's posture resonates with another image: the thousands slaughtered in gender warfare in the interest of restoring patriarchal subordination and control. The spilt blood stains the cane field as the primary site of oppression. The clenched blood-red fist of resistance becomes, at the end of Annaise's journey of discovery, the hand of the artist.

The journey of the Caribbean people clearly exemplifies the pitfalls inherent in modes of belonging and quests for homelands based on the primordial pull of blood and land. Transcending ethnicity and nationalism as primary forms of belonging, Mahabir (who dedicates her book to her husband, an African-American musician and activist) points to a space beyond. This narrative is rooted temporally in the unearthed ancestral and national histories of the oppressed; spatially in cartographies of natal lands, journeys and diasporas; and culturally in the hybridized cultural space epitomized by the resistance of Jouvert. Mahabir revels in her own version of Rawle Gibbons's formulation of its mysterious, elusive release of human energy and Burton Sankeralli's notion of the *leela* – the shared Indo- and Afro-Trinidadian dance of energy and ethos of play. Projecting its power transnationally and beyond the ethnic divides which have proven so resistant within Trinidad and Tobago, Mahabir affirms in turn that Jouvert spaces of resistance are and have been for a long time recreated in enclaves by artists and activists throughout the globe – "spaces of maroonage and alternative cultures, grounded in the earth hidden from Babylon", communities bound together by "deep appreciation they had for all people who shared their radical values regardless of race".[30]

These mobile and fluid spaces, though rooted in an African diasporic ethos as evoked in Gilroy's conception of a Black Atlantic, readily gather resonances of a diverse range of ancestral and natal cultures.[31] For persons of numerous ethnicities and homelands living in more than fifty metropolitan cities world-wide who remain under siege in the lands of their migration, Carnival has created underground subcultural spaces. It is a source of cathartic relief and cultural affirmation and a buttress against the daily erosion of petty and insti-tutionalized racism. Jouvert, calypso, jazz, blues, soca, chutney – all resonate with the same chord. They all point to a triumphant affirmation of the human spirit in what Rawle Gibbons terms "a theatre of self-liberation".[32]

NOTES

1. Carol Boyce Davies defines the complexities involved in the process of "writing home": "Migration creates the desire for home, which in turn produces the rewriting of home. Homesickness or homelessness, the rejection of home or the longing for home become motivating factors in this rewriting. Home can only have meaning once one experiences a level of displacement from it. Still home is contradictory, contested space, a locus for misrecognition and alienation. . . . The woman as writer then doubly disrupts the seamless narrative of home and so of nation. Further, her location in a variety of social and political contexts allows her internal critiques of new inscriptions of postcoloniality and imperial-ism." See Carol Boyce Davies, "Writing Home: Gender and Heritage in the Works of Afro-Caribbean/American Women Writers", in *Out of the Kumbla: Caribbean Women and Literature*, edited by Carol Boyce Davies and Elaine Savory Fido (Trenton, NJ: Africa World Press, 1990), 54.

2. Arjun Appadurai, *Modernity at Large: Cultural Dimensions of Modernism* (1996; reprint, Minneapolis: University of Minnesota Press, 2000). Reconstructed pri-mordialism as defined by Appadurai yokes constructs of ethnic belonging and pull of blood in the service of contemporary politics.

3. The novel's epigraph, drawn from Derek Walcott's 1992 Nobel lecture, reads: "And here they are, all in a single Caribbean city, Port of Spain, the sum of history / Trollope [sic] non-people. A downtown babel of shop signs and streets, mongrelised, / polygot, a ferment without a history, like heaven."
    The epigraph points to the major themes of the novel and the impact of cultural

change, which drives people through a Sargasso Sea without the benefit of a compass. Ultimately the major casualties of the process are the women. This issue can be seen as a radical loss or as an opportunity to reassemble the fragments into a coherent form.

4. Ramabai Espinet, *The Swinging Bridge* (Toronto: HarperFlamingo, 2004), 15.

5. Brij V. Lal, in "People In-Between: Reflection from the Indian Indentured Diaspora", in *The Construction of an Indo-Caribbean Diaspora*, edited by Brinsley Samaroo and Anne Marie Bissessar (St Augustine, Trinidad: University of the West Indies School of Continuing Studies, 2004), 4.

6. Aisha Khan, *Callaloo Nation: Metaphors of Race, Religion and Religious Identity among South Asians in Trinidad* (Kingston: University of the West Indies Press, 2004).

7. The general perception remains that ownership of the nation is substantively the preserve of the Afro-Caribbean populations, with other ethnic groups variously located on the continua of marginalization. This notion was subtly expressed in the ruling party's 2007 election tagline, "Trinidad and Tobago is PNM country".

8. The expression "people of Indian origin" is itself exemplary of the ambivalent relatedness, because the term as used in Trinidad up to this day excludes persons of mixed Indian and African ancestry. The less valued African antecedents are held to have cancelled out the Indian origin.

9. George Lamming has explored the permutations of this experiment in *Enterprise of the Indies* (Port of Spain: Trinidad and Tobago Institute of the West Indies and Trinidad and Tobago Review, 1999).

10. Characters like the French Creole landholder Mr Guillame are littered throughout literature. Cases in point can be found in Jean Rhys's representatives of the planter class who live in decaying homes, in overgrown fallen paradises, much in need of youth and currency to revitalize and bring them back to life. See Jean Rhys, *Wide Sargasso Sea* (1966; reprint, Harmondsworth, UK: Penguin, 1996).

11. This is the pattern of Olive Senior's "Arrival of Miss Coolie". Miss Coolie arrives in Mount Rose village clothed in sinuous saris and carrying a few spices and seeds. By the end of the narrative, as a result of her diligent shop-keeping entrepreneurship she takes over the decaying great house of the Creole overlords. In the process she supplants the African Mother Miracles, for whom the crossroads had been a significant spiritual location. It is commerce, not spirituality, which becomes the dominant ethos of the emerging social order.

12. Michael V. Angrosino, "Sexual Politics in the East Indian Family in Trinidad", *Caribbean Studies* 16 (1976): 21.

13. The details of the case were reported in a *Newsday* special report as follows: "Dr. Chandra Narayansingh was working at the Langmore Health Foundation in South. She lived in Buena Vista Road, St. Joseph in the lovely family home which she once shared with her husband, highly respected surgeon Dr. Vijay Narayansingh and their five-year-old daughter, Anamika. But she and Vijay had been separated for 18 months and he lived in another house. Reports indicate that they were going through legal process with respect to property and alimony settlements and such matters that are usual when a marriage has broken down. Her death was a severe shock not only to the people of the Langmore Foundation but to the public in general and speculation was rife as police began investigation . . . Among the many mysteries that remain unsolved is the fact that the killing was witnessed by several people but the police seems incapable of getting information. Rumours and speculation were rife until police eventually focused on a man by the name of Shaun Parris. But he had long skipped the country apparently as much afraid of the police as of the people who had ordered the contract. He had good reason to be fearful for the two men who gave him the contract were themselves eliminated in 1996." The eminent surgeon and his second wife were eventually tried for the murder and released, but not before the then chief justice intervened to influence the outcome of the trial.

14. Brinsley Samaroo, "Asian Identity and Culture in the Caribbean", in *The Enterprise of the Indies*, edited by George Lamming (Port of Spain: Trinidad and Tobago Institute of the West Indies and Trinidad and Tobago Review, 1999), 44.

15. In the chapter "Language and the Politics of Ethnicity", in *Beyond Borders*, edited by Jennifer Rahim with Barbara Lalla, 17–33 (Kingston: University of the West Indies Press, 2009), Lamming laments the deleterious impact of divisive African–Indian relations on the nation. Among the divisive elements he cites the fact that Indians were legally granted land which they in turn used to create breadbaskets for the nation, while Africans were given no legal title to land and ultimately no reparation for their enslavement. In his analysis of Lovelace's *Salt*, he comments on the manner in which this land issue fed the fear of interethnic rivalry, which positioned Indians as supplanters of Afro-Trinidadian privilege in popular cultural expressions and particularly in calypsos, which mischievously mocked the Indo-Trinidadian's quest for integration and upward mobility.

16. This construction is a radical departure from that proffered by Lakshmi Persaud's *Butterfly in the Wind*. Writing from an orthodox Hindu perspective, Persaud portrays Carnival as a prolific and criminal waste of time and resources. The grandeur, productivity and creativity which Maharaj celebrates are presented in Persaud's novel as exemplifying idleness, loss, frivolity and a too lush sensuality

and sexual aggressiveness. Much in the same manner as the spate of kidnappings in contemporary Trinidad tend to be interpreted as aggression and hostility of Afro-Trinidadians against Indo-Trinidadians, the robbery and murder of prominent Indo-Trinidadian businessmen at Carnival time are seen as a them-against-us offence – particularly as the willingness of lazy black good-for-nothings to steal for the sake of a Carnival costume and the delusions of grandeur conferred by mask and costume, notwithstanding the looming poverty and insignificance of Ash Wednesday.

17. Rawle Gibbons, "Room to Pass: Carnival and Caribbean Aesthetics", in *The Enterprise of the Indies*, edited by George Lamming (Port of Spain: Trinidad and Tobago Institute of the West Indies and Trinidad and Tobago Review, 1999), 153.

18. Patricia T. Alleyne-Dettmers, "The Relocation of Trinidad Carnival in Notting Hill Land and the Politics of Diasporisation", in *Globalization, Diaspora and Caribbean Popular Culture*, edited by Christine G.T. Ho and Keith Nurse (Mona: Ian Randle, 1995), 334.

19. Joy Mahabir, *Jouvert* (Bloomington, Ind.: Authorhouse, 2006), 28.

20. For a full discussion of historical and contemporary violence against Indian women in the home, see Paula Morgan and Valerie Youssef, "Gendered Inscriptions of Indo-Caribbean Family Violence", in *Writing Rage: Unmasking Violence through Caribbean Discourse* (Mona: University of the West Indies Press, 2006).

21. Mahabir, *Jouvert*, 38.

22. Toni Morrison, *Conversations with Toni Morrison*, edited by Danielle Taylor-Guthrie (Jackson: University Press of Mississippi, 1993).

23. Erna Brodber, *Myal* (London: New Beacon, 1998).

24. Mahabir, *Jouvert*, 41.

25. Ibid., 39.

26. Keith Nurse, "Globalization and Trinidad Carnival: Diaspora, Hybridity and Identity in Global Culture", in *Identity, Ethnicity and Culture in the Caribbean*, edited by Ralph Premdass (St Augustine, Trinidad: University of the West Indies School of Continuing Studies, 2001), 82.

27. I am indebted to Merle Hodge for this notion. On hearing this paper read at a UWI Department of Liberal Arts seminar, she expressed her own concern about overuse of the term *Caribbean*, as if belonging can be invoked through much repetition.

28. Frank Birbalsingh, *From Pillar to Post: The Indo-Caribbean Diaspora* (Toronto: TSAR, 1997), 214.

29. Espinet, *Swinging Bridge*, 15.

30. Burton Sankeralli, "Carnival: Trinidad Folk and Indian Presence", in *The Enter-*

prise of the Indies, edited by George Lamming, 154–60 (Port of Spain: Trinidad and Tobago Institute of the West Indies and Trinidad and Tobago Review, 1999).

31. Rawle Gibbons, commenting on the significant role played by Carnival in metropolitan city centres, identifies its capacity to shift what may be peripheral to the centre. "The attraction of the North to cultures of resistance that have survived and spiritually triumphed over their own (the North's) genocidal ambitions, bears testimony to other forces at play in the drama of remaking of the contemporary world"; "Room to Pass", 153.

32. Gibbons, "Room to Pass", 150.

Contributors

Rosanne Kanhai is Professor of English and Director of Women Studies, Western Washington University, Bellingham, Washington. Her areas of research and teaching are Caribbean women, post-colonial studies, feminist theory and criticism, and post-colonial and global studies. Besides creative nonfiction and journal articles, her publications include *The Green Face Man*, *Rage and Renewal* and, as editor, *Matikor: The Politics of Identity for Indo-Caribbean Women*.

Anita Baksh is a doctoral student in English, University of Maryland and a lecturer, St John's University, Queens, New York. She has a certificate in women's studies and is a recipient of fellowships and various grants. Her research and teaching focus on Caribbean Indian and Indian diasporic literatures, post-colonial theory and feminist theory.

Brenda Gopeesingh is an independent researcher, business entrepreneur and community activist. She is a founding member and ex-president of the Hindu Women's Organisation of Trinidad and Tobago. She has served on the board of the Network of NGOs for the Advancement of Women and was its assistant coordinator from 2002 to 2004. Gopeesingh has co-authored a workbook, *The Dynamics of Family Violence and How to Plan Workshops* and initiated publication of the *Hindu Women's Organisation Magazine*. She is company secretary and a director of Regal Products Ltd, a manufacturing company in Trinidad.

Gabrielle Jamela Hosein is Lecturer, Institute of Gender and Development Studies, University of the West Indies, St Augustine, Trinidad. Her research and teaching focus on Caribbean feminism, sexualities and governance. Hosein's publications include contributions to *Anthropology and the Individual: A Material Culture Perspective* (edited by Daniel Miller), *Fieldwork Identities: Self* *and Subject in Ethnographic Methods* (edited by Eric Taylor), *Gender in the Twentieth Century: Caribbean Perspectives, Visions and Possibilities* (edited by Barbara Bailey and Elsa Leo-Rhynie) and *Gender Issues and Caribbean Scholarship: Interdisciplinary Perspectives* (edited by Eudine Barriteau).

Shaheeda Hosein is Assistant Professor and Coordinator, Department of History, University of Trinidad and Tobago. Her research and teaching focus on Latin American and Caribbean relations and women and gender in Latin America and the Caribbean, with emphasis on the shaping of the female self. Her publications include articles in the *Caribbean Review of Gender Studies* and *Oral History Journal*.

Halima Sa'adia Kassim is Deputy Programme Manager (Gender and Development), CARICOM Secretariat, Georgetown, Guyana. Her research interest is changing gender relations within Muslim communities. She has taught history and sociology at the College of Science, Technology and Applied Arts of Trinidad and Tobago. Her publications focus on CARICOM's Millennium Development Goals, gender-based violence (including cyber-violence), poverty, changing age structures, child protection and migration.

Kumar Mahabir is Assistant Professor, School for Cognition, Learning and Education, University of Trinidad and Tobago, a cultural anthropologist, co-curator of the Indian Caribbean Museum, and chairman of the Indo-Caribbean Cultural Council and of Chakra Publishing House. His publications include *Caribbean East Indian Recipes, Medicinal and Edible Plants Used by East Indians of Trinidad and Tobago* and *Indian Caribbean Folklore Spirits*.

Paula E. Morgan is Senior Lecturer and Head, Department of Liberal Arts, University of the West Indies, St Augustine, Trinidad. She also coordinates the graduate programme in cultural studies. Her primary areas of research and teaching are gender issues in the literatures of the Caribbean and the African diaspora. She is the author of four books, the most recent being *Writing Rage: Violence in Caribbean Discourse*, co-authored with Valerie Youssef. Forthcoming publications include contributions to *Teaching Approaches to African American Literature* (edited by Gina Whisker) and the Modern Languages Association Options in Teaching Series (edited by Supriya Nair).

Sherry-Ann Singh is Lecturer in Indian History and the Indian Diaspora, Department of History, University of the West Indies, St Augustine, Trinidad. Her areas of research and teaching include social, religious and cultural transformations among Indians in Trinidad and other parts of the Indian diaspora. Her publications include articles in the *ICFAI Journal of History and Culture* and *Man in India: A Quarterly International Journal of Anthropology*; forthcoming is *The Ramayana Tradition and Socio-Religious Change in Trinidad, 1917–1990*.

Valerie Youssef is Professor of Linguistics, Department of Liberal Arts, University of the West Indies, St Augustine, Trinidad. Her primary areas of research and teaching are Caribbean sociolinguistics, language acquisition and discourse analysis, at both the undergraduate and postgraduate levels. Her publications include *The Languages of Tobago*, co-authored with Winford James, and *Writing Rage: Unmasking Violence in Caribbean Discourse*, co-authored with Paula Morgan. Forthcoming publications include contributions to *Sociolinguistics around the World: A Handbook* (edited by Martin Ball), *Variation in the Caribbean: From Creole Continua to Individual Agency* (edited by Lars Hinrichs and Joseph Farquharion), *Annotated Research Methods in Caribbean Research* (edited by Tony Bastick and Lorraine Cook) and, as co-editor with Barbara Lalla, Nicole Roberts and Elizabeth Walcott-Hackshaw, *Research Methods in the Caribbean: Cultural and Literary Studies*.

www.ingramcontent.com/pod-product-compliance
Lightning Source LLC
Chambersburg PA
CBHW021858020426
42334CB00013B/385